AMERICAN SPY

AMERICAN SPY

WRY REFLECTIONS ON MY LIFE IN THE CIA

H. K. ROY

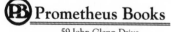 Prometheus Books

59 John Glenn Drive
Amherst, New York 14228

Published 2019 by Prometheus Books

Cover image © Shutterstock
Cover design by Nicole Sommer-Lecht
Cover design © Prometheus Books

"Chapter 1: Betrayal in the Balkans" accounts originally published in and adapted from "Betrayal in the Balkans," *World & I Magazine*, August 2001.

"The Closer You Get," track 1, on Alabama, *The Closer You Get*, RCA, 2000, compact disc, originally released in 1983. Used with permission by Easy Song Licensing.

Trademarked names appear throughout this book. Prometheus Books recognizes all registered trademarks, trademarks, and service marks mentioned in the text.

The internet addresses listed in the text were accurate at the time of publication. The inclusion of a website does not indicate an endorsement by the author or by Prometheus Books, and Prometheus Books does not guarantee the accuracy of the information presented at these sites.

All statements of fact, opinion, or analysis expressed are those of the author and do not reflect the official positions or views of the Central Intelligence Agency (CIA) or any other US government agency. Nothing in the contents should be construed as asserting or implying US government authentication of information or CIA endorsement of the author's views. This material has been reviewed by the CIA to prevent the disclosure of classified information. This does not constitute an official release of CIA information.

Inquiries should be addressed to
Prometheus Books
59 John Glenn Drive
Amherst, New York 14228
VOICE: 716–691–0133 • FAX: 716–691–0137
WWW.PROMETHEUSBOOKS.COM

23 22 21 20 19   5 4 3 2 1

Library of Congress Cataloging-in-Publication Data

Identifiers: ISBN 978-1-63388-589-9 (ebook)
ISBN 978-1-63388-588-2 (hardcover)

Printed in the United States of America

To the men and women of the CIA, past, present, and future.
To NA, SC, and MS.
To FJ and ML.
To SJ, CM, and JF.

CONTENTS

PART IV: RUSSIAN SPIES

PART V: CIA FAMILY

PART VI: HOT AND COLD RUNNING WAR: YUGOSLAVIA

PART VII: IRAQ: IT SEEMED LIKE A GOOD IDEA AT THE TIME

PART VIII: BRUSHES WITH CELEBRITY

PART IX: THE SPY WHO CAME DOWN WITH A COLD

PREFACE

As I watch a squadron of brown pelicans cruise by in formation, stall, then splash down into the warm turquoise waters of the Sea of Cortez, I receive an email reporting that an Iranian-backed Shi'ite militia has arrested my company's key man in Basra, Iraq. The de facto intelligence service of southern Iraq, the Hashd al-Shaabi, is demanding a laughably huge "fee" from my company in exchange for a "license" to continue to operate.

The Shi'ite intelligence service is unaware of the fact that a former CIA operations officer—yours truly—founded, owns, and operates the business they are attempting to shake down. They are also ignorant of the fact that their Iranian spymasters once targeted me for kidnap, torture, interrogation, and assassination (in that order) when I served as the CIA's first chief of station in war-torn Sarajevo.

Come to think of it, they are also in the dark about the fact that my company's natural access to individuals of their ilk has been exploited—with deadly effect, I might add—by relevant US authorities and coalition forces.

So, it could be worse.

But the Hashd still poses a real threat to my company's very existence. And to my colleague and his family.

What's my reaction to this latest dispatch from Iraq?

Meh.

The tide is out, the breeze is warm, and endless Baja beaches and tide pools beckon. I can deal with Iraq, or I can hang out on my patio, sip tequila and sangrita, and listen to another *cumbia* by Los Ángeles Azules.

Truth be told, I'm all Iraq'd out. Traveling in and out of Iraq, Syria, and elsewhere in the Middle East and wrestling with issues like this, seven days a week for fifteen years, have taken its toll.

To clarify, I love the unpredictable start-up phase of a risky venture, especially in a challenging place like Iraq. I'm just not crazy about the "running the established business" part.

I'm also tired of dealing with Shi'ite militias, Daesh (ISIS), and al-Qaeda in Iraq (precursor to ISIS), not to mention the impossible Iraqi government and equally impossible Western multinationals who rely on my company's services in Iraq. And don't get me started on the Bank of America, perhaps the most aggravating challenge of them all.

Before gambling on a business start-up in Iraq, I spent thirteen years as a CIA operations officer (aka case officer). For most of those thirteen years, I could not believe they actually paid me to do the job. I wasn't the only young ops officer blessed with that sense of wonder. The CIA mystique, culture, and way of life really are that intoxicating. Like most of my colleagues, I believed in the mission—I still do—and loved every bit of the experience. At least until I reached the ranks of middle management.

An unconditional commitment to the career is a good and necessary thing because the job demands unending hours and unquestioned 24/7 devotion to duty. It's a commitment I eagerly made, from intensive training assignments in the DC area to equally intensive, risky, and exhausting assignments in Latin America, the Balkans, and elsewhere.

The lengthy CIA training process was one of the greatest adventures of my life, and it alone generated enough memorable and hilarious stories on which to base an entire book.

Once I was posted abroad, employing solid tradecraft skills learned during training was essential to success and survival, whether on the streets of Latin America or while being followed by the Yugoslav "KGB" en route to a midnight agent meeting in Belgrade. Overseas, I frequently (and intentionally) crossed paths with Cold War nemeses, like Soviet and Cuban spies.

Post–Cold War CIA service allowed me and my family to bear witness to the breakup of Yugoslavia as it slid out of Communism and into a horrific, bloody civil war. I served on and behind the front lines, dispatching reports and influencing events in Croatia, Bosnia, and Kosovo. My wife and daughters experienced CIA life from a somewhat different perspective.

Because of the urgency of the Bosnia crisis, my raw intelligence reports, sent via secure satellite phone from Sarajevo during the siege and Srebrenica massacre, were passed directly to the White House and secretary of state—unfiltered and without the usual CIA headquarters analysis.

It doesn't get any better than that if you're a CIA operations officer in the field, even if the "experts" in Washington are initially skeptical of your 100 percent accurate report that the Bosnian Serbs slaughtered eight thousand Bosnian Muslim civilians over the course of a few days.

It's why the CIA exists: to report the unvarnished truth to policy makers.

I was also fortunate enough to support the mission even after resigning from the CIA. I found that I could actually do *more* for the US government (and my country) as a private citizen, since I wasn't bound by bureaucratic or chain of command restrictions that necessarily constrain staff employees. If I want to enter Kosovo—or Iraq, or Syria—midwar to set up a business, no one inside the CIA can stop me. Not that they didn't try. But since I was free to take more risks as a civilian than as a CIA officer, I was also able to provide even greater results in furtherance of America's global national security mission.

The unfortunate reality is that policy makers do not necessarily do the right or smart thing, even when they have spot-on intelligence to guide them. Presidents George H. W. Bush and Bill Clinton alike both ignored the CIA's prescient intelligence on the former Yugoslavia, and as a result their well-intentioned but misguided policies contributed greatly to the bloodshed during the protracted and largely avoidable Balkan wars.

Later, the administration of President George W. Bush chose to ignore my reporting that Saddam Hussein's intelligence service did *not* meet with al-Qaeda in Prague, one of the false justifications given for invading Iraq. That same administration ignored valuable input from seasoned US intelligence and military professionals before launching the invasion. Iraq had nothing to do with 9/11 and nothing to do with al-Qaeda. But the Bush administration was determined to invade Iraq, regardless of what the intelligence showed or failed to show.

After overthrowing Saddam (to the benefit of Iran), the White House continued to ignore its own experts and made a series of monumentally bad decisions, from firing the entire Iraqi military to implementing an ill-conceived de-Ba'athification policy. Iraq, the United States, and the world all pay the price to this day.

Later, President Obama's government foolishly pulled the plug on an extremely valuable collaboration with my company that might have helped prevent the ISIS surprise takeover of Mosul in summer 2014.

But politics trumped intelligence. In 2011, the Obama administration abandoned the Iraqi disaster that the Bush administration created, without even trying to renegotiate the status of forces agreement. Only to redeploy troops to Iraq, predictably, a few years later. The saga continues.

Yugoslavia. Iraq. ISIS. These were not intelligence failures. On the contrary, these were, for the most part, intelligence successes. But intelligence professionals and the CIA do not make foreign policy. Politicians do. They have the power to ignore intelligence, ignore the best options presented, and recognize only a single, unified Yugoslavia rather than accept reality and help the country break apart peacefully. They have the power to invade Iraq, despite a lack of intelligence linking Iraq and 9/11. And when things go badly because of their policies, they often blame the intelligence community.

For better or worse, I can personally attest to this, at least regarding Iraq and the former Yugoslavia. I'm not alone in believing that the ill-advised invasion of Iraq was the single largest foreign policy miscalculation in recent American history.

To date, that is. As we are witnessing once again, an American president has almost unfettered power and cannot be stopped once he decides (often impulsively) to do something in the arena of defense and foreign policy. In fact, I believe there's a very good chance President Trump may outdo President George W. Bush in terms of intentionally committing blunders of historic and catastrophic significance.

Equally ominous, there are serious indications that Trump is at the very least a witting collaborator of the Russian intelligence service. As of this writing, almost every foreign policy move made by Trump has directly served Vladimir Putin's strategic interests. Starting with Trump's shattering of alliances and withdrawal of America from its traditional global leadership role. The list of Trump's pro-Russian policies grows daily.

My hope is that these "street level" spy stories, in addition to providing entertainment and immersing the reader in my world, will illuminate why intelligence is essential to our national security and to our very survival as a nation. American spies sacrifice in the shadows to report the truth to power. If US presidents and policy makers continue to ignore or politicize the CIA, the "American empire" may be very short-lived.

Bad foreign policy decisions are a bipartisan problem. This is one reason I remain apolitical and independent of either party. It's fair to say I don't care for most politicians, and, although I'm not proud of this fact, I can't remember the last time I voted. A good spy must remain an apolitical seeker and speaker of truth.

As I mentioned, despite (or maybe because of) the never-ending adventure, I'm all Iraq'd out. Of course, I also once said, "I'm all CIA'd out." After which I learned it's sometimes easier to get in than to get out. Or as the Serbs would say, *"Dala baba jedan dinar da udje u kolo, a daje dva da izadje,"* meaning "Grandma paid one dinar to get into the *kolo*, and two to get out." For those of you unfamiliar with Serbian folk traditions, a *kolo* is a fast-paced circle dance, not for the elderly or faint of heart.

So, the time has finally come for me to spend more quality time at my Mexican safe house and write down some of the stories I've accumulated along the way. I haven't forgotten the details of what transpired long ago, since my long-term memory is almost photographic. Although not "photogenic," which is how an otherwise reliable source on North Korea once described her memory.

As for my short-term memory, that's another story. Fortunately, I have thousands of emails and other electronic files that serve as my unblinking memory bank of all essential details, not to mention dozens of Iraqi friends and colleagues who can also help to refresh my more recent, post-CIA memory. So, I can (and will) tell you the exact date and circumstances surrounding al-Qaeda's kidnapping of three of my employees in Mosul, for example. And how two of them (both Shi'ites) escaped with their heads because one of them was too fat to be stuffed into the trunk of his car.

The good news is by the time I finish writing this book, several more as-yet-unforeseen adventures will undoubtedly play out, and I'll have the makings of a second book. *Insha'Allah.*

ABBREVIATIONS

AQI	al-Qaeda in Iraq
BREN	brief encounter
CA	covert action
CE	Central Eurasia
CI	counterintelligence
commo	communications
COS	chief of station
CT	career trainee
det	detonation
exfil	exfiltration
helo	helicopter
MOIS	Ministry of Intelligence (Iran)
NODs	night-vision goggles
PCS	permanent change of station
PT	physical training
SDB	Yugoslav security service
SDR	surveillance detection route
SE/IO	Soviet–East European Internal Ops
SERE	survival, evasion, resistance, and escape
TDY	temporary duty

PART I

BALKAN TRILOGY

CHAPTER 1

BETRAYAL IN THE BALKANS: HILLARY SENT ME, BUT BILL NEARLY GOT ME KILLED

When the Central Intelligence Agency (CIA) selected me in mid-1995 to lead an all-volunteer team to war-ravaged Sarajevo to carry out a highest-priority mission, I had mixed emotions. One year earlier, my team and I had made it most of the way to Sarajevo on a similar mission but were turned back at the last minute due to the "deteriorating security situation" in the besieged city. In layman's terms, it was too dangerous. By 1995, the situation in Sarajevo had worsened, but possible NATO intervention required an immediate CIA presence on the ground in Bosnia's shattered capital. In fact, according to my division chief, First Lady Hillary Clinton made the call that the CIA should open up its first ever station in Sarajevo.

In mid-1995, the Bosnian Serbs were shelling the once-picturesque city of Sarajevo around the clock from the surrounding hilltops, and random sniper fire made it impossible to walk down its cobblestone streets in safety. Just getting into the city, which was cut off and surrounded by hostile Serb forces, was next to impossible. But this was the reason I'd become a CIA operations officer. I loved the adventure, believed in the agency and its mission, and always jumped at the chance to return to my old stomping ground in the Balkans. Despite the obvious risks, I was honored to be named the CIA's first chief of station (COS) in Sarajevo.

On the other hand, what was I thinking? I was back in the United States, on a relaxed rotational assignment after two overseas tours. I relished my nine-to-five American routine and being "Mr. Mom" to the two most wonderful little girls on the planet. The thought of being away from my daughters for a month or more was beyond difficult. And I couldn't shake the haunting notion that this time I might not be as lucky as I'd been during previous assignments. This time I might not return to my daughters at all.

Still, something about the Balkans kept drawing me back, even though every time I traveled there I was repulsed by what I witnessed and couldn't wait to get back out again. This war—like others before and since—was wicked, both literally and, perhaps less understandably, in the Boston "cool" sense as well. But as one of the agency's few experienced Serbo-Croatian-speaking "Yugoslav hands," I also considered it my duty to return when called. At least that was how I rationalized the decision when my daughters asked me why I'd agreed to take the assignment.

I'd already served in Belgrade, witness to the breakup of Yugoslavia as it slid out of the Cold War and into civil war. The CIA tapped me to go into Croatia during the height of the war there in late 1991, to report on the first armed conflict in the heart of Europe since World War II. The agency dispatched me to the region again in 1992, to do some poking around the front lines in a then little-known place called Bosnia and Herzegovina. I'd also covered Kosovo, where events unfolded much as we forecast in the early 1990s.

What I didn't know when I accepted this latest mission was that the Bosnian Serb shelling and sniper fire would end up taking a back seat to an equally deadly but much more personalized threat to my security in Sarajevo.

✳ ✳ ✳

Prior to my temporary duty (TDY) assignment to Sarajevo, I was required to stop off at CIA headquarters in Langley, Virginia, to plan the operation's specifics and update my lapsed medical clearances. This "highest-priority" TDY to Sarajevo ended up being put on hold for several days until I'd jumped through all of the requisite medical, legal, and administrative hoops.

First, there was the mandatory physical exam. I'd managed to avoid mine for years, but this time there would be no exceptions. Apparently, the agency didn't want any *unhealthy* CIA officers getting themselves killed in Bosnia.

Then, I had to sign a waiver of responsibility, agreeing that I was going to Sarajevo of my own free will and would not hold the agency liable if my physical appearance was altered by an explosive device. (As you will see, lawyers have taken much of the fun out of being a CIA officer.)

Finally, I had to meet with a young CIA psychiatrist, who was tasked to determine whether I was psychologically fit to travel back to the war zone. A recent graduate from an Ivy League medical school, the attractive blond doctor tried to get a handle on my motivation.

"You must be either crazy or suicidal to want to go back there!" she declared, apparently oblivious to the nature of the agency's mission.

"If you knew my ex-wife the way I do," I countered, "you'd realize that my suicidal tendencies are perfectly normal."

This argument did the trick, since I obtained her official blessing (and her secure phone number) and thought I was finally on my way to Sarajevo.

I soon learned that no one at headquarters had a clue how I was supposed to infiltrate Sarajevo. So, I decided to travel to Split, Croatia, on my own and improvise from there. I knew the country and the language, and, besides, that approach had always worked before.

Meanwhile, my team, which was to have included several armed security escorts, had now dwindled down to two officers: myself and John Garcia (not his real name), a gregarious senior commo (communications) officer who'd already proved his mettle in hot spots like Somalia. John managed to get his hands on an encrypted briefcase satellite phone, and the two of us made travel arrangements to leave that night for Europe.

At Washington's Dulles airport, John's wife of ten years came to see him off. With tears in her eyes, she kissed him goodbye and begged me to bring him back alive. I smiled and promised he'd be back. I was hoping I wouldn't let her down.

John and I talked all night on the flight to Zurich and discovered that we had a lot in common. We'd both been born and raised in the American Southwest, loved Jerry Jeff Walker's *Viva Terlingua* album, and regularly craved real Mexican food. More importantly, we both had families who meant the world to us.

After arriving in Zurich, we killed time by strolling around the Old Town, then spent another sleepless night at the airport Hilton. The next day we flew across Italy to the balmy Adriatic coastal town of Split, Croatia, a hub of activity during the war.

In Split we met up with two US military special operators who drove over from Zagreb in a brand-new armored Jeep Cherokee. Over ice-cold Dalmatian *pivo* (beer) that night in the smoke-filled restaurant of the Communist-chic Hotel Split, we reviewed our plan for entering Sarajevo the next day. We thought we'd decrease our odds of being shot by inserting our vehicle into a UN convoy that was scheduled to bring relief supplies to the isolated city, by way of Mostar and the deadly Mount Igman road. Although we were now armed, our light weapons and armored Jeep would serve little defensive purpose against the antiaircraft guns the Serbs might use to attack us.

My own weapon, incidentally, was "illegal" in the eyes of the agency's lawyers, who explicitly forbade me to carry a gun in Sarajevo. Every living creature in Bosnia—not to mention a few dead ones—was armed to the teeth at the time. It was, after all, a chaotic, war-torn city. Saigon, 1995. Regardless, the agency's risk-averse bureaucrats decided they'd rather deal with a dead officer than chance having to explain why one of their own shot someone in a war zone.

Not surprisingly, one year later, when agency officers were serving side by side with thousands of American troops in newly pacified Bosnia, the lawyers mustered the courage to permit our officers to carry weapons. After all, by that time, the likelihood that a weapon would ever have to be used for anything other than plinking *pivo* bottles was about as low as their own tolerance for risk.

* * *

The final leg of our journey to Sarajevo began when we left Split in the early morning hours of July 10 for the sleepy farming village of Tarčin, on the Bosnian-controlled side of Mount Igman. Along the way up the mountain's dusty back, we heard artillery shells whistling by overhead. There was also sporadic small-arms and machine-gun fire. This was our first real taste of the live-fire zone we were about to enter.

On our long drive in, our secret military escorts (dressed in civilian clothing) were all business. It's what you'd expect from the best of the best. Heavily armed, they sat up front, and we sat in back. There wasn't a lot of chitchat other than to brief contingency plans (e.g., review the game plan in the event we were attacked).

I asked if they spoke any Serbo-Croatian. They did not. So, I taught them some useful phrases. *Dobar dan* ("Good day"). *Hvala* ("Thank you"). And *puši kurac*, which had them laughing for the rest of the ride. (Search it on Google.) My language skills also came in handy that day while I mediated checkpoint disputes between nervous Bosnian soldiers and the various nationalities who comprised the UN contingent, since they typically did not share a common language.

Not long after dark, the UN convoy began winding its way down the face of Mount Igman and into Sarajevo. Like the city itself, all vehicle lights were blacked out to avoid being targeted, and the drivers used night-vision goggles to see. It was pitch black under a quiet, cloudless summer sky. For a moment it struck me that the moon and stars shone just as brilliantly over Bosnia as they did in the tranquil Sonoran Desert.

We knew that the Serbs could kill us at any time. Racing down the bumpy mountain road in the dark, inches from the edge of a steep, rocky drop-off, was in itself risky. Within a few weeks of my trip, three American officials were killed on this very road while attempting a similar entry.

After sixteen hours and several close calls, we made it to the newly opened official compound, a renovated villa in the heart of Sarajevo. There the security officer, Mike, welcomed us by providing detailed guidance on when and when not to flush the villa's toilets. We understood why the water was rationed, but after our exhausting trip it took several explanations by the exasperated security officer before we were able to straighten out our (feigned) confusion over what constituted a flushable act.

Mike then led us to the downstairs laundry room, which would be our living and working quarters for the next month. Since there was nothing to eat, we tried to sleep on the dusty and bug-infested floor. After three nights with no sleep, one more couldn't hurt.

The next morning, we bid a grateful farewell to our quiet military colleagues. They returned to Zagreb via the same risky route, having safely delivered us to ground zero. I later heard their superior officer was not pleased that his new Jeep Cherokee required extensive repairs after the round trip over the brutal Mount Igman road.

My primary mission in Sarajevo was to provide intelligence on the military situation in Bosnia, and on Bosnian Serb Army (BSA) military targets and capabilities, in advance of the expected NATO intervention.

One month later, I learned of successful NATO air and missile attacks on dozens of BSA positions, including radar and antiaircraft sites, command centers, and communications facilities, whose locations I had pinpointed in July. I was heartened that my mission to Sarajevo contributed at least in a small way to shortening the duration of the cursed war.

Since I'd previously served in Belgrade, where I ran traditional Cold War "denied area" operations, I was also tasked to perform an operational survey to determine whether or not the CIA could securely handle agents inside Sarajevo, using denied area tradecraft. I quickly determined that we could *not* handle or meet assets inside Sarajevo, at least not during summer months. No matter where in Sarajevo you walked or drove, locals were not on the streets, because of the danger. Sarajevans remained indoors but typically were hanging out open windows and balconies to relieve boredom and be cooled by fresh air. It would be almost impossible to meet with someone on the street without the meeting being observed and reported by residents, who were already skittish.

Dead drops, which we used successfully in Soviet bloc and other denied area countries in order to avoid direct contact with agents, would also be problematic in Sarajevo. A dead drop is a classic means of "impersonal" tradecraft for the exchange of communications and other materials (money, microfilm, etc.) between agent and handler. For example, an agent might leave secret documents in a predetermined hollowed-out log for his handler to retrieve later. "Concealment devices" such as fake rocks are often used to disguise and protect the secret material. The people of Sarajevo were literally starving, so even a dead drop inside a rat carcass risked being retrieved by a hungry resident.

While in Sarajevo, I also covered the Serb capture of UN-declared "safe areas" Srebrenica and Žepa, which fell during my assignment there. Madeleine Albright, then US ambassador to the United Nations, was especially keen to know the number of Bosnians killed. When I reported that, according to my reliable Bosnian security service sources, between six thousand and eight thousand Bosnians were slaughtered by the Serbs during the initial takeover of Srebrenica, Washington was skeptical. After all, Srebrenica was a "safe area," and even the Serbs would not so flagrantly violate international law.

Of course, having recently honed their mass-murder skills, the Serbs did not permit any outsiders near their killing fields. All non-Serb witnesses were killed. Or so they thought.

As is always the case, one or two intended victims would play dead or otherwise use their wits, luck, and determination and manage to escape. In the early 1990s, the US government helped set up the Refugee Debriefing Center in Croatia to question these survivors and collect evidence for use by the future War Crimes Tribunal in The Hague.

Initially I tended to believe Serb assertions that the Bosnians exaggerated or fabricated their tales of Serb torture and murder. Sometimes they did. Over time, however, I became convinced of the veracity of the Bosnian Muslims' seemingly implausible claims. When two refugees would show up at different sites, relating identical details of a particularly ghoulish act committed by identified Bosnian Serbs in a particular village on a particular date, we knew it was impossible for them to coincidentally fabricate the same unique details.

To this day I am awed by the Serbs' evil creativity when devising methods of torture and humiliation for their Bosnian Muslim and Kosovo Albanian victims. A small sampling of their grisly crimes against humanity, which turn the stomach and are literally inconceivable for most civilized human beings, are discussed in chapter 3.

Incidentally, it was later confirmed that over forty thousand Bosnians were "ethnically cleansed" from Srebrenica, and at least eight thousand men and boys were indeed executed or gunned down by the Serbs as they attempted to flee through the woods. The fall of Srebrenica was the final straw for the Clinton administration, and it led to the long-overdue NATO intervention to stop the Serb rampage in Bosnia.

✷ ✷ ✷

My daily meetings, at the oft targeted Bosnian interior ministry building at ground zero in downtown Sarajevo, were intense. I would drive at high speed to and from the meetings to decrease my chances of being hit by sniper fire. Seat belts were left unused in Sarajevo in case you needed to make a hasty escape from your vehicle. Random artillery shells were a constant threat, shattering the calm just when you got comfortable with the quiet.

My Bosnian security service colleagues worked night and day in stressful wartime conditions. They prowled around the office like caged animals, desperately attempting to gather intelligence and counterintelligence on the encroaching BSA. Dressed in camouflage fatigues, they smoked foul-smelling Balkan cigarettes at all hours, as did their Serb and Croat enemies in other parts of the country.

As the new Croatian security service had done a few years earlier, the Bosnians pleaded with me to relay to Washington their request for US military intervention. Their arguments were compelling, but my job was to obtain as much intelligence as possible, without promising any action in return. At the same time, following headquarters' guidance, I always held out the possibility that eventually the United States might intervene militarily on the side of the Bosnians. Ironically, I found myself in a similar position when discussing "guaranteed US noninvolvement" with Ibrahim Rugova and the Kosovo democratic leadership in the early 1990s.

During my meetings I also attempted to learn more about the growing Iranian presence in Bosnia. After the war started in 1992, the Iranian government moved in to fill the vacuum left by the West's inaction and, with the collaboration of the Clinton administration, provide military support to the dying Bosnians.

Through my recent work with the head of the new Croatian security service, I knew that the White House was facilitating Iran's illegal arms shipments to Bosnia. Details of this shocking revelation are covered in chapter 2. In the Bosnians' view, America stood by and allowed the slaughter of innocents, whereas Iran provided real life-saving assistance.

Against this backdrop, it is easy to understand why the Bosnians made it clear to me that they considered the Iranians to be close allies. By the time I showed up in Sarajevo in July 1995, the war had been raging for three years. The Iranians were dug in, thanks in part to the secret influence of the White House. My Bosnian colleagues refused to discuss Iran's role in Bosnia with me, other than to say Iran was welcome there. Soviet-made cars bearing symbols of Iranian private relief organizations were omnipresent, and some were involved in conducting harassing surveillance of official US government vehicles. The Iranians considered Bosnia to be their "backyard," and the few Americans present were not welcome.

Besides Iran, so-called *muj* influence in Sarajevo was palpable. Foreign fighters with insurgent experience targeting the Soviets in Afghanistan traveled to Bosnia to fight alongside their Muslim brethren. Between battles with the Serbs, these mujahedeen wandered the empty streets of the city. Many married local women.

Prior to the Bosnian War, Usama bin Laden had been funding mujahedeen fighters in Afghanistan.[1] As had the CIA. But American refusal to directly intervene in Bosnia to protect the Bosnian Muslims from Serb slaughter convinced bin Laden that the United States did not care and was, in effect, complicit through its inaction. Al-Qaeda's current leader, Ayman al-Zawahiri, and 9/11 mastermind Khaled Sheikh Mohammad both visited Bosnia, and bin Laden himself was in Sarajevo in November 1994.[2] In addition to his opposition to the presence of "infidel" American troops on sacred Saudi soil, Bosnia, I believe, was another genesis of bin Laden's hatred for America, and 9/11. I'm not alone in that assessment.[3]

Although cognizant of the Iranian threat in Sarajevo, I, like most people, was more concerned with surviving the daily wartime hazards in the city. The Iranians were a threat, to be sure, but they were a secondary threat under the circumstances. So, when my counterpart "Marko," the head of the Bosnian security service, called me into a room occupied only by him and a tall, bearded Middle Eastern man in fatigues—and then dismissed me—I took note but was not overly concerned by the strange incident.

✳ ✳ ✳

The day after Marko "showcased" me to the Middle Easterner, I learned from an unimpeachable source that the bearded man was none other than the head of Iran's intelligence office in Sarajevo. My source allowed me to read an English translation of the Iranian's secret ops cable sent to his Ministry of Intelligence (MOIS) masters in Tehran. In his classified cable, the Iranian intelligence chief explained how he had tasked Marko to bring me into the office so that he could see the new CIA chief in the flesh. His physical description of me was accurate, although he incorrectly reported that I had a military background.

The MOIS chief wasn't just looking me over out of professional curiosity. I also learned that he was in fact planning an operation to kidnap, torture, interrogate, and kill me. Probably in that order.

It was nothing personal. In the Iranian's eyes, I was a high-payoff target of opportunity. It's not every day that a lone, enemy CIA officer shows up and declares himself in true name to a security service controlled by Iran. As *Los Angeles Times* journalist James Risen would later report, by July 1995 the Bosnian interior ministry was under the control of the Iranian intelligence service.[4]

After I learned of this very personalized threat to my life and most if not all of my limbs, my whole perception of danger in Sarajevo was turned upside down. I was now focused more on not being snatched off the streets than avoiding the random barrage of mortars and sniper fire. I vowed not to make it easy for the Iranians to take me. Since I was alone behind enemy lines, I knew that brains, not firepower, would be my only chance of survival in this situation.

My mind immediately flashed back to the horrific kidnapping, torture, and murder of my colleague William Buckley, our COS in Beirut, by Iranian-backed terrorists ten years earlier. A savage act of terror the CIA avenged over twenty years later when, according to the *Washington Post*, the CIA and Mossad killed Hezbollah mastermind Imad Mughniyeh with a targeted car bomb in Syria.[5] The headrest bomb vaporized Mughniyeh's head, and part of his face was found fifty yards away from his vehicle.[6] I knew from the Buckley case that a CIA officer captured by the Iranians would never be traded or released, since the MOIS would never allow their deadly hand to be exposed. Capture by Iran meant certain torture and death.

The next morning, I conferred, via a secure satellite phone, with my CIA superiors in Washington. We agreed that the prudent thing to do would be to get out of Sarajevo as quickly as possible. Just getting back out under "normal" wartime conditions without being killed by the Serbs would be challenge enough. But now I also had to come up with an exfiltration plan for getting John and myself out without falling into the hands of the Iranians or their Bosnian collaborators.

In devising my exfiltration plan, I had to consider what I knew and didn't know about the situation. I also had to plan my escape based on a worst-case scenario. I knew that the Iranians were planning an operation against me. I now knew that Marko and his Bosnian interior ministry colleagues followed orders given by the Iranian intelligence service. The Bosnians and Iranians both knew my vehicle and me by sight. They also knew the location of our villa and had our office and phones monitored.

There was only one immediate way out of Sarajevo, and that was back over the Mount Igman trail. Unfortunately, my "friends" in the Bosnian security service controlled all of the police and military checkpoints between Sarajevo and Tarčin.

I then learned that one of our villa's local Bosnian employees was a spy for the Bosnian service, and he too could report on my comings and goings. In a worst-case scenario, the Bosnians and Iranians would know when and how I planned to escape and would intercept me before I was able to leave Sarajevo. They had me covered from every angle.

I discussed the various exfiltration options with Washington via a secure satellite phone. I was heartened when Washington laid out several impressive exfil options of its own, including some that involved sending in US forces via helicopter to extract me. The future CIA and National Security Agency director, and highly respected, General Michael Hayden was J2 at US European Command at the time. Hayden would have been involved in any helicopter extractions from Bosnia.

After careful consideration, however, I rejected Washington's tempting proposals. Since there was no air traffic in the skies over Bosnia, a helicopter attempting to enter Sarajevo might draw fire from all sides. Moreover, the military's plans would require up to a week of preparation. I knew I had to get out as quickly and quietly as possible before the Iranians and Bosnians realized that I was on to them.

I decided that the best exfil plan was for us to go out on our own, in a high-speed two-vehicle convoy. Without hesitation, the villa's courageous security officer Mike and his heavily armed colleagues (including a plainclothes military specialist detailed to the office) agreed to escort us out. We could depart for Split the next night.

Washington was not pleased that I had rejected all of its options, but it ceded to my decision, since I was in the best position to assess the situation. I also conferred with John, who backed my decision as the one most likely to get us out alive.

Hoping for the best but preparing for the worst, we created fake ID cards for John and me, in the event the Bosnian police were alerted to detain us on our way out of town.

Just before our escape, though, I discovered that the Bosnian mole was planning on getting out of Sarajevo with our convoy. If he learned that I was joining the convoy, he could alert his masters and they'd be able to pull me out at a roadblock, fake ID or no fake ID.

We decided that once the Bosnian spy entered our escape vehicle, we would disarm him and not allow him to exit until we'd made it over Mount Igman. We didn't want to give him any opportunities to alert the Bosnian security service of my unscheduled departure.

The night before bugging out, I briefed the newly arrived senior-ranking civilian on the situation. We talked up on the flat, tiled roof of the villa, to ensure our conversation could not be electronically monitored. The glow from burning buildings, garbage dumpsters, and flares was the only thing illuminating the blacked-out city at night. The locals had a name for their eerie, incandescent sky: Sarajevo Red.

As I was wrapping up my briefing, tracer rounds began to whiz by, no more than ten feet above our heads.

"Isn't that a beautiful sight?" the senior civilian mused.

"No, it's a dangerous sight," I replied before ducking back downstairs.

We left the villa at 2:30 a.m., as planned, in an armored Toyota Land Cruiser. As we pulled out of the silent, darkened compound, I was alert to any signs of surveillance. The entire city was without power and blacked out, and there were no cars on the road. We made it through several Bosnian and UN checkpoints near Sarajevo's airport without incident and without any indications of surveillance. Our unarmed Bosnian spy was buckled in and not going anywhere.

Then, just as we prepared to ascend Mount Igman, we were delayed for two more nerve-wracking hours in the dark while incoming Bosnian Army traffic cleared the checkpoints. By the time we were permitted to proceed over Igman, the sun had begun to rise and with it the risk of attracting Serb antiaircraft fire on the exposed dirt road. Because of this peril, Mike considered heading back to the villa to try again the next night.

I wasn't keen on turning back. To do so would permit the Bosnian spy to report my attempted escape, which would likely prompt the bad guys to accelerate their move against me.

Luck was with us, however. That morning the city and mountain were shrouded in a light haze, so visibility was poor. The Serbs would have difficulty targeting us. Moreover, we knew the frequently inebriated BSA soldiers were least attentive just before daybreak.

We decided to make a run for it. We raced to the heavily sandbagged French Battalion on top of the mountain without drawing fire. Along the way, we sped past the smoldering hulks of several UN vehicles that had been hit by the Serbs just hours earlier.

Throughout our escape from Bosnian territory, we were extra alert with our weapons at the ready. If the Iranians made contact or gave chase, we were prepared to do battle with them. I made John promise that he'd shoot me before letting any bearded fanatics haul me off for one of their notorious torture sessions. I was dead serious. I did not want to meet the same unspeakable fate as Buckley.

Knowing that John would have a tough time explaining to CIA lawyers why shooting me was actually in my best interests, I was as pleased as he was that he did not have to make good on his promise.

After our safe arrival in Split, we bade farewell to fearless security officer Mike and his military colleague, as well as the now harmless Bosnian spy, and made our way by taxi to the airport. From the airport pay phone, I called our nervous colleagues in Washington (collect) to let them know that we had made it out alive. My headquarters friends were relieved that we were safe and sound. And I'm sure there were more than a few bureaucrats who breathed a sigh of relief at the thought of all the paperwork and explaining they *wouldn't* have to do, thanks to our successful exfiltration.

As the adrenaline ceased coursing through my system, I could not resist the urge to sleep. With my duffel bag as a pillow, I passed out for an hour on the floor of the bustling Split airport, soldiers and passengers stepping over and around me as I slept. John reacted with his usual aplomb, drinking warm Cokes and watching military relief flights land and take off as though nothing had happened. He woke me when our flight was called.

The next day in Vienna I briefed Director of Central Intelligence John Deutch on our Bosnian mission. In Vienna for a regional chiefs of station meeting, he'd been following our travails and was eager for a full report.

A few days later I gave a similar classified briefing to a US congressional intelligence committee in Washington.

Although these high-level briefings were perhaps the most dangerous aspect of our trip, I survived them unscathed and thankful to be alive.

* * *

After my escape from Sarajevo, I learned that Marko, the head of the Bosnian security service who had betrayed me to the Iranians, and the Iranian MOIS agent, who had betrayed the teachings of the Qur'an by planning to kill me, both died under bloody and mysterious circumstances inside Bosnia.

CHAPTER 2

CIA LEAK

On January 15, 1997, the *Los Angeles Times* published a front-page article by renowned national security correspondent James Risen, entitled "Bosnia Reportedly Told Iran of US Spy."[1] Although the article did not identify the spy by name, I was the CIA "agent" exposed to attack in 1995 because my Bosnian counterpart betrayed me to the head of the Iranian intelligence service in Sarajevo.

I was shocked when I read the *Times* article, since the details of my mission to and escape from Sarajevo were classified. While I felt relief that at least my name did not appear in the article, it was clear that someone inside the CIA had leaked classified information to Risen. Why? Apparently for geopolitical motives: to lay the groundwork for the United States to pressure Bosnia to expel the Ministry of Intelligence (MOIS), Iranian Revolutionary Guard Corps, and Quds Force operatives from the country. In fact, expulsion of the subversive Iranian agents was a precondition to finalizing the Dayton Accords, which finally brought peace to Bosnia.[2]

Curious about who'd leaked "my" story, I tracked down James Risen and had a pleasant telephone conversation with him.

"Mr. Risen, I'm the CIA officer who was betrayed by the Bosnians to Iran. Would you mind telling me who leaked my classified story to you? Just between us, of course."

"Yeah, right."

It was worth a shot.

I then reasoned that since my secret mission was now public knowledge, I should be able to secure approval from the CIA's Publications Review Board to publish my own (unclassified) version of what really transpired. Chapter 1 is the updated version of my 2001 magazine article about my Sarajevo adventure, entitled "Betrayal in the Balkans."[3]

Looking back, the irony of the situation is enough to make my head spin. This unique but true spy story sheds a bright light on a much broader issue: how presidents from both political parties ignore intelligence and make disastrous foreign policy decisions. Decisions that adversely impact millions of people, often for generations. Including spies like me who risk their lives collecting and reporting this intelligence in the first place.

To be clear, the CIA does not go out and collect secrets willy-nilly. The CIA only seeks information that directly addresses specific intelligence "requirements" or questions, which are generated by the White House and other key intelligence consumers in the US national security apparatus.

Why were deadly Iranian operatives in Bosnia in the first place? Not just physically located in the heart of Europe but officially welcomed and completely in control of the country's minister of interior and the head of its security service?

The first underlying reason is because the George H. W. Bush administration ignored CIA intelligence (including my own reporting) and refused to recognize objective reality and help manage the fait accompli, the breakup of Yugoslavia into independent states. The US government's unbending and Tito-esque 1991 policy of forced unity helped light the fuse on the Balkan powder keg.

Predictably, the following year, the Bush administration flip-flopped and reversed its original ill-fated policy. Now, the United States decided, the Serbs were the bad guys and we would only recognize the independent republics. These US policies not only created confusion, but they also enabled years of bloodshed. I'm not suggesting the United States is to blame for the civil war in Yugoslavia, but our ever-changing policies made things worse than they needed to be.

The war in Croatia had begun to heat up in March 1991, followed by Slovenia's brief but violent war of secession in late June and early July 1991. Secretary of State James Baker visited Belgrade that summer and urged all parties to reject the inevitable independence movements and maintain a unified Yugoslavia. The CIA knew his effort was in vain, since it was contrary to the will of the people. In fact, the CIA's October 1990 *National Intelligence Estimate* was "stunningly prescient," unambiguously predicting, "Yugoslavia will cease to function as a federal state within one year and will probably dissolve within two."[4]

The enormity of his ill-advised position did not seem to faze Secretary Baker, however. I still recall overhearing him, as he exited his suite at the recently opened Belgrade Hyatt, slowly drawl, "Anybody got a breath mint?"

In the summer of 1991, I met my sensitive Yugoslav agent during a trip to Greece so that I could debrief him in a relaxed and secure setting on the situation unfolding in Yugoslavia. My agent was himself a professional intelligence officer and one of the CIA's most valuable sources on Yugoslavia. Lengthy debriefings in the course of my multiple, long-term temporary duty assignments (TDYs) to Yugoslavia were impossible because of Yugoslav security service monitoring and surveillance of the both of us, although I was able to meet him occasionally for a "brief encounter" late at night on the streets of Belgrade. (I describe how these risky internal meetings were planned and conducted in chapter 17.)

Over several days, in a suite rented in alias at the luxurious St. George Lycabettus hotel in Athens, I spent hours discussing various scenarios with my agent. These productive debriefings were exhilarating, since I knew the reporting was anxiously awaited in Washington and was critical to help guide US policy during this historic crisis in progress.

Equally enjoyable was my brief escape from my TDY to dreary, Communist Belgrade. Athens was a chance to experience a lively, brightly colored environment and spectacular food. I took advantage of my time in Greece to buy several CDs by my new favorite musical artist, Italian pop star Eros Ramazzotti. I also relished my daily hikes up Mount Lycabettus and seeing the Acropolis for the first time with my own eyes.

Generally speaking, it's impossible to get unbiased information out of a Serb, Croat, Bosnian, or Kosovar, since they have all been effectively brainwashed since birth in their own cultures and identities. Ancient hatreds have been passed down for generations; they harbor (sometimes) legitimate grievances against each other, and in the end, they will convincingly spout their "tribe's" party line or latest conspiracy theory. They are typically intelligent and highly educated people, but in the end, they always revert to their roots.

I later witnessed a similarly troubling tribal phenomenon in Iraq, between Sunnis, Shi'ites, and Kurds. More on this in chapter 24.

My agent was different. He considered himself a true Yugoslav first and foremost, and he was also a seasoned professional who was able to separate fact and analysis from his own personal opinion. He knew his job, and he performed like a pro. He was an invaluable agent and source of intelligence for the CIA. Our policy makers were fortunate to have access to his information and analysis, which, in theory, should have guided them to making enlightened policy decisions.

The most pressing scenario for discussion in Athens was to predict as best we could how events would unfold in the various republics in light of clear American insistence on recognizing only a single, unified Yugoslavia. Slovenia made a clean break, but that was not surprising since there were few ethnic Serbs in Slovenia, and President Slobodan Milošević was not going to expend too much treasure, blood, or effort to keep Slovenia in the Yugoslav fold.

Croatia was another story, and everyone expected that war to be bloody and violent. Sadly, our expectations were regularly met or exceeded until that war ended four years later.

But in the summer of 1991, Bosnia was not really on anyone's radar, except for those of us paid to steal secrets and look into the future in Yugoslavia. Many people were familiar with Sarajevo—it had hosted the 1984 Winter Olympics. Those who lived in Yugoslavia viewed Sarajevo as a charming, multicultural city on the top of everyone's weekend getaway list. But most of the world (including most of the US government) knew little to nothing about Bosnia or how it fit into the scheme of things in volatile Yugoslavia. They were about to find out.

After our meetings concluded, flights from Athens to and over Yugoslavia were canceled for two days because of the war and threat to civil aviation. I was unable to return to Frankfurt prior to resuming my Belgrade TDY. I took advantage of this forced delay by relaxing at the Astir Palace Hotel in Vouliagmeni, on the "Athens Riviera" just south of the capital. I felt as if I'd won the lottery. The anonymity and freedom from surveillance along with the peaceful seaside setting were refreshing and rejuvenating. My handful of stress-free days on the Aegean Sea provided a much-needed calm before the storm.

When I finally made it back to Belgrade, I sat down in the station's tiny, cramped, windowless office to write my forecast of what we could likely expect in Yugoslavia in the coming months and years. These occasional "think pieces" reflecting a station's candid war zone analysis were called *Aardwolfs* and were different from typical nuts-and-bolts intelligence reports. Aardwolfs contained fact along with informed analysis and fore-casts, and they were a useful adjunct to normal station reporting.

I laid out in detail, based in large part on my agent debriefings in Athens, how I believed events would unfold in Bosnia, as well as the rest of Yugoslavia. Specifically, I predicted that the ethnically motivated blood-shed in Bosnia would be horrific and would overshadow that in Croatia. Mine was just one voice. CIA Balkan analysts generally made the same case, providing the Bush administration with highly reliable intelligence on what was happening and what to expect in Yugoslavia.

Unfortunately, Secretary Baker and the Bush administration refused to heed CIA reporting. Baker's declaration that the United States would only recognize a unified Yugoslavia essentially gave the green light to the Serbs to violently suppress the genuine and inevitable independence move-ments in Croatia and Bosnia. In my view, had the United States accepted the reality that these movements were irreversible regardless of our policy, we could have helped Yugoslavia to break apart in a much less violent way.

Once the Bosnian War was underway, the United States did nothing to intervene in the predictable Serb slaughter of Bosnian Muslims for three long years. Simultaneously, the US government imposed an arms embargo on the former Yugoslavia, which only disadvantaged the Bosnians. The aggressor Bosnian Serbs were unaffected by the embargo, since they were able to obtain as many locally manufactured weapons as they desired from the Serb-dominated Yugoslav People's Army.

Like the rest of the world watching the Bosnian nightmare on the nightly news, the new Clinton administration was fully cognizant of the suffering of the Bosnian people. Bosnia was in this desperate situation in part because of US policy, and Bosnians were hoping and praying for a savior.

That savior turned out to be Iran, who recognized this unprecedented opportunity to gain a foothold in Europe under the guise of assisting des-perate, fellow Muslims.

Shi'ite Iran provided some humanitarian aid, but most of its support to the Sunni Bosnian government was lethal in nature. Iran sent Bosnia tons of arms, as well as mercenaries and military trainers. In the fall of 1992, during one of my TDYs to Zagreb, the Croatian government inter-cepted an embargo-busting Iranian 747 "relief" flight hauling weapons, hired killers, and a few samovars to Bosnia.

But later, in July 1994, I learned that Peter Galbraith, the US ambassador to Croatia, had quietly suggested to Croatian president Franjo Tudjman that he should permit Iranian arms shipments to transit Croatia en route to Bosnia. This suggestion violated official US policy, as well as the UN arms embargo on the whole of the former Yugoslavia, but since the orders had apparently come from President Clinton and National Security Adviser Anthony Lake, Galbraith complied in implementing this secret and arguably illegal policy.

I inadvertently found out about this secret order from my principal contact in Zagreb, who was then head of the new Croatian security service. A philosophy major in college, "Ivan" was a quiet, mousy, sad-eyed "bookworm" who mumbled so softly when he spoke that I had to lean in to within inches of his face in order to understand him. This was especially challenging if our meeting was held in a noisy, smoke-filled Zagreb restaurant or when driving in a car.

Our conversations were in Croatian, which is nearly but not quite identical to Serbian, which I spoke fluently. When Ivan became head of the security service, he automatically became a general in the Croatian Army, so the professorial Ivan was typically and incongruously attired in a military uniform. He was bright and capable, and always kind and hospitable to me (as were all of his Croatian security service colleagues), but it struck me that if ever there was a fish out of water, it was General Ivan.

During one meeting in Zagreb in the summer of 1994, when I was there TDY for a few weeks, Ivan dropped a bombshell. He trusted me—I was his first CIA contact when we established our first official relationship during the war. The CIA also educated the new Croatian service in how to operate a security service in a democracy, a novel concept for the former Communist and generally authoritarian Croatians.

"H. K., there's something I need to tell you," Ivan whispered in Croatian one night during a car meeting. "Remember how we worked together to intercept that Iranian arms shipment? Well, Ambassador Galbraith just told our president [Franjo Tudjman] that Croatia should now quietly permit Iranian arms shipments to pass through our country to Bosnia, undisturbed."

"Ivan," I said, "I believe there must be some misunderstanding. Our ambassador would never recommend a policy that was not only illegal, but idiotic. Is it possible President Tudjman misunderstood?"

"No, H. K. There was no misunderstanding. Believe me, this is what Galbraith told the president. What should we do? Should we permit Iranian weapons shipments to continue on to Bosnia?"

"Uh, I'll have to get back to you on that, Ivan."

My mind was racing. What should I do? It is not the job of CIA officers to report on the activities of other US officials. But this was potentially illegal activity.

I did not immediately report it in official channels, but I shared it with my colleague when he returned to Zagreb to relieve me a few days later. It fell to him to deal with the matter in official channels, and with the local aftermath. I did not envy him, and I heard afterward that CIA-Galbraith relations in Croatia were soured for a very long time as a result. In fact, according to a subsequent US congressional investigation into Iranian arms shipments to Bosnia, Galbraith later improperly retaliated against the CIA for quite properly unmasking the harebrained scheme.[5]

My understanding was that only three American officials (besides me) knew of this secret policy: President Clinton, National Security Adviser Anthony Lake, and Galbraith. Lake's subsequent nomination to be CIA director was derailed at least in part because of his involvement in this ill-conceived policy.

At the time, several moderate, pro-US governments (like Turkey and Saudi Arabia) had indicated a willingness to provide arms to the Bosnians. While this would strike some as duplicitous—we impose an arms embargo and then violate it with arms shipments—there were compelling humanitarian reasons to arm the Bosnians. Common sense would dictate that *any* country would be preferable to Iran in this situation. Yet the Clinton administration, for reasons that are still not credible, decided that Iran was to be the supplier of arms and influence in Bosnia.

By the time I showed up in war-torn Sarajevo in July 1995 to make initial contact with the Bosnian security service, two US administrations—one Republican and one Democrat—had ignored my intelligence and made disastrous policy decisions, which directly led to the malignant Iranian influence and my brush with death in Bosnia. After which the CIA leaked classified information to James Risen about Bosnia's betrayal of me to the Iranians, in order to pressure Bosnia to kick out the Iranians. Dizzy yet?

* * *

What did James Risen's article about my Sarajevo adventure miss or simply get wrong? Note that this was through no fault of his own, since he relied on his not entirely reliable CIA source(s) for the secret details of the story.

For starters, the CIA didn't "pull me out" of Sarajevo. As revealed in chapter 1, I rejected the CIA's recommended options and exfiltrated Bosnia on my own, with the help of my brave American colleagues.

The CIA feigned surprise that Iran had this kind of influence over the Bosnian security service. This should not have been a surprise to anyone paying attention. We enabled and ignored the Serb slaughter of Bosnian Muslims for three years, and then we facilitated, rather than obstructed, Iranian influence in Bosnia. It would have been surprising if this had *not* been the outcome.

Marko, the head of the Bosnian security service, did not just provide my identity to the Iranians. Obeying Iranian tasking, he set me up and "introduced" me to the head of the Iranian intelligence service in a private, three-way meeting in a small room in the Ministry of Interior. After which the Iranian MOIS chief wrote up his detailed description of me and his ops plan for kidnapping and interrogating me, along with other measures. Fortunately, I was able to read what he had planned for me and exfiltrate Sarajevo before he could execute his plan. And me.

The good news is the US government made removal of the Iranians and Bosnian interior minister (and Iranian agent) Bakir Alispahić a condition to the Dayton peace accords. In this sense, my close brush with death was not for nothing and may have actually contributed to the eventual life-saving peace accord.

Ironically, President Clinton—who had enabled Iranian influence in Bosnia—had to certify that Bosnia had expelled all Iranians before Congress would approve funding to train the Bosnian Army.

Two consecutive White Houses didn't just ignore the CIA, but they ignored reporting from this specific CIA officer. And because they ignored my intelligence, I almost paid the ultimate price. When US policy makers ignore intelligence, it's not just an academic question. There are real consequences, for millions of people and, in this case, for me personally.

CHAPTER 3

SREBRENICA MADNESS

Y ou are about to read a fictional but realistic cable exchange between a lone CIA operations officer, behind enemy lines in Sarajevo, and CIA headquarters, in the wake of the horrific Srebrenica massacre of July 1995. The exchange is based in part on actual secure satellite phone communications I had with CIA headquarters during my TDY to Sarajevo before, during, and after the fall of Srebrenica, and also on other actual cable exchanges throughout my CIA career. I reported on the Srebrenica massacre from Sarajevo, relying on Bosnian sources. "Cables" are what the CIA calls secret, encrypted "emails" between/among field stations and CIA headquarters. The CIA has utilized cables since long before the internet and email were available to ordinary civilians.

I do not possess and cannot publish actual CIA cables, but I've created this exchange for two reasons. One, the first cable's reported details of what transpired at Srebrenica are largely factual and not widely known or remembered by the public. This will serve as a reminder and shed some unpleasant light on the worst atrocity committed in Europe since World War II. (For those readers who want a visual reminder, a New Zealand–based Bosnian rapper known as Genocide captured the horror in a music video called "Srebrenica—Never Again.") Two, the cable exchange is realistic, in form and in substance, and illuminates the bureaucratic madness that often accompanies covert operations of historic importance. Sure, you may be risking your life in a war zone to report critical intelligence to Washington, but you'll need to go back and get a receipt if you want reimbursement for the black-market gasoline you purchased from a roadside vendor en route to the killing fields.

What follows, then, are the two cables.

The first cable is from the chief of station (COS) in Sarajevo to CIA headquarters, reporting on the Srebrenica massacre. The "tear line" is the intelligence portion of the cable. The cable also includes operational details that are not part of the intelligence report, explaining how, when, and from whom the COS obtained the intelligence. Finally, the cable includes administrative details, discussing what money was spent and why.

The second cable is headquarters' response to the COS's cable.

Welcome to my world!

S E C R E T

DATE: 19 JULY 1995 2347 ZULU

TO: IMMEDIATE DIRECTOR.

CITE: SARAJEVO 1813

WNINTEL INTEL OOTRIBE

SUBJECT: SITREP—MASSACRE AT SREBRENICA

REFS: A. DIRECTOR 74598
      B. SARAJEVO 1812

1. ON 8 JULY, FOLLOWING THREE-HOUR SDR TO CONFIRM NO SURVEILLANCE, COS CLARKE DROVE STERILE OPS VEHICLE FROM SARAJEVO TO SREBRENICA, TO COVER ANTICIPATED BOSNIAN SERB ARMY (BSA) ATTACK ON THE U.N.-DECLARED "SAFE HAVEN." COS WAS ON THE GROUND IN SREBRENICA FROM 8–18 JULY 1995, UNDER IRISH PHOTOJOURNALIST COVER. COS OBSERVED EVENTS DESCRIBED BELOW, OR OBTAINED INFO FROM U.N., BOSNIAN SERB AND BOSNIAN MUSLIM SOLDIERS, EYEWITNESSES AND SURVIVORS. COS RETURNED SAFELY TO SARAJEVO ON 18 JULY BY INSERTING HIS VEHICLE INTO MILE-LONG CONVOY OF RETREATING DUTCH U.N. SOLDIERS.

2. FOLLOWING IS TEAR LINE REPORT ON FALL OF SREBRENICA.

------------------------TEAR LINE------------------------

1. ON 8 JULY 1995, BOSNIAN SERB ARMY (BSA) GEN. RATKO MLADIC BEGAN FINAL ASSAULT ON U.N. SAFE HAVEN OF SRE-BRENICA, WITH MORTAR, ROCKET, AND ARTILLERY ATTACKS AGAINST THE REFUGEES. ON 10 JULY, BSA FORCES OVERRAN SEVERAL U.N. POSTS SURROUNDING THE ENCLAVE, AND TOOK HOSTAGE SEVERAL DOZEN DUTCH U.N. SOLDIERS. NATO BOMBED ONE BSA TANK, AFTER WHICH GEN. MLADIC IMMEDIATELY THREAT-ENED TO KILL ALL U.N. HOSTAGES. ACCORDING TO A DUTCH U.N.

OFFICER, THE FRENCH COMMANDER OF U.N. FORCES, GEN. BERNARD JANVIER, MADE A SECRET AGREEMENT WITH GEN. MLADIC TO STOP NATO AIR STRIKES AGAINST THE SERBS, IN EXCHANGE FOR SERB RELEASE OF U.N. PEACEKEEPER HOSTAGES. BY 13 JULY, THE BSA HAD KILLED OR "ETHNICALLY CLEANSED" APPROXIMATELY 50,000 REFUGEES FROM SREBRENICA AND NEARBY POTOCARI.

2. ON 12 JULY, GEN. MLADIC ENTERED SREBRENICA AND POTOCARI AS BSA FORCES SEIZED CONTROL OF THE ENCLAVE. ACCOMPANIED BY A TV CREW, HE ADDRESSED A GROUP OF PANICKY MUSLIM REFUGEES. SWAGGERING IN FRONT OF THE CAMERAS, MLADIC PATTED A YOUNG BOY ON THE HEAD AND ASSURED THE CROWD, "DO NOT BE AFRAID, NO ONE WILL DO YOU ANY HARM." AFTER THE CAMERAS WERE TURNED OFF, MLADIC PERSONALLY OVERSAW THE ENSUING HORROR. A COMMON THREAD THROUGHOUT THE SO-CALLED ETHNIC CLEANSING OPERATION WAS GEN. MLADIC'S SOOTHING WORDS TO THE REFUGEES JUST PRIOR TO BSA COMMISSION OF ATROCITIES AND/OR EXECUTIONS.

3. MLADIC DIRECTED THE NAZI-LIKE SELECTION PROCESS THAT BEGAN ON 12 JULY. SERB SOLDIERS SEPARATED MEN AND BOYS FROM WOMEN AND CHILDREN, WHILE U.N. SOLDIERS WATCHED. THE SELECTION PROCESS WAS CARRIED OUT IN ALMOST COMPLETE SILENCE, SAVE FOR THE OCCASIONAL SHOUTS OF BSA SOLDIERS ORDERING MEN AND BOYS OUT OF THE LINES THEY HAD BEEN FORCED TO STAND IN. BSA TRANSPORTED REFUGEES IN BUSES AND TRUCKS TO THE FRONT LINES, THEN FORCED THEM TO CROSS MINEFIELDS AND WALK FOR DAYS TO THE MUSLIM CITY OF TUZLA. THIS MASS EXODUS OF REFUGEES TOOK PLACE FOR SEVERAL DAYS.

4. THE SERBS DROVE THE MEN AND BOYS WHO REMAINED IN SREBRENICA TO NEARBY WAREHOUSES AND SOCCER STADIUMS AND EXECUTED THEM. ASSEMBLY/EXECUTION POINTS INCLUDE HANGARS IN BRATUNAC AND KRAVICA; SOCCER FIELDS IN KASABA, KONJEVIC POLJE, KRAVICA, AND VLASENICA; A SCHOOL IN KARAKAJ; A MEADOW BEHIND THE BUS STATION IN SANDICI; AND OTHER FIELDS ALONG THE BRATUNAC-MILICI ROAD.

5. SERB SOLDIERS WERE FREQUENTLY INEBRIATED WHILE THEY TAUNTED, ABUSED, ROBBED, RAPED, TORTURED, AND MURDERED THEIR VICTIMS. FOLLOWING ARE SPECIFIC EXAMPLES:

-- BSA SOLDIERS ROUNDED UP ABOUT 1000 REFUGEES AND FORCED THEM INTO A LARGE INDUSTRIAL HANGAR AT KRAVICA. SERBS OPENED FIRE THROUGH THE OPENINGS IN THE HANGAR, KILLING MOST OF THOSE INSIDE.

-- ON 13 OR 14 JULY, BSA PACKED APPROXIMATELY 2000 MEN AND BOYS INTO CLASSROOMS AND A GYMNASIUM AT KARAKAJ. BSA TOOK PRISONERS OUT BLINDFOLDED TO TWO FIELDS, SEPARATED BY A ROW OF TREES, AND EXECUTED THEM. KILLING FIELDS ARE LOCATED TEN MINUTES FROM THE GYM, NEAR THE RAILROAD TRACKS. BSA TOOK OTHERS OUT IN GROUPS OF 20-30 AND EXECUTED THEM NEAR A WASTE DUMP NEAR THE ALUMINUM OXIDE FACTORY. TWO MEN WHO SURVIVED AND ESCAPED TOLD COS THAT THEY HEARD SHOOTING ALL NIGHT LONG. THE NEXT DAY, THEY SAW A BULLDOZER LOADING DEAD BODIES ONTO TRUCKS THAT WERE DRIVEN AWAY. A DIFFERENT SURVIVOR SAW GEN. MLADIC AT THE EXECUTION SITE NEAR THE RAILROAD TRACKS.

-- SERBS ROUNDED UP ONE GROUP OF APPROXIMATELY 300 ELDERLY AND INFIRM MUSLIM MEN AND EXECUTED THEM.

-- SERBS CHOPPED OFF VICTIMS' NOSES, LIPS, AND EARS, AND OFTEN SLIT VICTIMS' THROATS. MANY BOSNIAN MUSLIMS REPORTEDLY COMMITTED SUICIDE IN ORDER TO AVOID THIS FATE.

-- A BSA SOLDIER APPROACHED A WOMAN AND ASKED THE SEX OF HER BABY. WHEN SHE SAID HE WAS A BOY, THE SOLDIER KILLED THE BABY WITH A KNIFE. ANOTHER WOMAN WAS STRUGGLING TO GET ON A BUS WHEN A BSA SOLDIER ASKED HER WHY HER BABY WAS CRYING. SHE SAID THE BABY WAS HUNGRY. THE BSA SOLDIER SAID, "WELL, HE WON'T BE HUNGRY ANYMORE," AND SLIT THE BABY'S THROAT.

-- BSA SOLDIERS FORCED AN ELDERLY MAN TO CUT OPEN A BOY'S STOMACH AND EAT PART OF HIS INTERNAL ORGANS.

-- A NAKED, BRUISED TEENAGE GIRL BOARDED A BUS, THE VICTIM OF MULTIPLE RAPES. SHE LATER HANGED HERSELF FROM A TREE WITH STRIPS OF A BLANKET. ONE FATHER HUNG HIMSELF RATHER THAN WITNESS WHAT THE SERBS WOULD DO TO HIS THREE DAUGHTERS.

-- THERE WERE NUMEROUS REPORTS OF SERBS DRAGGING WOMEN AWAY AND RAPING THEM. ONE YOUNG MOTHER OF THREE WHO WAS RAPED SAID THAT THIS WAS THE SECOND TIME SERB SOLDIERS HAD RAPED HER. THE FIRST TIME THE SERBS RAPED HER AT BRCKO, IN FRONT OF HER CHILDREN. AFTER RAPING HER MULTIPLE TIMES, THE SERBS URINATED INTO HER CHILDREN'S MOUTHS.

(FIELD COMMENT: THE USE OF RAPE AS AN INSTRUMENT OF TERROR HAS BEEN OFFICIAL POLICY OF BOSNIAN SERB LEADERS RADOVAN KARADZIC AND MLADIC SINCE THE START OF THE WAR. BOSNIAN SERBS SET UP "RAPE CENTERS" WHERE SYSTEMATIC RAPES OF MUSLIM WOMEN TOOK PLACE. THERE ARE REPORTEDLY THOUSANDS OF YOUNG BOSNIAN WOMEN AND GIRLS NOW SUFFERING SEVERE PSYCHOLOGICAL AND GYNECOLOGICAL PROBLEMS.)

-- BSA SOLDIERS IN STOLEN U.N. UNIFORMS AND VEHICLES TRICKED AT LEAST ONE GROUP OF REFUGEES TO COME OUT OF HIDING IN THE WOODS. THE SOLDIERS THEN LINED UP THE REFUGEES AND MACHINE-GUNNED THEM TO DEATH.

-- NEAR THE VILLAGE OF MECES, BSA USED AN EXCAVATOR TO DIG A LARGE PIT. SERBS ORDERED APPROXIMATELY 260 MUSLIMS INTO THE PIT AND BURIED THEM ALIVE.

-- THERE WERE SEVERAL UNCONFIRMED REPORTS THAT THE BSA USED CHEMICAL WEAPONS AGAINST THE REFUGEES, SOME OF WHOM SAID THE AIR SMELLED OF ROSES AND PEOPLE ACTED AS THOUGH THEY WERE DRUGGED. (FIELD COMMENT: THE YUGOSLAV ARMY (JNA) IS KNOWN TO HAVE AN INCAPACITATING AGENT CALLED "BZ," WHICH MAY HAVE BEEN USED IN BOSNIA.)

6. SEVERAL WITNESSES REPORTED ON GEN. MLADIC'S DIRECT INVOLVEMENT IN THE EVENTS AT SREBRENICA. ONE WITNESS OVERHEARD MLADIC SAY TO A COLLEAGUE, AS HE SURVEYED THE SCENE, "THERE ARE SO MANY (MUSLIMS), IT IS GOING TO BE A 'GOZBA' (LONG, DELECTABLE FEAST). THERE WILL BE BLOOD UP TO YOUR KNEES." ANOTHER WITNESS OBSERVED MLADIC NODDING AT THE WOMEN IN THE CROWD, SAYING TO HIS TROOPS, "BEAUTIFUL, KEEP THE GOOD ONES OVER THERE. ENJOY THEM."

7. (FIELD COMMENT: IN COS'S ESTIMATION, GEN. MLADIC AND HIS MEN KILLED BETWEEN 6000–8000 OF SREBRENICA'S UNARMED REFUGEES AND SOLDIERS, AND DROVE THE REMAINING 30–50,000 REFUGEES FROM THE AREA. ASIDE FROM OBVIOUS HUMANITARIAN IMPLICATIONS, GEN. MLADIC HAS NOW SUCCEEDED IN "ETHNICALLY CLEANSING" MAJORITY OF EASTERN BOSNIA, OPENING UP AN ALL-SERB CORRIDOR BETWEEN BOSNIA AND SERBIA/YUGOSLAVIA. COS BELIEVES GEN. MLADIC PLANS TO MILITARILY OVERRUN THE OTHER TWO REMAINING U.N. "SAFE AREAS" OF ZEPA AND GORAZDE IN THE COMING WEEKS. IF MLADIC SUCCEEDS IN "CLEANSING" THESE REMAINING TWO MUSLIM ENCLAVES—AND UNLESS NATO INTERVENES, HE WILL SUCCEED—COS BELIEVES MLADIC WILL THEN MOVE AGAINST HIS ULTIMATE OBJECTIVE: THE CAPITAL CITY OF SARAJEVO. ACCORDING TO REPORTING PROVIDED BY AN ADVANCED STATION DEVELOPMENTAL, THE BOSNIAN SECURITY SERVICE IN SARAJEVO SHARES COS'S ASSESSMENT OF BSA'S PLANS AND INTENTIONS.)

------------------------TEAR LINE------------------------

3. OOTRIBE/1 (T/1) IS ADVANCED STATION DEVELOPMENTAL IN PARA 7 FIELD COMMENT.

4. COS WILL REPORT WITNESSES'/SOURCES' NAMES AND BIO DATA SEPARATELY. COS WILL POUCH DATED/CAPTIONED PHOTOGRAPHS FOR HQS ANALYSIS AND FOR POSSIBLE FUTURE USE AS EVIDENCE IN WAR CRIMES TRIBUNAL AT THE HAGUE. COS CAUTIONS HQS IN ADVANCE THAT PHOTOS DEPICT HIGHLY DISTURBING, GRUESOME SCENES AND SHOULD NOT BE VIEWED BY THE SQUEAMISH.

5. STATION COMMENT: COS CONSIDERS HIMSELF A RATHER SEASONED "WAR CORRESPONDENT," HAVING COVERED WARS IN NICARAGUA, CROATIA, AND BOSNIA. HOWEVER, IF COS HAD NOT PERSONALLY WITNESSED AND PHOTOGRAPHED THE HELLISH SCENES THAT TRANSPIRED AT SREBRENICA OVER PAST SEVERAL DAYS, HE WOULD NOT HAVE BELIEVED HUMAN BEINGS CAPABLE OF CONCEIVING, MUCH LESS CARRYING OUT, SUCH MONSTROUS ACTS. COS BELIEVES HISTORY WILL RECORD THE MASSACRE AT SREBRENICA AS THE MOST BARBARIC ACT OF GENOCIDE IN EUROPE SINCE WWII.

6. ADMIN: COS INCURRED THE FOLLOWING REIMBURSABLE EXPENSES DURING HIS 8–18 JULY 1995 TDY TO SREBRENICA AREA:

-- PER DIEM: SINCE COS SLEPT IN HIS CAR AND ATE U.N.-SUPPLIED RATIONS, HE INCURRED NO FOOD OR LODGING EXPENSES.

-- GASOLINE: $250. NO RECEIPTS. PURCHASED ON BLACK MARKET.

-- FACILITATION PAYMENTS: $1000. NO RECEIPTS. PAID TO BOSNIAN AND SERB GUARDS AT ROADBLOCKS.

-- ONE (1) SHEEP: $50. PAID BY COS TO BSA SOLDIER WHO WAS ABOUT TO SHOOT THE SHEEP. COS RETURNED SHEEP TO RIGHTFUL OWNERS, A HUNGRY GROUP OF REFUGEES. NO RECEIPT.

-- LICENSE PLATES: $25. PAID TO ENTERPRISING YOUNG FACILITATOR IN SARAJEVO. COS REQUIRED TAGS FOR TRAVEL INTO BSA-HELD TERRITORY. NO RECEIPT.

-- 7.65MM PISTOL (USED) WITH AMMO: $50. PAID TO BSA SOLDIER AFTER COS'S BORROWED PPK WAS CONFISCATED AT GUNPOINT DURING STOP AT BSA ROADBLOCK NEAR SREBRENICA. NO RECEIPT.

-- PHOTOJOURNALIST VEST (BANANA REPUBLIC): $75. RECEIPT ATTACHED.

-- NY YANKEES BASEBALL CAP: $18. RECEIPT ATTACHED.

7. FILE: SREBRENICA MASSACRE; OOTRIBE/1.

S E C R E T

S E C R E T

DATE: 20 JULY 1995 2137 ZULU

TO: IMMEDIATE SARAJEVO.

CITE: DIRECTOR 78465

WNINTEL INTEL OOTRIBE

SUBJECT: SITREP—MASSACRE AT SREBRENICA

REF: SARAJEVO 1813

1. HQS COMMENDS COS CLARKE FOR REF DETAILED ACCOUNT OF
EVENTS AT SREBRENICA. FYI, YOUR REPORT WAS PASSED INFOR-
MALLY TO WHITE HOUSE, PENTAGON, AND NATIONAL SECURITY
COUNCIL. INITIAL FEEDBACK INDICATES WASHINGTON ANALYSTS
ARE SKEPTICAL BSA COULD HAVE KILLED AS MANY AS 8000 REFU-
GEES OVER COURSE OF A FEW DAYS, AS REPORTED REF. SUCH A
FEAT WOULD REQUIRE AROUND-THE-CLOCK MASSACRES OF LARGE
GROUPS OF PEOPLE. WE SUSPECT AT LEAST SOME OF COS'S
MUSLIM SOURCES EXAGGERATED EXTENT OF KILLING IN PART TO
INFLUENCE U.S. POLICY AND COMPEL NATO INTERVENTION.

2. OVERHEAD IMAGERY TAKEN OVER EASTERN BOSNIA IN
LAST FEW DAYS IS STILL BEING ANALYZED. STATE DEPART-
MENT REPORTING FROM EMBASSY SARAJEVO SUGGESTS U.N. WAS
TAKEN BY SURPRISE BUT DID ADMIRABLE JOB OF FACILITATING
ADMITTEDLY UNPLEASANT EVACUATION OF REFUGEES FROM SAFE
HAVEN OF SREBRENICA. EMBASSY ALSO PROVIDED TRANSLATION
OF RADIO PALE BROADCAST THAT CHARACTERIZED THE SREBRENICA
INCIDENT AS "NECESSARY TO EXPEL ARMED TERRORISTS AND TO
SAFELY EVACUATE WOMEN AND CHILDREN FROM WAR ZONE." WHILE
HQS SINCERELY APPRECIATES COS'S EFFORTS, UNFORTUNATELY
AT THIS TIME WE CANNOT DISSEM REF INTEL REPORT SINCE IT
DOES NOT TRACK WITH WHAT HQS AND OTHER COMMUNITY ANALYSTS
ARE REPORTING.

3. REGARDING COS'S USE OF IRISH PHOTOJOURNALIST COVER TO ENTER SREBRENICA: HQS IS PUZZLED AS TO WHY COS WOULD KNOWINGLY VIOLATE LONG-STANDING AGENCY PROHIBITION AGAINST USE OF JOURNALIST COVER. GIVEN EXIGENCIES OF SITUATION, IN THIS CASE WE PLAN TO SEEK DDO APPROVALS FOR A RETROACTIVE WAIVER OF PROHIBITION. IN FUTURE, HOWEVER, COS WILL RISK DISCIPLINARY ACTION, INCLUDING TERMINATION OF EMPLOYMENT, IF HE REPEATS THIS MISTAKE.

4. RE ADMIN EXPENSES REPORTED REF PARA 6, FOLLOWING ARE HQS COMMENTS:

-- PER DIEM: HQS REGULATIONS REQUIRE THAT COS SUBMIT PER DIEM CLAIM, EVEN IF NO FOOD AND LODGING EXPENSES WERE INCURRED. PLS RESUBMIT.

-- GASOLINE: HQS CANNOT REIMBURSE COS FOR THIS EXPENSE SINCE NO RECEIPT WAS OBTAINED.

-- FACILITATION PAYMENTS: HQS CANNOT REIMBURSE COS FOR THIS EXPENSE SINCE NO RECEIPT WAS OBTAINED.

-- ONE (1) SHEEP: ALTHOUGH THE EXPENSE WAS UNDER $75 AND NO RECEIPT IS REQUIRED, HQS MUST NONETHELESS DISALLOW THIS EXPENSE. HQS DEEMS THE PURCHASE OF THE SHEEP PURELY DISCRETIONARY ON COS'S PART, AND NOT ESSENTIAL TO COS'S COVER OR MISSION.

-- LICENSE PLATES: IF COS IS UNABLE TO RETURN THE LICENSE PLATES TO REF A FACILITATOR FOR A FULL OR PARTIAL $25 REFUND, HQS WILL REIMBURSE THE UNREFUNDED PORTION OF THIS EXPENSE. NO RECEIPT REQUIRED AS UNDER $75.

-- 7.65MM PISTOL (USED) WITH AMMO: HQS WAS CHAGRINED TO LEARN OF COS'S PURCHASE. COS IS FULLY AWARE OF HQS PROHIBITION AGAINST AGENCY PERSONNEL CARRYING WEAPONS IN BOSNIA. HQS REQUESTS COS DESTROY REF WEAPON AND CERTIFY SAID DESTRUCTION IN WRITING. COS WILL HAVE A LETTER OF REPRIMAND PLACED IN HIS PERSONNEL FILE, SINCE HE WAS

WARNED ABOUT THIS IN A RECENT STU-III CALL AND IN CABLE TRAFFIC. REIMBURSEMENT DISALLOWED.

-- PHOTOJOURNALIST VEST: UPON RECEIPT OF COS CERTIFI-CATION THAT HE WILL NOT WEAR PHOTOJOURNALIST VEST EXCEPT WHILE PERFORMING OFFICIAL DUTIES, HQS WILL REIMBURSE THIS EXPENSE.

-- NY YANKEES BASEBALL CAP: PLS SEE COMMENTS ON VEST.

5. FILE: SREBRENICA MASSACRE.

S E C R E T

The following legend is to help the reader decipher some of the terms used in these realistic CIA cables:

"ZULU" is Greenwich Mean Time.

"IMMEDIATE" means the cable is of high priority; lower levels of precedence include "ROUTINE" and "PRIORITY." There are higher levels of precedence as well.

"DIRECTOR" is CIA headquarters.

"CITE" means "from," where the cable originated (in this case, Sarajevo Station).

"WNINTEL," et al., are internal "slugs" or key words used to route the cable to the correct recipients.

"SITREP" means "situation report."

"REFS" are cables that were sent previously and that relate directly to the cable in question.

"SDR" is "surveillance detection route," an elaborate, preplanned route run by a case officer to ensure (s)he is not under surveillance before performing an operational act, such as meeting with an agent.

"COS" is the chief of station, the CIA's highest-ranking employee in-country.

"CLARKE" is the pseudonym of the COS. CIA employees do not use true names in cable traffic. They are assigned randomly generated pseudonyms that are used throughout their careers in cable traffic.

"00TRIBE/1" is a cryptonym used in lieu of true name to identify a particular foreign agent, or in this case an "advanced developmental" (someone who is not yet a formal agent but is taking steps in that direction). "00" is a digraph that refers to the geographic division in charge of the case, and "TRIBE" is the randomly generated word assigned to the agent to protect his/her true identity.

DDO is the CIA's deputy director of operations.

STU-III is a secure encrypted landline.

In CIA terminology, "agent" refers to the foreign national who agrees to spy for the CIA. The US officer who handles spies is called "case officer" or "operations officer" (aka "ops officer").

PART II

THE MAKING OF A SPY

CHAPTER 4

DON'T GET ME STARTED

"Are you a CIA agent?"

I've gotten that question a lot over the years. My response is always the same: "If I am, no one told me."

It's the perfect cover story, if you think about it.

In fact, I was a staff CIA operations officer for exactly thirteen years. Despite almost constant friction between myself and the CIA bureaucracy, I loved the agency and received numerous awards during the course of my career. For the record, I'm not usually one to toot my own horn (although I probably would if I could). And in fairness to the humorless CIA bureaucracy, it's likely this irreverent attitude that has generated much of the friction.

To this day, I can't believe they paid me to do that job. I also can't imagine a more challenging and fulfilling way of life. Since resigning from the CIA, I have continued to support the US government and military mission, initially via a business intelligence consulting company and, since 2003, via my ongoing business operations in Iraq.

The Balkans. The Middle East. Latin America. Los Angeles.

When I first landed, infiltrated, or in some other fashion arrived at each of these garden spots, they were at peace. All were apparently vying for the title of World's Most Insane Drivers, but at least they were relatively stable. Shortly after I set foot in each of these places, though, all hell broke loose.

A conspiracy theorist friend of mine is convinced there's a connection, that I am somehow responsible for the insurgencies, civil wars, fires, floods, earthquakes, race riots, and ethnic cleansing that erupted after my arrival in each of these hot spots. But as far as I'm aware, it was purely coincidental. I can't help it if I'm always in the right place at the right time. (That same friend once characterized me as "the half-wit love child of

James Bond and Forrest Gump," a ridiculous assertion since I look nothing like either of them.)

I wasn't born with a burning desire to cross enemy lines and enter war-ravaged Sarajevo in the dead of night. I didn't grow up longing to traverse the Iraqi desert enveloped in an epic sandstorm to help rebuild modern-day Mesopotamia. I really, truly did not want to set foot in Los Angeles. Ever. And yet somehow, I spent most of my adult life in war zones and other challenging environments.

For whatever reason—probably a combination of internal "wiring," training, and experience—I've always been pretty good at assessing and minimizing risk. When I travel to Middle East conflict zones, for example, I am not putting myself into as much danger as it appears to my friends and family, because of how I go about it. I'm also genetically blessed with unusually low blood pressure, which apparently helps a person to remain calm in almost any situation.

In case you have preconceived notions about the kind of person who joins the CIA and ends up in foreign hot spots, you should know that I've never been the macho, aggressive type who seeks out conflict. On the contrary, I prefer to avoid it. Give me too much to drink in a crowded, noisy bar and I don't want to start a fight. I want to start a family.

✷ ✷ ✷

Growing up middle class in the idyllic 1960s and 1970s American Southwest, I assumed that after high school I'd go to US Army basic training and then ship off to the war in Vietnam, like all the older neighborhood kids did. I knew from the nightly news reports that our young soldiers had to tread silently through the steamy, verdant jungles in order to avoid detection by the wily Vietcong. As a sufferer of seasonal allergies, I envisioned my future eighteen-year-old self on patrol in the sweltering tropical bush, forced to blow my nose on a banana leaf. The incessant honking and sneezing would of course betray my squad's position to the Vietcong, who would then kill us all.

This is the kind of thing that kept me up at night. So, when I learned over the radio in 1973 that the Vietnam draft had ended, I was surprised and relieved. It had never occurred to me that the wicked war would ever end. I figured I was off the hook and life would be pretty much smooth sailing from that point forward.

How did this former Catholic altar boy and (nondenominational) Boy Scout end up not only working for the CIA but also landing in multiple conflict zones no less? Upon reflection, I realize that much of my childhood was unknowingly devoted to pursuits that would later serve me well both during CIA training and in the field. And in some ways, my all-American upbringing, personal belief system, and curiosity about the world around me also led me to this unusual but fun and exciting way of life.

As a seventh grader, I never considered that smuggling contraband switchblades and low-grade explosives into the United States from Mexico (for resale to my classmates at very reasonably marked-up prices) would actually condition me to one day cross international borders in alias and smuggle banned equipment into Iraq. My unwitting parents had no idea I'd stashed my illicit merchandise under their vinyl car seats, or that I was operating an unlicensed import-export business. My siblings and I would feign sleep in the station wagon in order to get us quickly waved through the hot, dusty border crossing into the United States. Border officials in those days were more concerned with painstakingly dismantling beat-up "hippie vans" in search of drugs than with harassing the Brady Bunch as we returned from a camping trip to the remote desert beaches of Sonora, Mexico.

Those early forays into Mexico left their mark on me and, although I didn't realize it at the time, influenced the course of my life. I was instantly hooked on the colorful sights, indecipherable sounds, and alien smells of the border and beach towns. Not to mention the exquisite food, the exotic culture, and the pretty girls. I especially loved the Spanish language. I studied Spanish in school, but conversing with willing native speakers on Mexican soil provided the best education. My love of Mexico is as strong today as it was when I was a kid. I make my own *frijoles de la olla*, listen to Latin pop and *cumbias*, and know my way around Baja better than most of the locals. It feels good when Mexican friends tell me I'm more Mexican than they are.

Other early experiences, seemingly innocuous or just plain idiotic one-offs when they happened, also served me well in my future life as a spook.

One of my earliest and most vivid childhood memories involves two neighbor kids who were my very first friends. Billy and Carlos, who lived in the cul-de-sac across the dirt alley from my house, approached me one blistering summer day and offered a plastic cup of lemonade. Despite my natural (and understandable) naiveté about almost everything in life, internal warning bells went off. I told them I'd drink it but only if they each took a sip first. They did, and I then told them I'd changed my mind. Not surprisingly, the lemonade was in fact urine.

In CIA-speak, those bells going off in my head were my "CI antenna"—counterintelligence warning signs that things may not be the way they appear.

Years later, when I "executed" my sister's beloved, oversized, pasty-faced doll Priscilla by hanging her from the date palm tree in our front yard, her giant plastic head covered in a black shroud, I was subconsciously laying the groundwork for my future efforts to help eradicate ISIS in Iraq. At least that's how I like to rationalize my behavior now. (Sorry, sis.)

When I finally cracked open the *World Book Encyclopedia* my parents bought to further our public school educations, I went straight to the formula for gunpowder. And proceeded to buy the components and make my own. It's no wonder that years later I literally and figuratively had a blast during my two weeks of explosives training on a secret CIA base located somewhere on the Atlantic Seaboard.

Growing up, I also loved poring over old-fashioned folding paper maps and planning fifty-mile "bike hikes" to the various mountain parks around the city in which I lived. My friends and I would leave the house before dawn, our bicycles laden with army surplus canteens, mess kits, and other gear as we set out on our memorable adventures. During that same carefree era, my brothers and I would hunt, catch, and kill doves and crawdads and cook them in our poor sister's Easy Bake Oven, thoughtlessly leaving the toy oven's insides splattered with blood and feathers. (To this day she refuses to cook.)

Who knew that bike hikes and backyard barbecues would prepare me so well for nighttime land navigation and jungle survival training during the CIA's paramilitary course?

I grew up with wonderful Palestinian and Lebanese friends and neighbors, and as a result I've always been predisposed to love Arabs, their food, and their culture. When years later I entered Iraq to kick off my business venture, I felt right at home with the warm Iraqi hospitality.

During high school and college, I worked long, hot summers on a large ranch, where I was able to pick up more colloquial Spanish with hard-working migrant farm workers from Mexico. I also spoke Spanish regularly with my best friend, a kind and brilliant foreign exchange student from South America. Spending a month in his beautiful Spanish Colonial hometown with his family just prior to starting college was not only an enriching experience; it also resulted in further improvement of my Spanish language ability. All of this served me well during my first CIA assignment in Latin America.

During college spring breaks, my friends and I would take a sleepless fourteen-hour Mexican train ride from the hilly border town of Nogales, Sonora, through Culiacán to the vibrant beach city of Mazatlán, Sinaloa. The American organizers of these low-budget college trips typically spoke no Spanish, so I'd translate and help the hordes of college students check in to the hotel. The harried but grateful hotel clerks would typically reward me with an upgraded room. A gringo speaking Spanish in Mexico will also attract free margaritas and generally royal treatment. (In contrast, I later learned that a gringo speaking fluent Serbian in Yugoslavia would often attract curses and insults, I suppose on the assumption that he'll better understand what they're saying than will your typical, monolingual gringo.)

In college, after I'd saved up enough money ($3,150) to buy my first vehicle—a 1972 GMC Jimmy with 150,000 miles—my friends and I would spend weekends camping, quail hunting, and four-wheeling, "Take it Easy" blaring over the SUV's stereo speakers. This experience came in handy when handling weapons and four-wheeling in the wilds of Bosnia, Croatia, and Iraq. In Latin America, my four-wheeling skills were put to good recreational and agent developmental use. We'd often take our red four-wheel drive Caribe off-road to the top of a local mountain, and to some of the country's most remote tropical Caribbean beaches.

In college I took one year of Italian and picked it up quickly because of the similarities to Spanish, and because of a phenomenal language professor from Italy. After two semesters of Italian, I spent a couple of months (ostensibly) studying Italian in Perugia, Italy. In fact, I spent most of my time traveling solo around the breathtakingly beautiful country by train. Although I hadn't spent much time in class, I returned to Perugia at the end of the course to score an A on the final exam, thanks to my recent real-world language immersion.

While fluency in foreign languages is not a prerequisite to working as a CIA ops officer, it's obviously a plus. At the very least it will help you avoid situations like the one I had in Rome when I tried to meet up with some

English-only Italian American friends from home who were there for the week. After dropping a *gettone* into an Italian pay phone, I called my buddy at his hotel to plan our get-together.

"What's the address?" I asked.

"I don't know," was his not entirely unexpected reply.

"Well, what street are you on? With that I can probably find you."

"Hang on, I'll go check."

After a minute or two, my friend got back on the phone. "We're on Senso Unico Street," he reported.

Senso Unico means "One Way" in Italian.

Many years of part-time work for that same family's catering company also paid dividends during my CIA career. I learned how to function comfortably in formal social gatherings, often among the "upper class" and scions of industry and government. Years later I felt right at home during my first official reception overseas.

* * *

In August 1980, I bid a tearful farewell to my girlfriend "Stacy" and my family, packed up my truck with clothes and music, and drove cross-country for five days to Washington, DC, to fulfill my dream of going to law school. The law had always appealed to me and my strongly held beliefs in fairness, justice, and equality. I am grateful to have been born free in America and never cease to be amazed by the wisdom and foresight of our Founding Fathers. I also grew up in an era in which we were inculcated with the simple but valuable concepts of fair play, following the rules, and knowing right from wrong. I tend to be trusting of others until they prove otherwise. An astrology-hooked friend of mine insists I'm wired this way because I'm a Libra.

Moving to climatically challenged Washington, DC, induced serious culture shock in this flip-flop-wearing, chicken-taco-eating kid from the sunny Southwest, but my experience during those first three years was transformative and directly informed my decision to join the CIA. I worked, clerked, and/or interned throughout law school, in all three branches of the federal government. I also bore witness to a number of impactful historic events that just happened to coincide with my new life on the East Coast.

Permitted to practice law through the school's immigration law clinic, I became interested in foreign affairs when handling asylum cases for clients from Iran and El Salvador. I learned a lot from my clients about the political realities in both troubled countries, and found it much more fascinating than studying torts or civil procedure. Working as a law clerk at the US Department of Justice, I studied classified case files involving foreign narcotics and organized crime figures. All of this peripheral exposure to foreign danger and intrigue was new to me, and it only whetted my appetite for more.

I moved to DC just in time to grab a ringside seat to history in the making. Ronald Reagan was elected president my first semester of law school, and I witnessed his inauguration parade down Pennsylvania Avenue. Exactly one week later, I stood again on Pennsylvania Avenue with thousands of other Americans, basking in the emotion of the "hostage parade" of fifty-two Americans just released from captivity in Iran. They rode in DC Metro buses along the same route Reagan had taken one week earlier, the joy and relief on their faces palpable. It was the end of a long ordeal, for the hostages and for our nation. Little did I know at the time that years later I'd face my own life-or-death standoff with that same fundamentalist Islamic regime. Observing the Iran hostage crisis unfold and wishing I could do something about it was the start of my long but hardly loving "relationship" with the Iranian government.

The following year, on Saturday, November 13, 1982, I took the Metro from Pentagon City to the Foggy Bottom stop and then walked to the National Mall for the official opening of the Vietnam Veterans Memorial. Thousands of veterans, some wearing uniforms, some in jungle fatigues, most with patches, insignia, and medals, made a cathartic pilgrimage to their memorial near the Lincoln Memorial. America's Vietnam veterans never got a welcome home parade for a controversial war they valiantly fought but were not responsible for. The atmosphere that clear, windy day was a little raucous but mainly somber. The Wall soon became the most visited memorial in Washington. I would learn more about the realities and horrors of that war during CIA paramilitary and survival, evasion, resistance, and escape (SERE) training, which was taught by CIA and military Vietnam veterans.

During law school I was also fortunate enough to work as an intern for former US congressman John J. Rhodes. Rhodes was a decent and honorable man. A Republican, he was "old school" in that he was able to disagree with his political foes without being disagreeable or disrespectful. Rhodes was House minority leader when he and two other Republicans informed President Richard Nixon that he needed to resign. Country before party. Rhodes left office in 1982 and was replaced by another man of honor, John McCain. I still recall the first time I saw John McCain, walking alone with a slight limp down the corridor of the Rayburn House Office Building, toward me and his new office and future in the US Congress. I was not the only one who, aware of McCain's heroics and love of country, predicted at the time that this unbreakable leader would go down in American history as one of our nation's most selfless and principled patriots.

Another highlight of my law school years was meeting future Supreme Court justice Sandra Day O'Connor just after her nomination. Making history as the first woman appointed to the US Supreme Court, O'Connor grew up on a ranch, graduated from Stanford, and became a prominent attorney and judge. She was a real-life role model and inspiration.

"Ma'am, I'm a law student, and I'm looking forward to reading your opinions," I said when I met her, hoping my palms weren't too clammy as we shook hands.

"And I'm looking forward to writing them!" she responded, looking me directly in the eye with a sincere smile.

It was a very brief encounter but one of the most memorable and meaningful of my life.

My tenure in law school also spanned less positive but equally historic events. On March 30, 1981, President Reagan was shot outside the Washington Hilton Hotel by a deranged young man named John Hinckley. I was grateful Reagan survived. I now wonder if we'd have won the Cold War when we did had he not.

* * *

By the time I reached my third year of law school, I had become hooked on the idea of pursuing a career other than the traditional one of working for a big law firm. I gained criminal law experience with the district attorney's office back home and with the Felony Trial Division of the US Attorney's Office in DC, and I briefly considered a career as a prosecutor with the Bronx district attorney's office. In the end I decided to forego the law altogether and pursue a career with the CIA.

I researched the CIA as much as was possible in those pre-internet days, by speaking with people in the government who knew something of the CIA and by reading books about the agency. I read several sources of information describing what CIA training at "the Farm" entailed. I concluded that serving my country, living a life of intrigue in foreign lands, and getting paid for it were preferable to working as a lawyer in an office.

But first I had to figure out how to contact the CIA. The days of your English professor serving as a CIA "spotter" on campus, quietly suggesting you meet his friend from the government, were long past. I could not apply online like applicants do today. I must have looked up the CIA's number in the phone book because I got the process started, and shortly thereafter received a brief typewritten letter in the mail with no return address. The letter directed me to show up on a certain date and time at an address in nearby Rosslyn (Arlington), Virginia. The address turned out to be that of a CIA recruitment office, although there were no outward indications that it was the CIA. It was a nondescript office with a phony name, in an unremarkable office building near the Rosslyn Metro stop.

After that initial contact, I received subsequent letters in the mail, all with no return address and with instructions for the next meeting. Sometimes we'd meet in a hotel room, other times in office buildings in nearby Ballston (Arlington).

After about six months of interviews, and intelligence, language aptitude, foreign language, and psychological testing, I was scheduled for the dreaded polygraph exam at CIA headquarters in Langley, Virginia. I had nothing to hide, but by nature and upbringing I was a guilt-ridden Catholic boy. (My next book will be entitled *Guilt without Sex*.) I was pretty sure that once I was strapped in and started answering questions, the machine would violently squirt ink all over the polygraph operator's white shirt. Much to my relief, there was "no deception indicated" to any of my responses to the series of yes or no questions. I had been successfully "boxed" (polygraphed) and could move onto the psychiatric evaluation.

Ironically, the longer you work for the CIA, the tougher it is to pass the polygraph exam, in part because of the company you necessarily keep in foreign lands.

Polygraph operator: "Have you ever had secret contact with an agent of a hostile foreign intelligence service?"

CIA officer: "Hell yes! It's my job, remember?"

Polygraph operator: "It's a yes or no question."

My psychiatric evaluation was also conducted at CIA headquarters, on the ground floor Office of Medical Services. The shrink and I discussed a number of mental health issues related to work as a CIA officer, but what the doctor could not wrap his head around was the fact that I liked tequila but had never smoked pot. Since I'd grown up in the seventies, he simply did not believe me when I told him I'd never even tried marijuana.

He then asked me some routine questions about any medications I took or any allergies I might have. This interview took place right after the highly publicized Tylenol scare of 1982, when several people died from taking adulterated Tylenol capsules.[1]

"I'm allergic to aspirin. I break out in hives," I explained, itching for the session to be over.

"Take Tylenol instead," the doctor suggested.

"I don't think so," I replied, the Tylenol scare fresh in my mind.

"Why not?"

"Better red than dead."

I was quite pleased with my clever, topical, and geopolitically relevant answer, but the psychiatrist did not even smile. He jotted down a few more notes, closed his notebook, and ended the interview. (For those readers too young to remember, a common Cold War expression, uttered by CIA types and others adamantly opposed to Communism, was "Better dead than red.")

The final step in the process was the in-depth background investigation. Besides checking multiple government databases for any derogatory information, CIA investigators also contacted my friends, neighbors, teachers, and coworkers in person, even knocking on doors in my hometown. They wanted to know what kind of person I really was. It was at this stage in the process where I was convinced my application would go off the rails.

Allow me to explain.

When I first moved to DC, my girlfriend Stacy and I decided that we loved and missed each other so much that the only way to ease the suffering was to get married. (Okay, it may have been my idea.) And so, we got married, just before my third year of law school. Manifesting symptoms of pre-wedding jitters, I sent out the extra wedding invitations as a joke to a number of celebrities, including the queen of England, Israeli prime minister Menachem Begin, and the aforementioned John Hinckley. By that time, the criminally insane Hinckley was confined in St. Elizabeth's psychiatric hospital for his recent assassination attempt against President Reagan.

We never did hear back from the queen or Begin, but John Hinckley mailed back our RSVP card with a very nice handwritten note stating that, regrettably, he'd be unable to attend our wedding. He added that he had other commitments—I never knew if this was an intentional pun or not—but he wished us a happy life together.

It's common knowledge that prison officials routinely monitor all incoming and outgoing prisoner mail and phone calls. While Hinckley was not in prison, he was criminally insane and was locked up for trying to kill a US president. It's safe to assume that his mail was being monitored, if for no other reason than it would be good to know of any other psychopaths out there who may pose a risk to the president. It's also reasonable to assume that Hinckley's known contacts would be entered into a government database, searchable by, say, CIA investigators who are trying to determine whether or not an applicant should be entrusted with access to explosives and our nation's most sensitive secrets.

Alas, I was pleasantly surprised when no one from the CIA asked me about the nature of my relationship with putative presidential assassin John Hinckley. (For the record, I have not heard from Mr. Hinckley since he was released from institutional psychiatric care in 2016.)

Satisfied with my clean background, the CIA offered me a job as a career trainee (CT) in the Directorate of Operations, the foreign clandestine service of the US government. The elite CT program was "spy basic training," and all CTs had to successfully survive and complete over one year of rigorous training courses prior to becoming certified as an operations officer and deployed overseas.

CIA training would start after I graduated from law school, and I was given my choice to enter on duty with either the June or the October class. I was eager to put the law books behind me forever and join the CIA as soon as possible, so I said I'd start in June. The CIA man who offered me the job advised against acting so hastily. He recommended I pass the bar exam before joining up. That way, in case things didn't work out, I'd have something to fall back on. Otherwise, he said, my only real job option with nothing but CIA experience would be with the Mafia.

This was possibly an indelicate nod toward my Italian heritage, but it was sound advice nonetheless. I studied, sat for, and passed the DC bar exam, then reported for duty as a CIA CT in October 1983. I was twenty-four years old, and I was never more ready for anything in my life.

* * *

By about age fourteen, I was practically preordained to become a CIA officer, even though I knew next to nothing about the agency. By the time I graduated law school ten years later, I was a solid candidate for CIA employment: I had a relatively unremarkable background and lifestyle, and had demonstrated some willingness and ability to take calculated risks to achieve objectives in foreign lands. I nurtured a genuine curiosity about the world around me and thoroughly enjoyed becoming immersed in foreign cultures and languages. The CIA apparently concluded I could be trusted to operate independently and keep my cool under pressure, and could be counted on to exercise sound judgment when off on a solo mission. The CIA also valued my ability to develop rapport and work well with people from all walks of life, from migrant farm workers to members of Congress, and everyone in between.

I joined the CIA at a good time in its history. The Office of Strategic Services (OSS) veteran William Casey was CIA director, and he embodied the OSS derring-do spirit. Like the OSS before it, the CIA tended to attract those who had a real disdain for bureaucracy but still wanted to serve their country. As they (and I) would find out in the future, I definitely fit the old OSS stereotype. Unlike the OSS and early CIA, however, the CIA in the 1980s no longer recruited most of its new officers solely from the WASP-y ranks of Ivy League universities. Lucky for me.

I believe the CIA also assessed me as someone who could comfortably and unobtrusively blend in almost anywhere. Years later, it occurred to me that although I could survive better than most Americans anywhere on earth, the flip side is I also don't completely fit in anywhere. Even at home. (The CIA's psychiatrist would have had a field day with that gratuitous bit of introspection.)

By the time I showed up on the CIA's doorstep, I was just what they were looking for: a person they could trust, train, and confidently deploy abroad, who no one would ever suspect exactly what he was up to.

CHAPTER 5

CIA PARAMILITARY TRAINING

Drifting in and out of consciousness in a dank solitary confinement cell, I was grateful for the brief escape from this living nightmare provided by some very convincing hallucinations. I reached out to touch the damp leaves on the cool forest ground, even though I was alert enough to know they weren't really there. My tiny, pitch-black cell was transformed through the voodoo of food and sleep deprivation into daytime in the forest. I could see each perfect twig, leaf, and tree, the mossy browns and greens vivid and alive. For a moment I felt as though I were free again, back in the rain-soaked woods where I'd managed to survive the previous week by scrounging for food while training anti-government guerrillas. When I noticed the woodland ground beneath me crawling with thousands of tiny lone star ticks, I snapped out of it.

My American colleagues and I were hunted down and arrested in the woods a day or two earlier by heavily armed Communist government security forces. They disarmed us, covered our heads in suffocating hoods, and tossed us in the back of a military truck for the bumpy ride to the makeshift POW camp. There we were searched, stripped naked, and given Vietcong-style pajamas, several sizes too big. There were no drawstrings. If you let go, your pants fell down. The hoods remained in place, although I'd discreetly tip mine up a bit to facilitate breathing and to ensure I didn't trip over anything. This also allowed me to scout for intel on the layout of the camp and the number of guards, for escape-planning purposes.

Once we'd been processed into the small, remote camp, the guards gathered us all into a dirty room with bare walls and a single light bulb in the ceiling. There we were forced to face the walls and stand for hours on end without moving. When one of us succumbed to exhaustion and moved or collapsed, they'd punish the rest of us. I once tested their vigilance by pretending to track and snatch an insect off the wall in front of me, lizard-like, quickly putting it into my mouth. Retribution followed and lesson learned. No more fake bugs for me.

The guards left a single, filthy "honey bucket" in the middle of this illuminated group room, which we were forced to use in front of our comrades. Male and female alike.

After a day or so of being abused and humiliated in the group cell, some of us were sent to solitary confinement. This was like being unexpectedly upgraded to first class. Solitary had its downsides and was uncomfortable as hell, but at least I could sit or lay curled up on the floor and be left alone with my thoughts. I also took advantage of the solitude to rehearse the details of my cover legend in my mind. Who was I, ostensibly, why was I there, and what was I doing? I could not admit I was a CIA officer. I knew it was just a matter of time before the interrogations would begin.

My muscles cramped up after hours on end on the concrete floor of my closet-like, windowless cell. The stench from my only companion, a honey bucket, began to overpower the nagging hunger pangs, at least temporarily. *Was it night or day? How many days had I been here?* The sadistic guards ensured our disorientation and sleep deprivation through around-the-clock harassment by yelling and banging on our doors, and by playing earsplitting heavy metal music over tinny loudspeakers. It was surreal. But it was really happening.

There was a method to their madness. They were trying to wear us down, break us both physically and psychologically, to soften us up for the inevitable interrogation sessions. This was a well-run intelligence operation.

At one point they squeezed someone else into my cell. I couldn't see who it was in the dark, and neither of us spoke to the other, even though we sat shoulder to shoulder on the floor for hours. I didn't know if he was cooperating with the bad guys, and he probably wondered the same thing about me. Eventually they removed the anonymous visitor from my cell.

✳ ✳ ✳

A guard banged on the door to my cell and jolted me out of a deep, ten-minute slumber. My head was pounding, and my body craved water. Two guards yanked me up and dragged me down the dark corridor, toward a smoke-filled interrogation room. As we made our way through the hall, the guards lifted my hood and forced me to look at a colleague of mine who had been given food and a blanket for her cooperation. They also made sure I looked inside another room where my friend "Jack" had been hog-tied face-down on the floor and was being beaten by angry, menacing guards.

My escorts shoved me into the stark interrogation room right next to the room where Jack was being abused. This was to be my second interrogation session since my arrival at the camp. The room was furnished with a small, rustic wooden table, a desk lamp, and two sturdy chairs. A uniformed, mustached interrogator sat on one side of the table, and I was shoved down in the empty chair opposite him. It felt wonderful to sit in a chair instead of on the damp, uneven concrete floor of my cramped cell. A Styrofoam cup full of dirty water and half-cooked rice sat on the small table between me and my interrogator, a Cuban military officer who somehow knew I spoke Spanish. A slack-jawed armed guard stood behind the Cuban, his AK at the ready.

"What's your name?" he asked calmly, in Spanish, between puffs on his cigar.

"David Martino," I lied. The alias matched the fake documents they'd confiscated at the time of my capture. And, just as importantly, it matched the name I'd provided during the first interrogation.

"What's your mission?" he asked, just as he had about twenty-four hours earlier. He was hoping I'd change my story from the last interrogation session. He wanted to catch me in a lie.

I was briefly distracted by the anguished screams of my buddy Jack in the room next door. The guards had apparently lost patience with his uncooperative attitude and were doing their best to make his life miserable. My athletic colleague with a dry sense of humor seemed intent on provoking them. No matter how much discomfort it caused him.

"What's your fucking name?" Jack's interrogator shrieked at him, for the third time.

"I don't remember, sir," was Jack's plaintive reply.

Jesus, Jack, tell him your fucking name!

"What's your mother's name?" was the futile follow-up question.

"It's coming to me, sir," Jack replied with fake earnestness. "If you could just give me a few more minutes, I'm pretty sure I'll remember."

Angry beatings and more cries of pain.

I fought to suppress a smile. On the one hand, Jack's unbending resistance to these goons was admirable. On the other, he was making it unnecessarily hard on himself. My approach was to give up minimal, insignificant data, live my plausible cover story without variation from one interrogation to the next, and generally try and stay off their radar. But, to each his own.

"What's your mission?" my cigar-chomping interrogator angrily demanded, banging his fist on the table to get my attention.

Before I could answer with my meticulously memorized cover story, two heavily armed men burst into the interrogation room and shot my Cuban interrogator and the inbred guard dead. The attack was lightning fast, deafening, and lethal. The killers were Americans. I could hear other American special operators moving down the corridor, clearing each cell in a similar fashion. It was loud and chaotic. And glorious. For some reason I noticed the cup of rice and water was still sitting, undisturbed, on the table.

It took a second for me to fully realize what was happening: a small band of American Special Forces had overrun the POW camp, killing our enemy captors and liberating all of the American prisoners.

After the dust had settled, the US troops herded the dazed, newly freed prisoners outside. They lined us up for a head count—we were filthy, smelly, exhausted, and still in our Vietcong-style pajamas. The sun hurt my eyes, which had not been exposed to daylight in God knows how long. The American soldiers stood in formation facing us and ran an American flag up the flagpole, replacing the enemy flag. They played "The Star-Spangled Banner" over the camp loudspeaker. Together we recited the pledge of allegiance. Tears streamed down the faces of most of the freed prisoners. I was grateful the ordeal was over.

Meanwhile, the vile guards stood off to one side and quietly observed the ceremony. They weren't actually dead. We weren't in the jungles of Latin America. We were in the humid, tick-infested woods on a secret CIA base somewhere on the Eastern Seaboard. This was all part of our survival, evasion, resistance, and escape (SERE) training.

Deep down we knew it was training, but it didn't feel like it. It was real. We hated those bastard guards, and many of us could not bring ourselves to shake their hands when the ceremony concluded. The guards were actually fellow CIA and former military colleagues whom we'd never seen before SERE, and they took their abusive, sadistic roles seriously.

The fact is they did their best to prepare us to survive the brutal, life-threatening reality that would await many of us overseas. In my case, that would be Sarajevo. They also subconsciously planted the seed of hope in us. If and when we were captured by the enemy, and if we were unable to escape, we'd never lose hope that one day we might be rescued. Again.

We owed our captors and guards a huge debt of gratitude. But at that moment, I sure as hell did not feel that way.

✻ ✻ ✻

Temporary SERE discomfort notwithstanding, the lengthy CIA training process was one of the greatest experiences of my life. In the early 1980s, new recruits in the CIA's clandestine service embarked on an intensive orientation and training process centered in the DC area and elsewhere on the East Coast. Our training included months-long paramilitary, as well as tradecraft and operational courses, in addition to interim assignments on "Country Desks" at CIA headquarters. A Country Desk refers to an office that manages clandestine operations in a particular country. Once we successfully completed basic training and were certified as case officers, we moved on to any foreign language or specialized surveillance or other training necessary to prepare us for our first overseas postings. Most new CIA officers spend at least two years in basic and specialized training before heading overseas on their first undercover assignment. Contrast this with State Department foreign service officers, who often find themselves overseas within a few months of coming on board.

CIA tradecraft training ("spy school") at the Farm has been covered extensively in other books. I will not get into the details of tradecraft training, which only serve to reveal CIA methods—methods that are essential to the CIA's success and America's national security. Suffice it to say that all CIA training and tradecraft can be boiled down to a very simple, life-saving bottom line: *don't get caught*. These three words were never far from my consciousness and would serve me well throughout my CIA career and beyond.

The most highly anticipated training for those of us with no prior military experience was the lengthy Special Operations Training Course (SOTC—pronounced "sot-see"), the CIA's paramilitary course for prospective American spies. Run by former US military personnel with CIA experience, SOTC gave us a real taste of military life, without having to actually join the military. The purpose of SOTC was not to mold America's future spies into Special Forces soldiers, although the focus of our training was indeed on Special Forces / guerrilla tactics and operations. We learned the fundamentals of asymmetric or unconventional warfare, from the insurgent's point of view. We conducted hit-and-run ambushes and made (and detonated) IEDs and plastic explosive shape charges. We saw how deadly det cord could be. We blew the hell out of semitrucks and anything else they'd let us blow up. I loved it. Looking back, I realize that SOTC was not unlike ISIS training, but without the messy distractions of Facebook and decapitation.

Unlike al-Qaeda trainees, we were not subjected to the dreaded monkey bars. I always wondered why al-Qaeda broadcast propaganda images of its recruits swinging on monkey bars. Were these comical video clips meant to terrify us? Or did bin Laden secretly harbor a twisted sense of humor? My five-year-old daughter, upon observing the terror group's monkey-bar antics on TV one day, rolled her eyes and said, "I could do that," before returning to her coloring book.

The purpose of our "basic training" was team and confidence building, as well as familiarization with a host of military and special warfare concepts. We were not required to have "high and tight" haircuts (although they were advisable), but we lived in Quonset hut barracks, ran PT, ate in a mess hall, wore camouflage fatigues, and spent days on end in the woods. After three years of city life, law school, and the DC bar exam, I found that SOTC was a very welcome change of pace. The fact that our CIA training was taking place near historic American battlefields, including the site of a seminal battle for America's independence, made it all the more meaningful.

We received intensive training and conducted day and night exercises in land navigation, amphibious (small boat) operations, conventional and specialized weapons, guerrilla warfare, and explosives and demolition. Besides the usual array of US small arms and assault rifles, we threw hand grenades and fired M60 machine guns, M79 grenade launchers, AK-47s, Uzis, WWII-era M3 Grease Guns, and, my personal favorite, a Czechoslovak Škorpion 7.65 mm machine pistol. I'd never shot trap or skeet before, but having spent my youth hunting quail, I hit every clay pigeon during trap and skeet drills with a well-worn twelve-gauge shotgun.

Although we didn't get to set one off, we learned about the unconventional "claymore on a stick," invented and first deployed along the Ho Chi Minh Trail, by our unforgettable SOTC instructor "Nate." The M18 claymore mine was designed to function as a directional mine on or close to the ground, but Nate would attach it to a bamboo stick so that it would rain down shrapnel on the unsuspecting enemy. A weapons instructor, Nate would repeat the same warning tailored to each exercise in his slow, Southern drawl: "If your claymore on a stick is pointed the wrong way, it'll likely ruin your whole day."

We also received black cache training. During the Cold War, the CIA would bury hidden (black) caches of money and weapons in the woods in Soviet bloc countries, to be dug up by our agents when signaled to do so. At the Farm we learned how to prepare the caches and the maps, which the agents would use at some future date. We also played the role of the agent so that we'd understand how critical it is to prepare an accurate and detailed map. Instructors gave us maps prepared by CTs several years in the past, and we headed out into the woods at some remote spot on the Farm at night and attempted to retrieve them.

Locating what we believed was the black cache site, my partner and I dug down at the designated spot until we hit metal. Holding red lens flashlights, we pulled out an old ammo can and struggled to pry open the lid. When we finally did, it made a loud whoosh sound, as though we were opening up a giant can of tennis balls. Much to our chagrin, the black cache contained a decomposed skunk, which our fun-loving predecessors had buried about five years previously. I don't fully understand the chemistry, but the can became vacuum sealed over time. The overpowering rotting skunk odor, which instantly blasted out of the can, was indescribable and clung to us and our vehicle for days. (Another team dug up a more civilized buried deer's head.) I am not at liberty to reveal what my partner and I buried in our cache, since I don't want any of my former colleagues tracking me down now for belated payback.

Preparing and dropping resupply bundles onto a designated drop zone while hanging out of a low-flying short takeoff and landing Twin Otter plane was especially fun and challenging. The Twin Otter is a popular cargo, medevac, and skydiving plane. Although it had little to do with our training, taking high-speed, deafening, roller-coaster nap-of-the-earth rides while half hanging out of a Vietnam-era UH-1 Huey helicopter was also a memorable experience. Like most of our SOTC instructors, the daredevil Huey pilots honed their skills years earlier in and above the jungles of Vietnam.

SOTC's final exercise culminated in the brutal but valuable SERE course. SERE is a rigorous program for high-risk military and the CIA. The experience is brutal and exhausting, but it is extremely valuable preparation for young CIA officers about to be deployed into a hostile world. SERE took place at the end of SOTC and at that time was based on the actual Vietnam experience of American POWs.

Our course was modeled after the original course, developed by the late US Army colonel Nick Rowe, who, according to multiple news reports, developed the SERE program for the army after his escape from a barbaric Vietnamese POW camp.[1] Rowe, who wrote the gripping book *Five Years to Freedom*, spent five years as a POW before escaping while being taken out for execution. Sadly, this inspirational American hero was murdered in the Philippines a few years after we took our course. The official version held that Rowe was murdered by Communist insurgents belonging to the New People's Army. However, a mutual friend and civilian colleague who worked with Rowe at the US embassy in Manila told me he and others are convinced Rowe was actually murdered by elements of the Philippines military, probably because Rowe was going to expose their illegal profiteering from stolen US military assistance.

Regardless of the actual circumstances surrounding Colonel Rowe's assassination, my fellow CTs and I were extremely fortunate to have received the benefit of his years of experience, suffering, and sacrifice.

✷ ✷ ✷

By the time we were "rescued" by American Special Forces from our POW imprisonment, I'd decided I'd had enough fun and games in the woods. I was all SOTC'd out. Paramilitary training was great, it definitely exceeded my expectations, but I was burned out. I think it ceased to be fun right around the first time I dropped my Vietcong drawers and perched myself on the honey bucket in front of my fellow prisoners. (My law degree didn't count for squat at that moment.) Although I'd volunteered for the two-week parachute jump school following SERE, I'd mulled it over and decided during my hours of solitary confinement there was no way I'd spend another two weeks running PT and jumping out of perfectly good airplanes. No thanks. After a weekend of R and R with my wife, I'd put on a suit and tie and begin my headquarters interim assignment two weeks early. A few months after that I'd be ready to return to the Farm for the "ops course"—the CIA's infamous spy school. As I told my good buddy R. J., another lawyer who for some inexplicable reason did not share my sentiments about skipping airborne training, "Fuck it, I'm outta here!"

CHAPTER 6

SECURE YOUR CHUTES

As we made our final preparations in the hangar and cross-checked each other's gear just prior to boarding the Twin Otter for our first CIA parachute jump, jumpmaster Charlie steeled our nerves by playing the Alabama song "The Closer You Get" over giant loudspeakers:

> The closer you get, the further I fall
> I'll be over the edge now in no time at all
> I'm fallin' faster and faster and faster with no time to stall
> The closer you get, the further I fall.[1]

Funny guy.

The CIA's army airborne–based jump school was the most fun of all CIA training. By the time jump school began, we'd survived paramilitary training, including the grueling SERE course. Our morale was high, as was our sense of camaraderie, and we were in top physical condition.

Jump school was purely voluntary, and although I'd contemplated skipping it after my honey bucket epiphany, a post-SERE weekend of R and R and a great Italian meal with R. J. and our wives at the old-school Pizza and Pasta restaurant on Wilson Boulevard in Arlington helped me to come to my senses. I'd been looking forward to this "icing on the cake" training from day one. I was also grateful for this unique opportunity to jump out of an airplane and get paid for it.

Week one was devoted to ground school, where we learned the fundamentals of jumping and, more importantly, landing. We'd run PT twice a day, including on full stomachs, following a frenzied food fest at midday in the mess hall. The course instructors did not give us much time for lunch, so we had to make it count.

In the 1980s, military chow halls weren't as nice as today's dining facilities (DFACs), like those found on bases in Iraq and Afghanistan. DFACs offer a variety of healthy food options and generally do a pretty good job of it under the circumstances. The Farm's mess hall featured typical Southern fare found on US military bases everywhere: lots of sugar- and salt-laden deep fat fried foods, and seconds were encouraged. I loved the mess hall. When I asked the "lunch lady" what scrapple was, she informed me that this tasty breakfast side dish from the mid-Atlantic states was "everything from the pig but the oink." Count me in!

Just as nothing from the pig goes to waste with scrapple, nothing else went to waste in the mess hall either. One of our more beloved and colorful colleagues was Big Dale, a "strapping buck" (his term) force recon US Marine. As we were finishing chow, he would loiter among the tables, politely asking in his northeast Philly accent, "Youse gonna eat those scraps?" He'd then grab and devour them as we headed out to PT. Big Dale's stated preference was for fresh pork. If we dallied on our way out of the mess hall, he'd announce, "Make a hole!" a split second before plowing through the middle of us.

I couldn't tell you what I had for dinner last night, but I'll never forget Big Dale's antics. One of the primary reasons we all have such fond memories of CIA training is because of the shared secret experience, camaraderie, and endless laughs with colleagues like Big Dale who remain trusted friends to this day.

In addition to relentless PT, we practiced basic "parachute landing falls," aka PLFs. Since we would jump using army-standard MC 1-1 Bravo parachutes, we would not touch down lightly, the way civilians do today during one-day commercial jumps. No, depending on the wind (or lack thereof), our descents could be fast and landings could rival those made when jumping off the roof of a two-story building. If you failed to land properly, you'd break bones. Mastering the PLF was essential to avoiding being hauled off the landing zone in the back of an ambulance.

To simulate exiting an airplane in flight, we jumped repeatedly out of a forty-foot tower. Just before jumping we had to shout our training alias and badge number, to demonstrate we still had rudimentary control over our mental faculties. It's not easy to make yourself jump out of a forty-foot tower, even with a safety harness attached to a cable. For fun, we got to rappel down the back side of that same tower. (It's also hard to convince your body to go along with leaning backward off the top of a tower.)

Big Dale led PT with some of his more inspired Marine Corps jody calls, such as, "This is a story 'bout a man named Jed, weird motherfucker wore a rubber on his head," but most of the traditional calls became boring and repetitive. There were only so many times we could enthusiastically chant, "I know a girl who lives on a hill; she won't do it but her sister will." To spice things up, I came up with a few jody calls of my own, some of which would probably get me booted from training in today's CIA. Besides being politically incorrect, they skewered some of the absurdities we were taught in jump school.

For example, we learned how to deal with a dangerous "towed jumper" scenario, in which a jumper is towed from the plane by a faulty static line that fails to release the jumper and deploy the parachute. The primary chute will not open under these circumstances, but the physics of the situation make it physically impossible for those on board to pull the towed jumper back inside the fast-moving plane. We were warned not to pull the rip cord on the reserve chute while still tethered to the plane, since that could bring the entire plane down.

The game plan—assuming the jumper is conscious—is for the jumpmaster to cut the static line with a knife once the towed jumper signals he's ready. After being cut loose, the jumper activates the reserve chute and safely returns to the earth.

So far so good.

The problem arises when the towed jumper is unconscious, either from banging his head repeatedly against the side of the plane, or from fainting from fear as he takes the leap into the abyss. In this scenario he cannot signal the jumpmaster and also cannot pull his reserve chute. The jumpmaster cannot cut him loose since he's unconscious. What to do?

Charlie's plan was as follows: After communication with the ground, the pilot would fly the plane low and slow over the runway with the dangling towed jumper aligned directly above a pickup truck, which would be moving along underneath the plane at roughly the same speed. Charlie would cut the static line, and the unconscious towed jumper would drop safely into the nurturing bed of the speeding pickup truck.

What could possibly go wrong?

We reviewed this scenario in detail over several beers one night in the Student Recreation Building (SRB aka CIA bar). "Girls Just Want to Have Fun" was playing on the jukebox for the third time that night, and someone was asleep on the pool table. It may have been Charlie. At any rate, the runway was not all that long, which was one reason we used the short takeoff and landing Twin Otter. Some quick beer math told us the odds of the plane and the pickup truck aligning perfectly, and at the same velocity in the middle of that very short runway were somewhere between "Yeah, right!" and "Ain't gonna happen!" Not that I had any better ideas for how to deal with an unconscious, towed jumper, but I was not going to crash and burn quietly.

I led the next day's PT with the following, morale-boosting jody call, specifically tailored to our training:

"Towed from a plane, PLF in a truck . . . sounds to me like a clusterfuck."

✱ ✱ ✱

"Secure your chutes!" became a popular catchphrase during paramilitary training and jump school, and it carried through to the more civilian (and civilized) ops course. This was undoubtedly another of Big Dale's gems, and I heard him yell it one night around midnight as fair warning before he wreaked havoc on the bachelor officers' quarters (BOQ) during the ops course. His modern-day "fee-fi-fo-fum" was immediately followed by the sound of slamming (and locking) doors up and down the BOQ's corridors. What provoked this outburst? When Big Dale returned from the SRB that night, he couldn't help but notice that someone had moved his bed, dresser, clothing, and belongings outside onto the grass. Set up exactly as it had been in his room.

So, besides its literal meaning regarding parachutes, the phrase also implied something along the lines of "Prepare to be screwed, anally." Its distant linguistic cousin, *Bohica*—"Bend over, here it comes again"—was also heard on a regular basis in elite CIA circles. Along with the infamous "Death by Roo-Roo!" joke, which involved American hostages, primitive jungle tribespeople, and buggery.

Why nonconsensual anal sex humor was so prevalent during CIA training (and beyond) is anyone's guess.

* * *

Despite the rigorous and repetitive training, many of us were still nervous about making our first parachute jump. In part because, as we were often reminded, jumping out of a perfectly good airplane is not normal human behavior. (Another Marine Corps classmate admitted he'd actually lost control of his bowels during his first jump. In addition, he said, his eyes were closed tight the entire way down, so technically it was a night jump.)

After we were awakened at "oh dark thirty" in our Quonset hut the morning of our first jump, the psyops began almost immediately.

Previously airborne-qualified Big Dale hopped down from his upper bunk and kneeled next to our half-awake classmate "Jesuit Joe" on the lower bunk.

"Hey, Joe, I just had a dream about your first jump. Your chute didn't open, so you pulled your reserve. The reserve didn't deploy, but dirty laundry flew out, along with a note that said, 'Fuck you.'"

Big Dale's wake-up call was met with nervous chuckles.

"Oh yeah," Big Dale added, more loudly, but almost as an after-thought, "and then you screamed in!"

During ground school, Charlie reassured us daily, "Your chute will open. I guarantee your chute will open." Predictably, one classmate's chute did not open. Fortunately, when the classmate, whom I'll call "the Interceptor," pulled his reserve, he wasn't met with dirty laundry and a thoughtful handwritten note but with a functioning and life-saving reserve chute. As you will learn in chapter 16, the Interceptor's luck would continue unabated throughout training.

We made the first two jumps out of a Twin Otter. On my first jump, I was seated on the left in the plane's doorway next to classmate "Carol." Our feet dangled out over the edge. Our jumpmaster was "Rodd," another colorful SOTC instructor with Vietnam experience. Just before we were tapped on the helmet to exit the aircraft, Rodd gave Carol a big "good luck" kiss.

I launched myself out the door before he decided to kiss me as well. Carol and I had been squeezed in pretty tight and could barely fit in the doorway together. As I exited the plane, I caught my left arm on the side of the opening and immediately found myself plummeting to earth upside down. The static line chute deployed, jerking me upright, but forcing my too-large helmet down over my eyes. *My first jump is going to be a night jump!* I pushed the helmet up but did not see the landing zone. I was headed toward the historic river that ran alongside the landing field and marked the boundary of the Farm. I toggled the chute and turned myself around.

After I'd endured nausea-inducing heat, noise, and fumes (and unwanted kissing) inside the plane, it was a relief to be outside and descending through the serene fresh air. The view of the Farm from above was spectacular. Unfortunately, there wasn't much time to enjoy it, since we jumped from only 1,200 feet and would be on the ground shortly. When I was about one hundred feet above the ground, I lined myself up with the X on the drop zone, turned myself into the wind in order to slow my final descent, and concentrated on not looking at the ground (that would cause your legs to bicycle and could result in injury). I then noticed that someone had just parked an ambulance about ten feet from the X. Afraid I might land on top of the ambulance, I broke protocol and turned to run with the wind for my final fifty feet. This sped up my descent, and I crash-landed on the unforgiving ground without any semblance of a proper PLF. Miraculously, I was not injured.

An instructor came running over to see if I was okay and then to chew me out for my crazy maneuver.

"What the hell were you thinking?" he shouted, incredulous.

"I was thinking I'd rather not land on top of the fucking ambulance, which some fucking genius just parked on top of our fucking X. That's what I was thinking."

My second jump and PLF went beautifully, and I was looking forward to our third jump, out the back end of a Chinook CH-47 helicopter. We'd shuffle down single file and jump off the ramp, which was sometimes slippery from hydraulic fluid, but otherwise it made for a nice and easy platform from which to take the plunge, sort of like diving feetfirst down a giant drain, and easier than forcing yourself out of a cramped Twin Otter doorway.

After another hot, nauseating flight and lots of circling the drop zone, I followed the guy ahead of me and exited the helicopter as planned. On the way down, I realized that there was no wind at all to turn into. Nothing to slow the descent the final hundred feet. I dropped fast and did my best to perform a proper PLF, but I landed hard, planting one thick-soled French paratrooper's boot about four inches into the hard, dry ground. I tried to pull myself up but had hurt one foot and was unable to gather my parachute and walk unassisted. I noticed that others from my stick (group of jumpers) had been similarly injured on this windless jump, including R. J. and a likeable classmate known as "Army Jim," whose leg bone was now visible to the rest of us.

Despite our injuries, Charlie assumed we were faking it and ordered us to remain standing to pack chutes. (He reluctantly believed Army Jim.) I was examined briefly by a young CIA medic but received no real medical care until returning to DC a few days later. My foot and ankle continued to swell. It turned out I had fractured my foot and would be in a cast for the next several weeks. Twenty years later, the CIA awarded me my paratroop jump wings.

After jump school at the Farm, I attended a course for US government employees at the State Department in Foggy Bottom. On crutches. There we learned esoteric government terms like "conal rectification," whereby a foreign service officer could request a transfer from, say, the Consular Cone (specialty) to the Political Cone. Naturally, I immediately took to "inadvertently" calling it "rectal conification," in secret tribute to our solemn CIA traditions involving sodomy jokes. Although the snooze-inducing course was tough to sit through after months of adrenaline-filled paramilitary training at the Farm, the experience at the State Department did serve to remind me that I made the right choice by joining the CIA.

PART III

LATIN AMERICA

CHAPTER 7

GOING OPERATIONAL

From inside the restroom stall, I could overhear a giddy, animated conversation between what sounded like two long-lost but equally inebriated Pakistani twins who had just been reunited moments earlier, right there in the men's room of the Quality Inn Skydome lounge in Crystal City, Virginia. Or were they Bangladeshi? There were several other loud, intoxicated patrons in the restroom, and I'd already had a bit too much to drink myself, but even in the fog of war (and fiesta) I'm pretty good at picking out accents. Nonetheless, as I exited the stall I was shocked to see that one of the two "Pakistanis" was my good buddy R. J. from CIA training. With blond hair, blue eyes, and as fair-skinned as my sister's martyred Priscilla doll, R. J. had somehow convinced his new best friend that he was from Rawalpindi. (R. J. had actually spent part of his youth in Bangladesh, hence my confusion over the accent.)

I washed my hands, broke up the budding bromance, and dragged R. J. back out to my going-away party in the dimly lit rotating lounge overlooking the Pentagon and the National Mall. Motown hits were spinning, and good tequila flowed freely. My wife Stacy and I had to catch a flight to Latin America early the next morning, and I wanted to spend as much quality time as possible with R. J. and my other close CIA friends before heading out on my first assignment.

I was one of the first to deploy from our group, but my fellow partygoing spy school graduates would soon be dispatched as well to the four corners of the earth as CIA operatives. R. J. was slated for South Asia, where he would bear witness to the real *Charlie Wilson's War*. My brothers and sisters in arms (and in trench coats) and I had grown very close in training at the Farm, and it would be years before we saw each other again.

* * *

Although I was headed to Latin America, the CIA initially earmarked me for a job in a pro-Soviet country in French-speaking Africa. Following graduation from CIA paramilitary training and the operations course, and certification as CIA operations officers, those of us who graduated eagerly awaited word of our first overseas assignments. When we joined the CIA, we agreed in writing that we would serve anywhere the agency sent us, based on the oft cited, always priority-taking "needs of the service." One unwritten exception to that rule was that the Directorate of Operations would not "draft" a new officer for Africa service if he did not list Africa Division on his overseas assignment "wish list." Although I had not requested Africa Division, I was still drafted for the number two slot in a two-man Africa station. My adviser at the Farm was from Africa Division, and he'd apparently recommended me for that challenging job. He must have thought I was the right kind of guy to go up against the Soviets on turf they controlled. Either that or he didn't really care for me at all.

Before deploying to Africa, I'd first have to master the French language during ten months of language school, and I'd require more advanced denied area surveillance training. The job would have been a rewarding and demanding first tour, but my new bride wasn't keen on the idea of contracting a flesh-eating disease on the front porch of our jungle bungalow. (Note to self: next time don't let her read the State Department post report until after we're wheels up.) Also, after three years of law school and a year and a half of CIA training, I was eager to get out of Washington and start working overseas as soon as possible. Training for Africa would delay me for another year.

I met with Ted Price, former CIA deputy director of operations who was then head of the career management staff, and told him about my predicament. I respectfully pointed out that I already spoke fluent Spanish and Latin America Division had so many slots to fill they were drafting officers who spoke no Spanish, including a very sharp classmate of mine who spoke fluent French (but no Spanish) and wanted to serve in Africa. Might not the needs of the service be equally met if my friend and I were to quietly swap divisions? That way we could both deploy immediately, without the added delay and expense of language school. I didn't say it out loud, but I was thinking, *Call me crazy, but this sounds like a win-win-win to me!*

I knew I was on shaky ground. I'd agreed to go wherever the CIA sent me, and the small Africa station was a good, tough first assignment. If I'd refused the offer, I likely would have been fired. It was not my place to question the CIA's personnel gods, especially so early in my career. But I'm a lawyer and a Libra, and sometimes I just can't help myself. It would not be the last time I'd try and buck the CIA bureaucracy.

Much to my surprise, after mulling it over for a day or two, Mr. Price called me into his office and told me he agreed with me, with the emphatic caveat that I'd better do one hell of a good job in Latin America. I thanked him and assured him I would not let him down. I immediately walked down the corridor to meet with the PEMS (personnel) officer for Latin America Division to tell her the good news. (But not before hazing a new CT by telling her she had to shout her badge number just before dropping a classified burn bag down the chute to the downstairs furnace. I did my part to ensure this fun CIA tradition lived on.) The PEMS officer was grateful to have a newly minted officer who already spoke Spanish, and she gave me my choice of assignments. I could go anywhere I wanted in Latin America.

My objective was to work in a station where I'd be given serious responsibility from day one. I chose a strategically important country with a medium-size station, run by a tough and respected COS. Since the CIA's current rules prohibit me from identifying the city or country where I was posted, I will refer to both the country and the capital city, where I lived, as "Palmera." In Palmera Station they'd expect me to hit the ground running, and if I kept up with the pace I would be assured of gaining a broad range of operational experience. I'd handle important existing agents; produce intelligence reports; spot, assess, develop, and recruit new agents; and also take on one of the CIA's largest and most effective programs. Palmera was a hard-target-rich and relatively benign operating environment, crawling with Soviet and other bloc officials, as well as Cubans, Libyans, Chinese, and Sandinistas. I'd also handle a sensitive asset from Nicaragua.

In other words, Palmera was manna for spies. Plus, it was a low-cost tropical paradise, with great restaurants, a nonstop social life, and lots of in-country travel opportunities. It was the perfect assignment for a first-tour CIA officer looking to make a name for himself.

After I took a month of operational and refresher Spanish at CIA language school with some native Spanish-speaking instructors, Stacy and I got our typhoid shots and our first of many official passports and made travel arrangements for our one-way flight to Palmera, Latin America.

After the dizzying and bittersweet late-night send-off at the Skydome lounge, we left DC early the next morning for Palmera via Miami International Airport.

✷ ✷ ✷

As the giant aircraft made its final descent into Palmera International Airport, it struck me that this was for real now. *I'm operational, and I'm officially in violation of another country's espionage laws.* Surveying my new country of residence for the first time through the plane's window, I was awed by the beauty of the country's green, rugged mountainous coastline, much of it engulfed in shadowy rain clouds. Ugly modern buildings and run-down but functional *ranchitos* dotted the hillsides. I was about to embark on my next adventure, and I was as happy as a dog with two tails. (As it turned out, in Latin America I rarely had a tail, but during my travels to Yugoslavia it was not uncommon to be dogged by two.)

In the mid-1980s, life in this large Latin American democracy was idyllic, for most locals and foreigners alike. It was more complex than this, but the life I led there can best be summarized as running covert operations around the clock for the CIA while living the good life, not unlike that depicted in the record-shattering "Despacito" music video. We moved from a one-bedroom apartment in Arlington to a large, two-story, station-provided villa in a leafy, upscale residential neighborhood of Palmera. Our backyard was a lush paradise, where we could pick bananas, mangoes, and papayas from our covered tiled patio, while watching colorful parrots swoop past between tropical rain showers. It did not suck.

My three-year tour was more productive, successful, and enjoyable than I could have ever imagined. But something that happened my very first week in-country knocked me off-balance and has me scratching my head to this day.

✷ ✷ ✷

Working my first official reception, I met a friendly but almost uncomfortably intense young Palmera government official named Luis. His job gave him phenomenal access to his government's secrets and policy makers. Strategic information the CIA required, for reasons I am not at liberty to reveal. A bachelor, he'd been educated in the United States and England and spoke flawless English. He was charming, well-dressed, and happy to talk to the new American official in town. Luis made a positive initial impression, clearly very sharp and sophisticated, but he also seemed almost unnaturally attuned to me.

Literally within a minute of exchanging business cards, he said, "H. K., I know where you really work, and I'm telling you right now, I won't ever spy for you." In so many words, he claimed he was able to read minds. My CIA affiliation was not apparent from my business card; on the contrary, most people with my job title were not secretly working as a CIA officer.

I laughed it off as a joke, but inside I was in turmoil. *How can this be? This was definitely not covered in training! Am I being set up by my colleagues?* It was like jump school all over again, where nothing went the way it was supposed to.

I never got an answer to those questions, but I shook it off because it made no sense and I do not believe in mind readers. (Stacy, on the other hand, was convinced he was just that.) I thought maybe he'd been unsuccessfully pitched in the past, but I traced him and there was no record of him ever having been met or pitched by another CIA officer. Over the coming months, my wife and I continued to develop a solid friendship with Luis, and I learned more about him and his access to information of interest to the US government. We entertained him at home, and he joined us on road trips to the beach.

Luis was the real deal in terms of his position and access and would have made a fantastic first recruitment. But anytime I attempted to broach the idea of him "educating" me about his country's strategic policies, he stopped me and reminded me what he had told me the moment we met. Luis was not offended, and we remained friends, but he somehow knew what I was up to. He was unwilling to cross that line and spy on his country for the US government.

It was a very rude introduction to the world of spying, and fortunately, it was the only time something like that ever happened.

CHAPTER 8

CUBAN OPS

had always hoped to visit Old Havana before Fidel Castro died. A leisurely sojourn to this Spanish Colonial marvel, frozen in time for the past sixty years, was high up on my bucket list. Savoring ropa vieja while sipping a mojito and grooving to the mesmerizing prerevolutionary boleros of the group Buena Vista Social Club in a dimly lit Cuban joint in Miami, while really nice, cannot possibly equal that same sublime experience in Havana.

I came close a couple of times. The CIA tasked me to TDY to Havana over Christmas 1995 to probe, survey, and generally mess with the DGI, the exceptionally competent and aggressive KGB-created Cuban security service. Since I'd be working there under the protective umbrella of Cold War rules, the most the DGI could do was rough me up a bit before tossing me off the island. In this sense, getting caught while screwing with the DGI as an American spy is vastly preferable to getting caught while screwing with ISIS as an American spy. Or as an American anything for that matter. There were definitely tangible benefits to operating under the unwritten but generally respected Cold War rules.

The CIA selected me for the Havana mission because of my Latin America tour, but primarily because of my recent denied area experience in Yugoslavia operating against real Communist thug surveillance. The DGI, like the KGB and others of their ilk, understandably fear agents and other representatives of democratic societies, and they do their best to protect their illegitimate, unelected masters from the threat posed by freedom by keeping us under their dirty, heavy thumbs.

But I digress.

I'd also successfully completed the CIA's intensive denied area surveillance training course. If I were under surveillance in Cuba—and I would be—I'd know it, and I'd be able to describe their modus operandi in great detail to my CIA superiors.

Unfortunately, Speaker of the House Newt Gingrich shut down the government over a personal slight just prior to my scheduled TDY, and so I never did make it to Havana. In 2014, two years before Castro's death, I traveled to Guantánamo Bay Naval Station on private business, but that trip doesn't really count since on Gitmo I was safely out of reach of his DGI goons. (In case you're wondering, no, I was not wearing an orange jumpsuit, and I was not shackled to the drink cart.)

Sure, I could explore Havana today as a private citizen on a tourist passport, but I have to assume my name and past CIA affiliation may be on the DGI's watch list. The truth is I don't want to risk spending my remaining years in one of Fidel Castro's notorious political prisons for the sake of an authentic puro Cubano. Interrogation by a Cuban during SERE was enough for me, thank you. As much as I'd love to sample an authentic daiquiri or two at El Floridita, one of Hemingway's favorite hangouts, I'll just have to make do with Miami.

Over the years I was involved in a number of operations against the Cuban regime, none of which was particularly successful. My most memorable took place during my tour in Latin America. Attending another official reception, standard issue Cuba Libre in hand, I spotted the local Prensa Latina rep standing by himself, also nursing a cocktail. (I don't remember what it was, but it was definitely not a mojito. Palmera produced some of the best rum on earth, but most of my contacts there inexplicably preferred Johnny Walker.) Akin to the Soviet TASS, Prensa Latina was Cuba's official state press agency, and it was widely speculated that the agency was used to provide cover for Cuban intelligence agents. A Prensa Latina official was ipso facto considered a priority target.

I worked my way through the buzzing crowd of networking journalists and spies, approached the Cuban agent, and introduced myself. "Carlos" was a stout, swarthy guerrilla turned journalist in a well-worn suit (and loosened tie) of dubious origin. He sported a convincing Fidel Castro beard and barely opened his mouth when he spoke. We exchanged business cards and pleasantries in Spanish, and after some small talk I invited him to lunch the following week at La Bussola, an Italian restaurant, ostensibly to discuss Latin American politics.

La Bussola was Palmera's first authentic, upscale Italian restaurant, and it was located in a popular middle-class shopping and restaurant district. If I was going to voluntarily subject myself to mind-numbing Latin American revolutionary bullshit for a few hours—and I was—I would at least treat myself to an authentic insalata caprese and some ravioli al pomodoro in the process.

Over time I developed a friendly but businesslike relationship with Carlos. I didn't come out and identify my actual employer, but Carlos knew I was CIA. No "normal" American in my position would waste his time meeting with a known Cuban agent, and in fact would probably be prohibited from doing so. Carlos and I would regularly debate Latin American and world politics, and we had shown a polite respect for each other's views. (Carlos, if you're reading this, turns out my stated fear of Cuba's destructive influence in Latin America was warranted. Witness Venezuela. Fidel's lackey Hugo Chávez—and his successor, drone-dodging conspiracy theorist Nicolás Maduro—destroyed Latin America's oldest, wealthiest democracy and millions of Venezuelan lives. Like Syria, Venezuela has been devastated by its own leadership, who value power more than country. Venezuela has become a country of poverty, refugees, and human trafficking.[1] Well done!)

Again, I digress.

While I was building a working relationship with Carlos, the CIA suffered a devastating hit to its sensitive Cuban ops program. In late July 1987, the Cuban government revealed on state television that a number of Cubans believed by the CIA to be unilateral agents were in fact double agents, controlled all along by the DGI.[2] Many of these agents had even passed CIA polygraph exams. A colleague and classmate of mine, assigned to Havana, was videotaped by the DGI while engaged in an operational act and had to leave the country. He was set up by a double agent himself.

A few months earlier, I'd personally run counter-surveillance while another CIA colleague met one of the doubled Cubans in Palmera. At the time, the CIA assumed the Cuban was good and not a double; we believed he was an agent who was betraying Cuba by providing secrets to the CIA. By the end of the evening, I knew the Cuban agent had "made" me in various locations around Palmera. I reported this to my colleague afterward and asked if the agent had mentioned seeing me. He had not. That struck me as worrisome, since a bona fide Cuban agent would be understandably nervous about attracting surveillance while meeting his American handler and would report any suspicions. His life was on the line. A bona fide Cuban agent would want to confirm I was exactly what I appeared to be: benign CIA counter-surveillance, there for his protection. Since the Cuban was in fact a double, he wasn't concerned by my presence, since he didn't need my protection. I reported this red flag in cable traffic.

Carlos and I continued to meet up from time to time at La Bussola, while the CIA's Cuban ops group engaged in damage control in the wake of the recent disaster. We were losing, badly; Cuba had outplayed us every step of the way. The CIA's natural tendency in situations like this—pre-9/11 anyway—was to circle the wagons, conduct in-depth CI investigations and damage assessments, and generally assume a defensive posture.

I had other ideas.

✱ ✱ ✱

I had recently helped Carlos to obtain a tourist visa to travel to New York "on vacation." This hard-core Communist revolutionary said he had never been to the United States and was eager to experience the Big Apple. What I did not ask or know, and what he would not tell me anyway, was whether or not he had any operational meetings planned while on Yanqui territory.

The timing was right. I drafted a detailed operational proposal to headquarters, one in which the CIA would remain on the offensive and in which we would come out on top no matter how things went down. We were desperate for a Cuban win, and I believed I could deliver one.

I reported Carlos's planned trip to New York so that at the very least we'd learn of his contacts there. This could help validate him as a target. The kicker was my recommendation that I travel to New York, where I would "bump into" Carlos and cold pitch him to work for the CIA. (Alternatively, to keep me clean, another CIA colleague could cold pitch him.)

Bear in mind, although Carlos and I had a good relationship, we were not trusted friends, and he had shown no real, exploitable vulnerabilities.

Absent this unique opportunity and calamitous moment in CIA-DGI history, it would have been foolhardy to recommend pitching him at this stage.

There was a method to my madness. In the unlikely event Carlos accepted the pitch, we'd have to assume he was still controlled by the Cuban government. Another double agent. We would immediately subject him to an intense, hostile interrogation and polygraph exam. An exam he might pass, as did the other Cuban doubles.

If he rejected the pitch, or accepted the pitch but failed the polygraph, we'd expel him from the country. Carlos would report everything to the DGI upon his return to Palmera or Havana, sending a clear message to Castro that despite our recent setbacks, we were not going to let up in our efforts to aggressively target and recruit Cuban spies. *We're CI-fucking-A, and we're gonna keep coming after you!*

If he accepted the pitch and passed the polygraph, we'd still have to assume he was a double, although we'd handle him differently. We'd fully debrief him and provide him with a basic communications plan and some benign intelligence collection requirements. Nothing we couldn't afford to lose to the DGI. Maybe these requirements would give the false impression we still had unilateral Cuban agents not controlled by the DGI. We'd send him back to Palmera to await further instructions.

In the highly unlikely event he turned out to be a legitimate agent, we'd handle him using denied area tradecraft. If our assumption that he was a double was proved correct, we'd confirm this over time, but without being embarrassed again. We'd run this operation on our terms and on our turf. In my view, the CIA had lots to gain and little to lose with my plan, including a much-needed morale boost.

As expected, headquarters rejected my proposal. They were in full-on defensive mode and were unable or unwilling to even consider this kind of counterattack. By enabling Carlos's trip to New York without any kind of monitoring or approach, we sent a strong message to Castro that he had won. Again.

CHAPTER 9

INTERNAL OPERATIONS: NICARAGUA

Hastily exiting my junior suite at the Palmera Hilton, I almost crashed into an overloaded housekeeping cart parked inches outside my door.

"*Buenas tardes,*" I said with a nod to the matronly hotel maid standing next to the cart, arms folded across her chest. I recognized her from the previous day. The uniformed woman remained motionless and stared at me, one eyebrow arched, an unforgettable *Oh no you didn't!* look plastered across her face. I shot her a weak smile, squeezed past the cart, and strode toward the hotel elevator.

I knew why she was less than pleased to see me again. This was the third day in a row I would leave the suite in bad shape. Worse, my exit came a couple of hours after a burly businessman who bore a striking resemblance to former Red Sox designated hitter David Ortiz, aka Big Papi, left the same room. A room that appeared to have been ransacked by a pack of hungry wolves. Bedsheets were draped over the desk and chair, and pillows were strewn around the room. Wet bath towels were everywhere. The TV was tuned to the local MTV station, blasting nonstop Latin pop hits, like "Humo del Cigarrillo" by Pastor Lopez, to mask our conversation.

* * *

In the mid-1980s, the CIA was running a not-so-secret war in Nicaragua, supporting the repressive anti-Communist Contras against the even more repressive Sandinista government. I spent nearly a quarter of my time in Latin America focused on Nicaraguan operations, which I ran from outside Nicaragua. I developed Nicaraguan political and media sources, and I also ran (handled) a very productive unilateral agent who was working in the capital city of Managua. My agent traveled from Managua to Palmera every few months for debriefings.

"José" was serving as his country's defense attaché inside his country's embassy in Managua. I won't identify his home country, but politically his government was sympathetic toward the Sandinista regime. Because of José's excellent natural access to senior Sandinista officials, he was one of the CIA's best sources of intelligence on the Soviet- and Cuban-backed Sandinista regime. Managua was a denied area, so it was difficult for CIA officers to meet with assets in-country. I handled José from outside Nicaragua, but for his protection and to maintain the secrecy of our contact, I practiced sound operational tradecraft for all meetings and communications. If either his own country or the Sandinistas were to learn he was an agent of the CIA, he'd be arrested, imprisoned, and possibly executed.

José was an imposing figure, over six feet tall and very strong and husky. He enjoyed good food and whiskey, and barely fit into his trademark blue suit and tie. A professional military man, José was a very disciplined and productive "natural" agent who was not afraid to take calculated risks. He believed in our mission, since he had witnessed firsthand the abuses inflicted upon the Nicaraguan people by the ruthless and corrupt Sandinistas.

I would meet José in temporary safe houses, hotel rooms in Palmera that I rented in alias. We typically met for several days in a row, each debriefing lasting several hours and resulting in multiple timely and important intelligence reports. I would not spend the night in the room. To ensure that the large, anonymous hotel did not assume I'd checked out early and rent the room to someone else, I'd mess up the bed and leave articles of clothing in the closet, and toiletries in the bathroom. After our meetings, José would leave the room first and I would wait another couple of hours before exiting the hotel. The door housekeeper had to clean up after our routine, although espionage is probably the last thing she suspected was afoot.

As the situation in Nicaragua worsened, the CIA decided we needed more regular reporting from José. We could not afford to wait three months or more for each successive batch of reports. Since it was too risky to meet him inside Nicaragua, where both he and any CIA officers would attract enemy surveillance, we decided to provide him with secure covert communications (COVCOM) equipment. This would allow him to regularly send his reports via satellite from Managua without running the risk of engaging in a personal meeting.

The COVCOM of choice at the time was the RS804 encrypted satellite radio, a big, bulky piece of communications equipment. The problem we faced was finding a way to physically deliver this suspicious-looking equipment to our agent in Managua, undetected. The KGB had gotten its hands on a set in 1983 when they arrested an officer in Moscow as he used the equipment in a park, so it was known to our enemies as spy gear. José could not carry the RS804 into Nicaragua personally, and he could not use his country's diplomatic pouch without exposing his role as a spy.

Headquarters was unable to come up with any solutions. José and I brainstormed extensively until we hit upon an unusual game plan. José would hold a birthday party and invite everyone from Managua's small expat community, including a CIA officer. I cannot reveal the details, but headquarters would securely deliver the RS804 to the officer in Managua before the party. After receiving the RS804, our officer would conceal the equipment inside a large box, wrapped as a gift. (S)he would then bring the gift to José's party and hand deliver it to our asset. Even if Sandinista surveillance had our officer (and the party) covered, the gift should not arouse any suspicions under these circumstances.

The ruse worked beautifully. We successfully delivered this incriminating but potentially productive spy gear to our valued agent under the noses of hostile surveillance. José had already been trained on the RS804 during our meetings in Palmera. He began to produce and transmit a steady stream of valuable intelligence reports, becoming an even more prolific reporter than before.

Once again, success depended upon thinking "outside the box" (or inside the box, as it turned out). Creative solutions to unique spy problems are required almost daily in the world of espionage, but the specifics are not something that can be anticipated or taught in advance at spy school.

CHAPTER 10

MESSING WITH CHINESE SPIES

In my experience, Chinese foreign intelligence officers can be brazen, at least by the relatively refined American standards of espionage etiquette. (I'm guessing our British cousins in MI6 say the same thing about their dreadfully less sophisticated CIA counterparts.) Chinese spies seemingly either cannot or will not make much of an effort at disguising what they're really up to, whether socializing or on the job. After learning this lesson the old-fashioned way, I managed to turn the tables on one particularly pesky Chinese agent in Latin America.

I first became aware of this Chinese proclivity for crude approaches at a CIA-financed bash my wife Stacy and I hosted one balmy Saturday night at our Palmera villa, to which we invited a select number of priority recruitment targets and fellow station officers. The entire affair was not unlike inviting fish to a party in a barrel. A station-orchestrated function like this provides much more bang for the buck than a typical reception, where you're as likely to bump into a talkative Canadian economics analyst as a sullen but priority East German spook. Our modern Spanish-style quarters and tropical garden were jammed with a happy throng of Soviet, Nicaraguan, Eastern European, and Chinese spies and officials, along with several local political figures of operational interest. (Our Palmera friends would typically show up around midnight and expected us to do the same when they invited us to an intimate dinner party ostensibly starting at 8:00 p.m.)

All seemed to be enjoying the open bar, tasty arepas, and live music provided by a phenomenal reggae band from the Caribbean. The weather was perfect—as always—and many of the normally button-down guests wore guayaberas and other casual dress to this scripted but informal affair. Spanish was the common language among most of the guests, and their language skills (and mine) improved greatly after several Cuba Libres, handcrafted (to use today's trendy vernacular) by a CIA bartender with generous pours of smooth Palmera rum.

As the band delivered another hypnotic tune by Toots and the Maytals, I welcomed a Chinese official and his wife to the celebration. I'd met the Chinese cultural attaché, whom I'll call Mr. Kang, a few weeks earlier at one of Palmera's many official functions. Around thirty years old and wearing black-rimmed glasses, he was one year into his four-year tour of duty in Palmera. Like all Chinese officials posted abroad, he and his dependent wife were forced to leave their only child in China, as human "collateral" to ensure they did not defect. Worse, they would not see their young daughter at all during their four-year overseas assignment. I felt truly sorry for them, but this inhumane policy was routinely applied for the same crude but effective reasons to most diplomats and spies from Communist countries.

Mr. Kang handed me a bottle of Chinese wine. He then asked (in broken Spanish) how much we'd paid for a piece of Haitian naïve art that was hanging on the wall next to us. He also wanted to know how much we paid our household staff and whether we paid in dollars or Palmera pesos. I fudged the answer, saying my wife would know but she was occupied at the moment. (I wasn't lying; Stacy was chatting up my priority KGB target and his wife in the garden, next to the mango tree. More on him later—the KGB man, not the mango tree.)

Mr. Kang then invited my wife and me to join him and his wife for dinner the following week at a large Chinese restaurant in an upscale commercial neighborhood of Palmera. I readily accepted, then pawned him off on my good friend (and Soviet access agent), an official from a country friendly to the Soviet Union.

As a CIA officer, why was I so eager to meet with the bumbling Mr. Kang, whose official title suggested his role in Palmera was limited to attending concerts and organizing cultural exchanges? It's simple: when a Chinese "cultural attaché" extends an invitation to an American official, there's no doubt about what's actually happening. We're not going to discuss Ming Dynasty vases. This is the first step in the "assessment and development" dance carried out by spies the world over. In fact, I made the first move when I invited him to our party. (I'd also made a mental "note to self" to offer him the standard college education for his child, if and when I pitched him.) Since Chinese intelligence officials were priority targets, and CIA officers were priority targets for the Chinese, we'd happily accepted each other's invitations. The fact that I'd accepted his invitation told him I was either a CIA officer who was allowed (if not tasked) to meet with Chinese officials, or I was a "normal" American official without such permission who was willing to run the risk and meet, for as yet undetermined motives.

✱ ✱ ✱

As planned, Stacy and I met Mr. Kang for dinner the following week at one of Palmera's best Chinese restaurants. His wife was a no-show, but several of his male colleagues (whom I'd never met) were there, all dressed in dark suits and ties. Mr. Kang greeted us in the restaurant's entrance and directed Stacy and me to sit down on an ornate wooden bench in the reception area. One of his colleagues promptly crouched down and snapped a photo of the two of us. Stacy shot me one of those *What have you gotten me into this time?* looks. I just shrugged and assured her the light and crispy lumpias (spring rolls) were well worth the indignity of it all.

We then proceeded like sheep being led to slaughter to a big round table in a beautiful private dining room. The ambience in the room was not unlike that in fine Chinese dining establishments throughout the United States, decorated with traditional Chinese vases and artwork, and a latticed ceiling. Chinese music played softly in the background, and the efficient restaurant staff was entirely Chinese. The only non-Chinese employee was a young local who provided home delivery in the vicinity of the restaurant on his *moto*. (I know this because he regularly delivered Chinese food to our villa.)

After ordering food for the table in Mandarin, Mr. Kang asked us (in Spanish) several basic biographic questions. He wanted to know where we were born, what colleges we had attended, and whether we had any children. There would be no small talk with this young spy, who clearly was eager to gather enough preliminary information on his American target to draft his first ops cable back to Beijing. His colleagues enjoyed the dinner but did not participate in the conversation. I assume they may have been his superiors and wanted to observe their young protégé in action.

When the dinner and informal interrogation ended, Mr. Kang and his colleagues stood and thanked us for coming. We shook hands all around, and they dismissed us with a bow.

As Stacy and I were leaving the restaurant, walking slowly across the parking lot to our Caribe, I was trying to process what had just happened. My thoughts were interrupted by Stacy grabbing my arm. She uttered just one word to me, phrased more as a rhetorical question: "Seriously?"

Since this was my first overseas assignment, it would be the first but far from the last time she would ask me that same question, in that same tone, and with that same look on her face.

✹ ✹ ✹

The following week, Mr. Kang called me at the office to invite me to a one-on-one lunch with him at another, smaller Chinese restaurant. Again, I accepted, happy to have an official Chinese developmental and grateful Stacy would not have to endure another round of *Jeopardy!*—*Espionage Edition* on behalf of spouse and country.

As discussed in chapter 9, in the mid-1980s, the CIA was running a semisecret war in Nicaragua, supporting the counterrevolutionary Contras against the repressive Sandinista government. (For what it's worth, as of this writing, "El Piricuaco," President Daniel Ortega, continues to kill and abuse his own people.[1]) The capital city of Managua was a dangerous place at the time, and China had an embassy there.

Over lunch, apparently confident that he now had me right where he wanted me, Mr. Kang pulled out his list of requirements. He got right to the point. What the Chinese government really wanted to know was whether or not the United States planned to escalate and invade Nicaragua militarily. Mr. Kang evidently believed that (1) I was privy to this sensitive information, and (2) I would share it with him over Chinese-government-funded hot-and-sour soup, now that we'd bonded in such a meaningful way.

In point of fact, Mr. Kang was standing on my last nerve. My patience had not only worn thin, but it was also as tattered as that last ISIS flag taken down by coalition forces in Mosul.

Rather than indignantly rebuff his request the way any normal "running dog" CIA officer would, I discreetly looked over both shoulders before leaning in, encouraging him with my body language to do the same.

"Mr. Kang," I whispered conspiratorially, "I am not authorized to share this with you, so please do not tell *anyone* this came from me. *Get your people out of Managua by next Tuesday!*"

I slowly looked over my shoulders one last time for good measure and then relaxed back into my chair, pleased to see that Mr. Kang was scribbling furiously in his notepad. I could literally feel my blood pressure dropping, and I felt an overwhelming sense of serene calm. I'm pretty sure it was my first Zen moment.

Once again, after wrapping up the meal and his mission, Mr. Kang stood, shook my hand, and sent me off with a bow.

∗ ∗ ∗

I never did hear back from Mr. Kang, so after a few months I tried to call him at the Chinese embassy. Had I considered him a promising developmental I would have stayed off monitored phones, but this call was simply to satisfy my morbid curiosity. The operator patched me through to the "Cultural" section. Someone picked up the phone and asked who was calling. When I gave my name, I could hear some frantic, suppressed discussion in Chinese in the background. The phone was then passed to another Chinese embassy staffer. Giggling nervously, she thanked me for calling and informed me that Mr. Kang was no longer in Palmera. Before I had a chance to ask why, she hung up.

We may never know why Mr. Kang left Palmera three years short of tour, but I like to believe that he was yanked home unceremoniously after his superiors in Beijing determined that his blockbuster intelligence report about the secret American invasion of Nicaragua turned out to be a load of crap.

Did China evacuate its embassy in Managua as I recommended, leaving only "essential personnel" behind to report on the impending war? Did they all bug out in a panic? How much money (and face) did this cost the Chinese government and all who found his report credible? Is this really why Mr. Kang was recalled to Beijing?

One can only hope.

This episode will not likely go down as a success in the annals of the CIA's storied history, but I did at least manage to amuse myself.

CHAPTER 11

MOON OVER LIBYA

O n April 5, 1986, Libyan agents operating out of the Libyan embassy in East Berlin planted and detonated a bomb inside the popular La Belle discotheque in West Berlin, killing two American soldiers and injuring 229 others.[1] Ten days later, the United States launched air attacks against select targets in Benghazi and Tripoli, in retaliation for Libya's involvement in this and other terror attacks against Americans. A full moon shone brightly on the night of the raid, potentially increasing the odds the American planes would be more visible and vulnerable to attack by Libyan antiaircraft batteries. One American aircraft was shot down during the air operation. Putative American ally France refused to allow US warplanes to overfly France en route to and from Libya, adding 2,600 nautical miles and considerable additional risk to the American pilots' mission.[2]

At the same time, the CIA was developing a number of "covert action" operations to quietly counter hostile anti-American actors worldwide. What exactly is covert action? In 1948, the National Security Council first directed the CIA to undertake covert action operations that were determined as acts "which are conducted or sponsored by this Government against hostile foreign states or groups or in support of friendly foreign states or groups but which are so planned and executed that any US Government responsibility for them is not evident to unauthorized persons and that if uncovered the US Government can plausibly disclaim any responsibility for them."[3] Covert action included psychological warfare and other "hidden hand" operations that fell somewhere between the two overt options of traditional diplomacy and direct military action.

Several months after the Berlin disco bombing, and as a result of a covert action operation I was running, the CIA was able to obtain positive strategic results in Palmera, which made life much safer for the "good guys" and much more difficult for the "bad guys" who sponsor terrorism. The story of how this successful op came to be does not reflect a textbook CIA operation and demonstrates what despots the world over instinctively understand: fake news works. Every now and then, it even works to the benefit of the good guys.

* * *

Although my primary objective during my three-year tour in Latin America was recruiting foreign agents who could produce foreign intelligence (FI), I also devoted considerable time and energy to running counterintelligence (CI) and covert action (CA) operations. The CI operations were typically designed to uncover intelligence fabricators and double agents on our payroll, while the CA work primarily targeted hostile, antidemocratic governments. As part of the Palmera station CA program, I ran a large network of CA assets, including a key, highly productive agent whom I recruited my first year in-country.

CI and CA are typically unrelated, but the two disciplines intersected in an astonishing way one year, with very positive results for US national security interests. Running CI operations won't always get a case officer promoted, but it is essential espionage work. The same is true of CA, where the results are not always easy to measure. Recruiting spies who produce FI is what gets a CIA officer promoted. As an example of the tension between CI and recruitment efforts, when I arrived in Palmera, my predecessor turned over to me the station's top FI producer, an agent he had recruited and for which he was likely promoted. A first-tour officer, I was warned not to screw up the station's most valuable case. Over time, I cross-checked this alleged superstar agent's intelligence against my own sources and realized that there were serious issues with his honesty and bona fides. I eventually concluded the agent was a fabricator, and I terminated him. Rather than acknowledge the importance of this "defensive" CI success, which uncovered the ugly truth about an agent who had been the source of hundreds of FI reports, my COS dinged me in my performance review for taking too long to fire him. (Interestingly, the CIA does not retroactively rescind promotions based on the recruitment of agents who turn out to be bad, but I believe they should.)

At the time of the Berlin disco bombing, I was handling another trusted Palmera station agent—an unobtrusive "utility" asset named "Manuel" who had been on the CIA's books for nearly twenty years. Manuel was good at his job and was a pleasure to handle. I knew I could count on him to deal with any "unusual" tasking that fell outside the areas of expertise of other station assets.

Not long after the American air attacks against Libya, Manuel reported to me that he happened to be near the US embassy one day and had observed two men who appeared to be "Arabs" photographing the American diplomatic compound. I was initially skeptical, but he provided their license plate number, which we traced and learned was connected to a local Middle Eastern man with ties to known extremists. The obvious implication was the "Arabs" may have been casing the American embassy in advance of a terrorist attack. In light of heightened tensions at the time between the United States and Libya, our best guess was that Libya might be involved. Libya could easily add the chaotic country of Palmera to their growing list of global venues in which they were targeting Americans for terrorist attack.

Based on Manuel's report, which we passed to the US embassy, the embassy requested and received an enhanced security presence from the government of Palmera.

* * *

During this same time frame, CIA headquarters conceived of a creative global CA campaign designed to disrupt potential threats to America. Headquarters tasked me to run the program in Palmera. The ingenious plan was risky but, if carried out properly and without detection, could produce valuable results. The campaign was cooked up by headquarters CA experts who were well versed in propaganda and intelligence operations. Unfortunately, I am not permitted to discuss the specifics of the CA campaign, but its objective was to counter potential terrorism activity and reduce the risk to Americans globally.

I really liked the clever idea and quickly responded with a detailed proposal for securely executing this promising CA operation. My job would be made easy by the fact that I was running a finely tuned CA network with a long track record of success, with no "flaps" or compromises. The network was intentionally set up in such a way as to protect American interests with minimal to no risk of exposure. I had tasked this unwitting team successfully numerous times in the past, and the US government hand would remain hidden. Guaranteed. It seemed like a no-brainer to me.

For reasons I never understood, headquarters rejected my plan and ordered me to execute the "fake news" op directly, without involving my network. Their reasoning seemed to be that they did not wish to risk revealing this sensitive op to my vetted and proven network. I pointed out that in the event I was caught in the act by the local security service, there would be no way to plausibly deny that the US government was behind the operation. This otherwise brilliant CA operation would be blown, and it would trigger a serious diplomatic incident with the government of Palmera. Worse, the flap would be made public, undermining other legitimate American efforts to counter threats globally. On the other hand, if we followed my recommended approach, the US government would not be implicated and would have plausible deniability.

It was clear that the headquarters plan greatly increased the odds of getting us into precisely the catastrophic situation we all wanted to avoid. But headquarters always has the last word. My COS and I reluctantly agreed to execute the plan one long Palmera night. We knew that if we were caught, the resulting catastrophe would result in us and our families being expelled from the country, and US-Palmera relations would suffer a serious and unnecessary body blow.

We set out shortly after dark, in a sterile ops vehicle untraceable to the station or official American interests. After ensuring we were free of surveillance, we drove to Palmera's bustling international airport, where the first part of the operation would unfold. As I was exiting an airport restroom, I noticed an airport police officer watching me. He began to follow me as I exited the airport arrivals area on foot. Our vehicle was parked right outside the terminal in the drop-off lane, and my boss was in the passenger's seat. I hopped in the driver's seat and sped off before the cop could catch up with me.

As we drove back toward the capital city, incriminating evidence of our "fake news" activity still in our vehicle, we approached an ad hoc police checkpoint that was stopping each car. Two gringos in a car late at night in this part of Palmera could understandably arouse suspicion. I did not want the police to search our vehicle and determine that we were who we were, doing what we were doing. The implications were monumental should it become known that American officials were involved in this particular activity. My worst fears were about to be realized.

My boss yelled at me to stop, but as I rolled up to the checkpoint, I smiled at the cop, waved, and drove on through. There was only the one police car there, and the cop was standing outside his vehicle, so I quickly calculated the odds were he would not pursue us. Luckily, my gamble paid off, although we heard a shot fired as I sped off into the darkness. After completing the remaining tasks for the night, we made it back to the station without further incident.

The next day (a Saturday), our CA campaign had already gotten the attention we wanted: there were multiple, breathless television news reports about what someone had done the previous night in multiple locations around the capital city. The local government and Foreign Ministry expressed immediate outrage at the actions they believed the "bad guys" had carried out in their country. This time the bad guys had gone too far.

The American ambassador, whom we had not briefed in advance—an exception to the rule in cases like this—summoned us to his office at the US embassy. He quickly and correctly surmised that the station was behind this. We "came clean," and happily, he had no objections, other than the lack of forewarning. He understood that our operation would make life in Palmera safer for all Americans, including those like him working at the American embassy.

In the end, the government of Palmera took the actions we had hoped they would take. The threat to Palmera and to US interests in Palmera had just been reduced dramatically. Mission accomplished.

Moral of the story: fake news works, if you're not caught in the process.

Which brings me back to Manuel, the long-time station asset who first set things in motion with his explosive report about Arabs photographing the American embassy. Although Manuel was an easy agent to handle, I had my doubts about his bona fides. Something didn't feel right. For example,

Manuel often requested an advance on his salary, a clear warning sign that money was maybe too much of an incentive. When I refused his requests for a pay advance, I'd tell him, "*Un mariachi pagado toca mal,*" meaning "A prepaid mariachi plays badly." Although the expression is Mexican, Manuel understood my point. The folk song "Guantanamera" is less likely to disappoint if you wait to pay until after the job is done. I wasn't going to play along with his wishful interpretation of the CIA acronym: *Cash in Advance.*

Always wearing my "CI hat," just as we had been instructed during training at the Farm, I continued to vet Manuel. I arranged a rather hostile polygraph session in order to pressure him to admit the truth about a number of things he had reported over the years. I did not and do not believe in the magical powers of the polygraph, particularly with a pathological liar—or trained agent, like those from Cuba and East Germany who passed CIA polygraph exams—but "the box" can be a useful tool with someone who believes it actually works. During the polygraph exam, I truthfully told Manuel I knew he had just lied about a particular question, and so he admitted he had lied about that particular report. But to my surprise, when asked, he also admitted making up the entire Arabs-casing-of-the-embassy story. It never happened. Manuel knew tensions between the United States and Libya were high, and he correctly surmised that a report like this would be well received and well compensated.

I met Manuel a few days later on the street and terminated him as an agent. Unhappy with him for so many reasons, I also took an unorthodox and unsanctioned measure to ensure he never wasted the CIA's time again. Although I had not recruited him, I had handled him for over a year, and we had a good relationship. Manuel had his hand in a number of important station operations, so I was very pissed off. I had him sign a statement that I'd typed up in Spanish, in which he agreed that he would not reveal his relationship with the CIA to anyone, ever. Moreover, he would never contact the CIA again in the future, for any reason. I told him that I would know if he did either, no matter how far in the future it may be. Finally, the document said that if Manuel ever violated this agreement, the CIA would take extreme measures against him and his wife and children. A visibly shaken Manuel signed the agreement, and we shook hands and said adios.

The agreement, of course, was completely bogus and unauthorized. It was something I came up with on my own as a means of ensuring Manuel went away for good. I shredded it when I got back to the station. Although my method was unorthodox, I'm sure he never bothered the CIA again.

Manuel's fake news worked. Until he got caught.

Looking back, I realize there were other CA, propaganda, and "fake news" moments throughout my CIA career, going all the way back to training at the Farm. During the ops course, my good "Pakistani" buddy R. J. and I created and printed up dozens of copies of an (unclassified) satirical newsletter we'd created, focused on training and life at the Farm. The *Onion*-like articles and photos were suggestive of some of the romantic and training shenanigans that went on among classmates, but they did not explicitly identify anyone. Since our training took place in a fictional country called Victoria, the newsletter was called *Victoria Daily—the VD You Won't Want to Get Rid Of*.

R. J. and I set our alarms for 3:00 a.m. one night, got up, and distributed the subversive newsletter under the doors of everyone's rooms. By 8:00 a.m., all of our classmates (and instructors), assembled in a lecture hall, were intrigued and trying to figure out who was behind the prank. *VD* was the talk of the Farm. Keep in mind, this took place in the halcyon days before cell phones, internet, and 24/7 news, and we were further cut off from the outside world by virtue of the fact we were all ensconced on an isolated base. This unsanctioned CA op was nothing less than semi-scandalous. To this day, no one knows that R. J. and I were behind it. We even lampooned ourselves in the newsletter to divert any possible suspicion away from us.

Many years later, I did much of the writing for an April Fools' edition of an American expat newsletter in the Balkans. One satirical segment was a list of books ostensibly written by various American personnel and their dependents. The titles were ironic or humorous riffs on that person's well-known and sometimes unflattering traits or characteristics. The wife of the defense attaché, for example, was always complaining to anyone who would listen that the American embassy didn't provide curtains for her bathroom, which overlooked the Libyan embassy. The title of her book was *Moon over Libya*.

PART IV

RUSSIAN SPIES

CHAPTER 12

CIA VS. KGB

As I wound my way back from the bustling open bar, a small plate of tapas balanced precariously on top of my Cuba Libre, I couldn't help but notice that Soviet first secretary "Boris Gudenov" appeared to be hitting on my beautiful wife, Stacy.

Yes!

I had never met Boris in person, although I knew more about him than he knew about me. Born in Moscow to educated parents, he had developed into a fast-track "golden boy" by a young age in the Soviet Foreign Ministry. He held a diplomatic rank in the Soviet embassy, but the CIA had concluded for a variety of reasons that Boris was in fact a KGB officer. I was up to speed on a lot of his biographical data after carefully reviewing his extensive CIA file. His wife accompanied him abroad. During his previous assignment to a sleepy Central American nation, Boris carried on an illicit affair with an attractive local Latin woman, who just happened to be on the CIA's payroll. Boris had a kind and intelligent Russian face, and looking back I realize that physically he very much resembled Vladimir Putin, but with a full head of wavy, sandy brown hair.

I learned in advance from one of our multiple sources of information that Boris would likely show up at this reception without his wife. I'd briefed Stacy on Boris and on the game plan for the evening, which included using her as "bait" to lure him into a friendly ambush. (It was the least I could do after the Chinese restaurant fiasco.) Her mission was to stand there in the kill zone while I loitered at the bar and observed the scene. Based on what I knew of Boris, I would not have to wait long for the scheme to unfold organically.

Our gambit worked like a charm. He went for the bait. I hustled back to my nervous wife, offered Boris a croqueta, and we were off and running. Up until that point, no CIA officer had ever met Boris in person.

* * *

During the Cold War, recruiting a Soviet KGB officer was the ultimate goal of every CIA officer. Penetrating the monolithic Soviet intelligence apparatus was the bane and basis of the CIA's existence. Aside from having natural access to valuable intelligence on Moscow's plans, intentions, and capabilities, KGB officers could also provide critical counterintelligence (CI) reporting. At the top of our list of CI requirements was whether the CIA was penetrated by a Soviet mole. A well-placed KGB officer working secretly for the CIA could have warned us, for example, that notorious CIA traitor Aldrich "Rick" Ames was a long-term KGB asset. This knowledge could have helped prevent the capture and execution of the CIA's indispensable agent Soviet general Fedorovich Polyakov, who along with many other agents was betrayed by Ames to the KGB. Code-named "Tophat," Polyakov passed secret intelligence to the CIA about Soviet missiles and nuclear strategy, and he identified Soviet spies living in the United States.[1] The Tophat operation is proof of the concept that a single KGB asset can save countless lives and significantly enhance the national security of the United States.

The CIA categorized Soviet and other bloc officials as "hard targets" precisely because it was next to impossible to recruit them to spy for the United States. In part because it was nearly impossible for CIA officers to meet and spend private "quality time" with them away from the prying eyes of their Soviet embassy colleagues. Soviet officials abroad were closely monitored by the KGB and were forbidden to have social contact with US officials. They were carefully vetted before being deployed overseas to ensure their loyalty to the USSR. A dissatisfied Soviet could always defect, but it was a rare and risky occurrence. The Soviet government would retaliate against children and other family members of defectors or spies back in the USSR, and this was another compelling incentive to Soviets living in other countries to avoid all contact with Americans.

Faced with this Sisyphean task, how was a hapless CIA officer ever to meet, much less recruit, a Soviet spy? Patience, luck, and meticulous operational planning, for starters.

The journey of a thousand miles begins with one step. That first step was headquarters validation of any particular Soviet target, based on his known access to intelligence of interest and other factors. The CIA had been monitoring Boris's career for years, collecting extensive biographical and assessment data, and had already validated this young KGB officer. In a nutshell, because of his access and potential vulnerabilities, he was deemed an extremely attractive operational target for assessment, development, and recruitment. Boris's adulterous affair in Central America told us he was one of those rare KGB officers willing to run risks and break Soviet rules. We knew he had an eye for the ladies, which could provide interesting opportunities to get next to him. He also seemed to have more freedom than most Soviet officials abroad, which might make meeting him privately a real possibility. He was a loyal, rising Soviet star, but one who liked to live on the edge. This made him an especially attractive target.

With the validation box checked, the next step was to orchestrate direct but discreet contact between a station officer and the target. This task alone might elude us for years if not forever. Fortunately, that difficult hurdle had been surpassed when my wife and I "happened" to meet Boris at the aforementioned reception, away from the prying eyes and ears of his Soviet embassy colleagues.

The next stage was the most challenging of all: find a way to have sustained and meaningful contact with the target in order to assess him while slowly developing a friendship and relationship of trust, without having that contact come to the attention of anyone from the Soviet or other bloc embassies. This was accomplished in part by building and tapping into an extensive network of human and technical sources that covered the target's personal and professional life without his knowledge. This kind of coverage would not only provide more valuable insights into a target's vulnerabilities, but it would also result in information on his movements around town that would enable a case officer like me to engineer a "chance" encounter with him on the street. These choreographed, seemingly random meetings would give me the opportunity to chat with him informally and set up the next meeting time/place, without touching the monitored telephones of his embassy.

* * *

Aside from the obvious professional and national security reasons for making sustained contact with Boris my top operational priority, I also had personal motivations for pursuing this Soviet developmental. Stacy and I were close friends with Scott and Amy, another station couple. They had told us about their own nasty experience with the KGB in Leningrad. The Leningrad KGB, known for being even more brutal than their Moscow counterparts, smashed Scott and Amy's car windshield and pulled Scott (a husky 220-pound man) through the jagged glass opening. They then handcuffed Scott and Amy and separated them from each other and from their small daughter and hauled them off for interrogation at KGB headquarters. Shortly thereafter the Soviet government declared them persona non grata and expelled them from the Soviet Union. After hearing of their family's unnecessarily horrific experience at the hands of the KGB, I was doubly motivated to turn the tables on the Russians.

Scott was senior to me, with extensive Soviet experience. He and I worked closely together to coordinate a slow, "natural," and deliberate cultivation of this potentially valuable asset. Amy worked relentlessly to monitor all Soviet/bloc activity in Palmera and one day tipped me off that Boris had a doctor's appointment in half an hour at a health clinic across the street from the station. I parlayed that timely heads-up into another "off the grid" lunch meeting with Boris.

All of our social contacts were either seemingly accidental or arranged in advance, and we studiously avoided monitored office telephones. Boris was remarkably relaxed during our encounters, which typically took place over lunch or at receptions, including his own national day reception at the Soviet embassy. Hundreds of locals and foreign expats were in attendance, so my presence there on that date was unremarkable. Although alcohol was officially banned by then president Gorbachev at all Soviet functions, Boris invited me to a back room where the "secret" embassy bar was hidden. There, under the watchful gaze of an airbrushed portrait of a blemish-free Gorbachev, we continued our good-natured but purposeful verbal sparring over several rounds of Russian vodka. Over time we developed a friendship and relationship of (relative) trust, something rather unusual between a CIA officer and his KGB counterpart. Much of our time was spent swapping jokes (and lies) along with accusing each other's service of clearly being the more heinous.

After one friendly lunch not far from the station, Boris gave me a lift back to the office in his dip-plated vehicle. He played some Russian pop music on the car's cassette player and translated the lyrics for me into Spanish. His favorite was a 1983 pop song called "Trava u doma" ("Grass by the Home"), about cosmonauts in space who are longing for the green grass of home. Boris also told me one of his favorite jokes, a version of which is translated here from Russian to Spanish to English:

> Many years ago, the Soviet foreign minister flew to New Delhi for meetings with his friend and counterpart, the Indian foreign minister. On their limo drive into Delhi from the airport, the Soviet noticed an Indian man squatting on the side of the road, defecating. The Soviet huffed, "You never see that kind of thing in Soviet Union." The Indian foreign minister was embarrassed but remained silent.
>
> A few months later, the Indian foreign minister flew to Moscow for a reciprocal meeting with his old friend. On their limo drive into Moscow, the Indian foreign minister saw a man defecating on the side of the road. "You see," he said, "the same thing happens here in the Soviet Union! Your society is not so superior!"
>
> The Soviet foreign minister was embarrassed and very angry inside. After their arrival in Moscow, he called the director of the KGB and explained what had happened, demanding that the KGB find and arrest whoever it was they'd seen on the side of the road. It was nothing short of an unforgivable national embarrassment to the Soviet Union.
>
> Less than one hour later, the head of the KGB called the Soviet foreign minister.
>
> "Comrade Foreign Minister, I have good news, and I have bad news."
>
> "What is good news, Comrade KGB Director?"
>
> "We found man making srat on side of road."
>
> "Bravo, Comrade KGB Director! Please to put him in gulag for life, or to execute him. What is bad news?"
>
> "Man making srat was Indian ambassador."

Despite our jokes and friendly banter, I never lost sight of the fact that there was no moral equivalency between the CIA and KGB, or between the United States and Soviet Union. Quite the contrary. The KGB was an instrument of control and tyranny, whose raison d'être was to ensure the survival and expansion of one of the most repressive regimes in global history. The Soviets also possessed a nuclear arsenal that threatened (and continues to threaten) the very existence of the United States. It was precisely for these reasons that penetrating the KGB was the CIA's primary mission.

✷ ✷ ✷

To augment the rather limited perspective gained from my own personal contact with Boris, I recruited two local access agents from a country friendly to the Soviet Union. They did not know each other, but both would give me additional insights into Boris that I was not likely to obtain on my own. One was a brilliant, soft-spoken senior diplomat in his country's embassy, who had excellent contacts within the Soviet embassy. The other was a gorgeous young dancer who was able to develop her own access to local Soviet social circles and, with luck, to Boris. Although I recruited the embassy officer because of his natural access to the local Soviet community, there were also peripheral benefits: he once told me about a meeting in the Soviet embassy where key personnel were informed of President Gorbachev's decision to begin withdrawing Soviet troops from Afghanistan. This information would not be public for some time, and my intel report on the subject was well received by Soviet watchers at CIA headquarters.

Because Boris was such a high-priority target, I faithfully documented every conversation between the two of us, recording every detail I could remember about our contact. If we were meeting over drinks at night, I'd sometimes retreat to the bar's bathroom stall to jot down notes, to ensure I did not forget a single salient detail. The fact that Boris was willing to continue to meet with me was another indication that he was different than most Soviet officials. My cables were followed closely at headquarters by Soviet experts, including American spymaster Burton Gerber, Soviet–East European Division chief. Headquarters would respond to every cable, often with their informed big-picture analysis of what was transpiring, along with suggestions for how to move the developmental forward. Headquarters did not typically micromanage non-Soviet cases to this extent, but because of the potential risks and rewards, they remained fully engaged in this case. Unlike some other cases I ran, headquarters contributions in this operation were welcome.

✷ ✷ ✷

Although I'd recruited and run several productive non-Soviet agents during my three-year tour in Palmera, my development of Boris was considered more important than any of those career-enhancing "scalps." It was difficult enough to meet a validated Soviet target, much less develop a real, long-term relationship with one. With the help of many team players like Scott, Amy, and Gerber who remained in the shadows in Palmera and at Langley, I'd managed to do both, and it was the most fun and rewarding *Spy vs. Spy* experience of my career. But after nearly three years of progress, the correct decision was made to stand down on making any kind of recruitment approach.

Why didn't I pitch him? We had a solid enough relationship and liked and trusted each other as much as was possible under these very unusual and restrictive circumstances. Boris was clearly a risk-taker who took advantage of his freedom. But the reality was he had never evinced any real vulnerabilities to indicate he would be amenable to a recruitment pitch. This was fairly evident right from the start. He was not your run-of-the-mill KGB officer, but on balance he was and always would be a loyal Soviet officer. Recruiting Boris, while a lofty goal, was not my real aim. My objective was to forge a strong relationship of trust with Boris so that if and when the day came that he had "mentally defected" and was ready to switch sides, he'd know whom to call.

CHAPTER 13

HOW—AND WHY—
TO RECRUIT A RUSSIAN SPY

n November 1989, the Iron Curtain parted and the Berlin Wall was demolished on the world stage, to stirring, thunderous applause. Repressive Communist regimes throughout Eastern Europe followed suit, crumbling one after another like so many decaying dominos. In Dresden, a young KGB lieutenant colonel named Vladimir Putin was frantically burning classified documents and single-handedly staving off an angry crowd of freedom-starved East Germans outside the city's dreaded KGB headquarters. A few months later, a disillusioned Putin would return to Mother Russia with his new East German washing machine.[1] The dissolution of the future Russian dictator's beloved Soviet Union would soon follow. The revolutionary movements gained momentum, liberating all of the Warsaw Pact countries and eventually shattering the hegemonic Soviet Union itself.

Less than two years after my final contact with Putin's colleague, priority KGB developmental Boris Gudenov, I found myself caught up in this historic change sweeping rapidly across Eastern Europe. After a year and a half of specialized surveillance and language training in the DC area, in October 1989 I made the first of many long-term TDYs to Belgrade, Yugoslavia. Yugoslavia's own unique brand of socialism was doomed to fail, but not before a long and bloody civil war engulfed the entire country. I wasn't the only CIA operations officer fortunate enough to be working in that part of the world. My predecessor in Latin America was covering the bloody Romanian revolution from Bucharest like a seasoned war correspondent, while my other CIA colleagues kept equally busy staying abreast of rapidly changing events in other Eastern European capitals. In late

133

1989, there was no better place on earth to be deployed as a CIA officer than Eastern Europe.

Not long after my arrival in Yugoslavia, a local contact introduced me to a man who wanted to speak with an American official. After a quick introduction, the man volunteered that he was a Soviet citizen who worked for the KGB. (The KGB was replaced by the FSK in November 1991, and the FSK was reorganized into the Russian State Security Service, FSB, in 1995; meanwhile, in December 1991, the KGB First Chief Directorate became the Russian Foreign Intelligence Service, SVR.[2]) I asked him what he wanted. Like me, the man got right to the point: in a hushed voice, he said he wished to work in place for American intelligence as a double agent against the KGB, in exchange for hard currency; alternately, he would submit to a full one-time debriefing and share all of his KGB secrets with me.

Having come of age in a CIA culture where recruiting a KGB agent—or anyone with access to the KGB—was a high-priority but nearly impossible task, I thought that I'd just hit the jackpot. Yes, the man could be a "dangle," sent by the KGB to identify CIA officers and see how far he could run with this double agent ploy. But that seemed unlikely in light of the turmoil engulfing the KGB at that moment in time. And yes, the Soviet Union was clearly headed for collapse, but Russia would always be Russia. Russian leadership would remain autocratic, and Russians would always suspiciously view America and NATO as an ongoing threat to their existence. I thought their Serb cousins in Yugoslavia perfectly summed up the changing political situation in nuclear-power Russia with one of their many folk sayings: "*Vuk dlaku menja ali ćud nikada*," meaning "A wolf changes its fur but not its temperament."

I photocopied the man's documents and jotted down a description of his current job and access, and we arranged to meet again in a few days. I wrote up an initial trace cable to learn if CIA headquarters had a file or any other information on the man, and a request for an expression of operational interest, thinking headquarters would be as intrigued as I was about this potentially valuable CI asset. Although this Soviet walk-in would have been even more attractive to us a year earlier, he still struck me as a tantalizing lead.

Instead of giving me the green light, headquarters responded with a curt "no operational interest" and refused to authorize any further contact.

They would not even agree to pay this confessed KGB agent for a potentially valuable one-time debriefing. The reasoning appeared to be that since we were on the verge of victory in the Cold War, the KGB was no longer an enemy target worth pursuing. My reading of the tea leaves turned out to be correct: the CIA's new Soviet–East European (SE) Division chief sent out a worldwide cable telling CIA ops officers to stand down on pursuing Soviet targets, since the threat from Russia had all but disappeared. (At the end of the Cold War, SE Division was renamed Central Eurasia [CE] Division.) Although somewhat reminiscent of the time headquarters shot down my proposal to aggressively pursue the Cuban spy, this lack of operational interest was on a much larger and more dangerous scale. I was flabbergasted by what I considered to be a naïve and shortsighted CIA approach to an enemy that would never go away.

I met with the Russian again a few days later. I told him that I had discussed his case with American intelligence officials and they were unwilling to take him up on his offer. He did not seem to be as surprised as I was by our lack of interest. He somewhat sheepishly asked if I would at least buy his Soviet paratrooper's watch for twenty-five dollars. I happily did so, collecting the first of many Soviet souvenirs that would come my way for years to come. (Enterprising Afghans made a small fortune selling items like belt buckles taken from dead Soviet invaders. Old friend R. J. gave one to me, but I rarely find the right occasion to wear it.) The rebuffed KGB volunteer still agreed to a full debriefing, even though I could not pay him anything else. I wrote up a thorough report, including names, dates, operations, and other details from his KGB career, but never received a response from headquarters. The CIA was apparently gearing up to cover what they considered more compelling espionage targets, like the Japanese auto industry.

* * *

Despite this egregious if temporary lapse in judgment, it did not take the CIA long to wake up to the fact that the Russia threat was not going away. Much to the relief of many CIA officers and analysts, we again began to focus on targeting certain categories of Russian officials for recruitment.

When not on lengthy TDY assignments from the Washington area back to the Balkans, I operated primarily in another persona, meeting and recruiting foreign officials who could provide the CIA with access to their country's most sensitive secrets.

One day over lunch, a trusted and well-traveled American buddy of mine named "Dave" told me about an interesting friend of his: a high-level Russian government official who was recently promoted into a position with access to information potentially of importance to US national security. Dave told me that he and "Sasha," besides enjoying a years-long working relationship, had also become close personal friends and golfing buddies.

I extensively debriefed Dave on his Russian friend Sasha and wrote up an initial trace cable. Headquarters responded with a surprisingly detailed trace response, while validating Sasha as a high-priority recruitment target. The CIA had an extensive file on Sasha and gave me the green light to proceed. The next step was to engineer a "chance" encounter with him under benign circumstances, not unlike the approach I took with Boris in Latin America. The difference was Sasha would not knowingly run any risks by meeting with me, since he would know me only as a friend of our mutual friend Dave. Neither Dave nor I would tell Sasha of my CIA affiliation. Sasha's guard would be down, and he'd have no reason to suspect I was in fact a CIA ops officer whose objective was to convince him to betray his country. At least not initially. The fact that our mutual friend vouched for me would bestow upon me almost instant bona fides in the Russian's eyes. This was the key to our initial contact.

In the early 1990s, when I was planning my approach to Sasha, the Russian government was in disarray and could not afford to pay its top nuclear, rocket, and other scientists basic living-wage salaries. Iran took advantage of the chaotic situation facing the former Soviet Union and successfully transferred significant amounts of nuclear technology from Russia to Iran.[3] Many economically desperate Russian scientists felt forced to sell secret Soviet technology to outlaw countries like Iran and North Korea. Although they could barely afford to pay their bills, Russian officials did enjoy greater freedoms than before when it came to foreign travel. I once met a top Russian stealth scientist for drinks at a dive bar in Washington, an unimaginable concept (for both of us) just two years earlier. He lamented the fact that the beer I bought him was the first he'd had in over a year, since he simply could not afford such luxuries. His five-hundred-dollar-per-month salary was barely enough to cover the basics. As "What's Going On" by Marvin Gaye played on the jukebox, I ordered another round.

After some planning sessions with Dave, we decided that a natural, non-threatening way for me to meet Sasha would be to join their foursome during an informal golfing get-together planned for later that winter in the Bahamas. Several of Dave's friends, colleagues, and family members would be there for a days-long, relaxing retreat at an upscale golf resort. Sasha would no doubt greatly enjoy his "escape" from Russia in the dead of winter to play golf in the warm Caribbean sun. Besides golf, there would be multiple cocktail parties and other social events where I could get to know Sasha. I hoped he'd be pleased to meet me, a trusted friend of our mutual friend Dave.

There was just one problem with our brilliant plan: I didn't play golf. I had played a few times in high school, but if golf and I agreed on anything, it was that golf was not my game. I had one month to get up to speed so that I'd be able to keep up with Sasha and Dave on the links without embarrassing myself too much. Since my ability to play golf was essential to my mission, I played as much as possible with a very patient colleague who had played team golf in college. By the time I showed up in the Bahamas to meet Sasha, I could fake it well enough to accomplish phase one.

Sasha and I hit it off instantly. He was unlike any other Russian I'd ever met, probably in part because I'd never met one under such happy or relaxed circumstances. He spoke decent English, although my Serbian came in handy when he got stuck on a word, because of the similarities between Russian and Serbian. (I told him my maternal grandfather was a Serb and I'd picked up a few words as a child.) After spending a few hours together on the golf course, I invited him to lunch the next day. He readily accepted. We were both "stuck" in paradise for several days, so Sasha had plenty of free time on his hands.

Over lunch at an outdoor ocean-view restaurant, Sasha and I discussed our backgrounds and how we'd come to know our mutual friend. He corroborated much of what Dave had already told me about his current job. I am not permitted to go into detail, but because of the circumstances, I was able to pitch Sasha to provide secret information to me in the future.

Without hesitation, Sasha said he'd be very interested. Because of the manner in which I had engineered our first meeting, Sasha had no reason to be suspicious and we could get right down to business.

I explained the way our arrangement would work, and Sasha never questioned my background or asked questions about how his information would be used. Like most of his fellow Russian professionals, Sasha was having trouble making ends meet on his meager salary. He was happy to work privately for me. We agreed to meet in another month in a third country when he was scheduled to travel outside of Russia again on business.

* * *

I formally recruited Sasha early on in the relationship. Over the course of the coming year, I met several more times with him during his business trips outside of Russia. As a Russian who had grown up in the repressive Soviet system, he innately understood why it was in everyone's best interests to keep our arrangement secret. I provided Sasha with long lists of headquarters-provided questions for him to answer. He wrote up dozens of detailed, well-organized reports in direct response to over 95 percent of the requirements. If he could not answer a question, he said so. CIA headquarters analysts and other intelligence consumers were extremely pleased with Sasha's access and with the accuracy of his reporting. The CIA deemed Sasha and his information extremely reliable and of high value to the US government.

* * *

This inexpensive operation was highly successful, yielding significant "bang for the buck" to the US government. The operation remained secret from start to finish. My Russian agent delivered volumes of invaluable secret intelligence directly responsive to CIA requirements. America's national security was enhanced thanks to one well-placed Russian spy.

PART V

CIA FAMILY

CHAPTER 14

REAL HOUSEWIVES OF THE CIA

T he life of a CIA spouse can be fun. It can also be lonely, confusing, terrifying, exasperating, and exhausting. And that's just during training.

Although this chapter is called "Real Housewives of the CIA," the title, while descriptive of what follows, was admittedly chosen in part for the sake of a cheap laugh. In today's CIA, the dependent spouse is just as likely to be a "real househusband." With that in mind, the following vignettes could apply equally to any CIA spouse.

My wife Stacy and I married young, just before my third year of law school and her senior year of college. Transferring to a school in Washington for her last year of college was the first of many sacrifices she willingly made over the years to humor me and my jealous mistress (the CIA). We both spoke foreign languages and had spent long periods of time overseas, so the idea of joining the CIA and living and working abroad appealed to both of us. Although since she had no desire to work for the CIA, that meant her career would take a back seat to mine, as long as we hopscotched around the planet every couple of years. Still, how bad could it be?

Stacy's first taste of what lay ahead came on day one of "our" new career, when I shared the CIA's clear directive that in the future, she would have to lie to her friends and family about where I really worked. Sadly, she couldn't brag about my acceptance into the CIA's secret spy school, where I'd jump out of airplanes and train for the exciting life of an American James Bond. If pressed, she could admit that I had some lofty if exaggerated title given to entry-level paper pushers who weren't able to pass the foreign service exam and become real diplomats. If cornered, she could reluctantly reveal that my specialty was compiling statistical data on soybean production in Paraguay. At this point, anyone interrogating her about my job would find his or her eyes glazing over, and all questioning would inevitably cease. (I sometimes used this effective method myself when responding to nosy relatives and acquaintances, although the old standby, "If I am a CIA agent, no one told me," also left them baffled.)

After I shipped off for several months of paramilitary and tradecraft training at the Farm, Stacy and I would see each other on most weekends back in DC. This meant that soon after leaving her family and moving to DC to be with me, she found herself alone all week at our apartment. But wait, I'm not as much of a cad as you think! Before abandoning my bride, I taught her how to use a tactical shotgun for home defense (and close-range quail hunting), and she put her new skills to good use one night (for home defense, not for quail hunting). Situationally aware, Stacy noticed that a man was kneeling down outside the door to our eighth-floor apartment, looking through the small gap between the floor and the bottom of the door. He didn't knock and silently stayed put when she asked who he was and what he wanted. Our moderately priced apartment complex had a front desk on the ground level, but no one answered her repeated calls for help.

At that point Stacy's training kicked in. She grabbed the twelve-gauge Mossberg riot gun from the closet, walked to the door, and confidently pumped it once. The unmistakable sound of a shotgun round entering the chamber was enough to convince the Peeping Tom to make like a sheepherder and get the flock out of there. He never returned. At least not to *our* apartment.

✳ ✳ ✳

Life as a CIA wife in Latin America was, for the most part, pretty sweet. We moved from our one-bedroom Arlington apartment to a large, furnished Spanish-style villa, complete with an outdoor shower. (I never actually used it, but for some reason I found it comforting to know it was there, just in case.) We even had a housekeeper; my mom insisted I needed one ever since those long-ago days when I was just a messy little kid, tricking my friends into drinking their own urine. Stacy landed a job as the US embassy's assistant commissary manager, taught aerobics, and later became the community liaison officer (CLO), a prestigious job normally reserved for more senior spouses. (Her merit-based selection over older and more experienced wives was semi-scandalous at the time.) The CLO would coordinate congressional delegations, organize weekend trips for American staff, and be involved in other morale, welfare, and recreation activities.

Outside of our work, we led a very active social life. Sure, I'd use her as bait to lure my KGB target at an official reception, and she'd also graciously help me to spot and assess other foreign recruitment targets, some of whom we'd otherwise have no interest in befriending. I can still recall hearing her pleading something along the lines of the following on more than one occasion: "I'm sure the Pakistani first secretary is a great guy, but must we invite him and all eight members of his family to the beach house for our only vacation of the year?" She also had to contend with the kinds of harassment that women experience every day, in every part of the world. One evening, we were at an informal expat party at someone's home. For some reason I was seated on the floor, and Stacy was standing next to me. She was approached by the Egyptian ambassador, who began to hit on her. I was too tired to get up, so I tugged on his pant leg. When he looked down, I wagged my finger at him.

But we also socialized with the American community, went to wild parties at the Marine House, and traveled extensively throughout the spectacularly beautiful country of Palmera and elsewhere in Latin America. We snorkeled with barracuda in the crystal-clear sea, canoed up a copper-colored river to one of the world's largest waterfalls, and hiked through cool, foggy green mountains. The Palmera restaurant and nightclub scenes were world-class (and affordable). Stacy even talked me into taking salsa and merengue lessons. To this day I can't sit still if I hear Wilfrido Vargas's "El Africano." In the late 1980s, life was good in Palmera.

Predictably, my job often rudely interfered with our dream life. Just before setting out one weekday morning on a "breaking and entering" technical op to plant a listening device inside a priority hostile target organization's beach house, located several hours outside the capital, my colleagues and I realized we needed one more vetted team member to provide counter-surveillance. Our counter-surveillant would park his car on the side of a remote jungle road to deal with "mechanical problems," a couple of kilometers away from the target beach house. Should any personnel from the target organization unexpectedly drive past in their diplomatic-plated car en route to their seaside villa, the counter-surveillant would alert us via secure radio and we'd abort the mission, getting out of the house before the hostiles arrived.

We needed a trusted "inside" person to assist, since this was a highly sensitive and risky operation, and we did not have enough cleared station officers or headquarters TDYers to cover all of the roles. My COS decided that my witting wife would do the job. I reminded him that Stacy was working as the assistant commissary manager and she couldn't just leave her post on a moment's notice. It would put her job in jeopardy and might also raise suspicions, since many embassy employees knew or at least suspected who my real employer was. My arguments fell on deaf ears, and he ordered her to assist. Stacy complied, and the operation went off without a hitch. It also earned me another *What have you gotten me into this time?* look.

It was then we both accepted the reality that the CIA got two employees for the price of one. The wife—and in those days it was typically a wife and not a husband—was an unpaid partner. The CIA expected the wife to participate in training and operations, especially entertainment and developmental work in which the case officer husband attempted to cultivate individual targets of operational interest. The practice was not necessarily fair, but that's just the way it was. I suspect it is less the case today, but it certainly was common in the "old days," including the late 1980s and into the 1990s.

This "two-for-one" phenomenon became doubly apparent after my Latin America tour, when we transferred back to DC for the grueling but phenomenal Soviet–East European Internal Ops (SE/IO) course prior to our upcoming series of long-term TDYs to Communist Yugoslavia. As my former CE Division chief Milt Bearden and the national security journalist James Risen revealed in their book, *The Main Enemy*, the SE/IO course was the CIA's equivalent of the US Navy's Top Gun school for fighter pilots.[1] It was hands down the best, most challenging, and most valuable training I ever received in my life. Although all CIA officers underwent solid surveillance detection training during the operations course at the Farm, those of us selected to operate in denied areas also had to successfully complete the much more intensive SE/IO course. The CIA had to be 100 percent certain the officer could detect hostile surveillance before deploying him to a denied area to run sensitive agents—agents who, simply put, would be arrested and executed if the case officer failed to detect surveillance. The ability to detect surveillance was a learned technical skill, like refrigerator repair, and either you got it or you didn't. Those officers who failed the course did not suffer any career setbacks, but they would not serve in denied areas.

Stacy and I had orders to report to the seven-week-long SE/IO course within a few days of touching down in DC following our enjoyable but exhausting three-year tour of duty in Latin America. When we departed from DC three years earlier we were living the free and easy life of newlyweds, but by the time we returned, we had an adorable and precocious one-year-old daughter, and no one to care for her during training. After we left our Spanish-speaking little one for the first few days with day care, our hearts couldn't take it any longer and we flew my mother-in-law to DC to babysit for the remainder of the course. (I won't bore you with the details, but trust me when I say that summoning my mother-in-law for help was an indication of just how desperate the situation had become.) The stressful course ran five long days per week, with lots of independent casing and other work required on weekends. We had to assume we were being monitored 24/7, in the car and even at home, for the duration of the course. The objective of the course was to replicate as much as possible what our lives would be like during our TDYs in Yugoslavia. If Stacy had been unable or unwilling to take the course alongside me, the CIA would have canceled my Belgrade assignment. The unpaid spouse was an integral part of the team for denied area operations, and we knew this when we accepted the job.

During the SE/IO course, we were trained and tested relentlessly by the best of the best—CIA officers who had gone through the training themselves and who had completed successful tours operating in hostile denied areas like Moscow. The instructors knew exactly what we would face once we were operational, and they quite correctly cut us no slack. They pushed us to the limit. By the end of the course, you either knew if you were "black" (surveillance-free) or you didn't. If there was any doubt at all, you'd fail the course and would find an onward assignment in a less hostile operating environment. The bottom line was the CIA owed it to our agents, who risked their lives for us and the United States, to run them securely and with minimal risk of compromise. The CIA's raison d'être, and mine, became Stacy's.

During the course, we went up against the best surveillance on earth, including a secretive US government unit I'll call Special Surveillance Squads (SSS). Indicative of how good SSSs are at monitoring a target without being detected, they are known within government security circles as Ghosts. SSSs are not law enforcement or intelligence officers, but they are separately trained undercover operatives who conduct counterterrorism and counterintelligence surveillance operations. They seamlessly blend in with their surroundings, making it next to impossible to detect them. Who suspects they may be under surveillance by a guy operating a backhoe, a harried woman making deliveries out of a florist's van, or identical twins with dwarfism in line at the airport?

While an SSS Ghost is a stealthy surveillant, in CIA parlance, a "ghost" is someone who you have mistakenly concluded has you under surveillance. As critical as it is to be able to detect surveillance, it is almost equally important to know when someone you suspect of surveillance is actually a ghost, in order to avoid aborting a rarely scheduled, critical agent meeting. Imagine failing to learn about an imminent terrorist attack against the United States because a CIA officer aborted a key meeting after mistakenly believing he was under surveillance. We had to know the difference between a ghost and actual surveillance. We had to trust our training.

The SE/IO course benefitted CIA officers in the "pipeline" for the Soviet bloc because we were able to face off against the kind of professional, almost invisible surveillance we could expect overseas. Monitoring CIA officers and their spouses in training exercises also helped the SSS operatives to better understand how a foreign spy or terrorist might operate inside the United States. The training was mutually beneficial and is an example of how the various agencies of the US government should and often do cooperate, for the good of our nation.

Stacy and I worked hard and passed the course. We always correctly determined if and when we were black, and we were also able to conduct operational acts undetected while under intense SSS surveillance.

Being able to detect surveillance does not preclude a CIA officer from being set up by a controlled or compromised agent, the way my friends

Scott and Amy were in Leningrad. One morning during training, Stacy and I were in the middle of our preplanned surveillance detection route (SDR) to ensure we were not being followed before committing a planned operational act near Hogate's, which was coincidentally one of our favorite restaurants. Hogate's was located on Maine Avenue in Southwest DC, near what is now the DC Wharf. A tall, imposing, apparently homeless man in a camouflage jacket approached us, acted as if he knew us, and tried to sell us drugs. (I'd lived and worked in DC for years, and this was not an uncommon occurrence.) We told him no thanks and tried to move past him, at which point half a dozen federal security officers appeared out of nowhere and converged on us, weapons drawn, shouting commands, arresting us both. The "homeless" man also pulled a gun; he was in fact a fellow officer. Curious passersby who witnessed our arrest got their jolt of excitement for the day. Looking back, I'm just grateful smartphones and YouTube had not yet been invented. Getting arrested with your wife by half a dozen police is not the kind of thing you want your mother-in-law to see on the local news while playing Ring around the Rosie with your one-year-old at home.

The arresting officers cuffed us and put us into two separate unmarked vehicles. Stacy did not look happy as they pushed her head down and buckled her up in the back seat of a dark sedan. I was pretty sure this was part of training, although I could not yet be sure, since we were in a semi-seedy part of town and we were observed talking to a drug dealer. Cops have been known to make mistakes. No one had warned us in advance that this might happen during the course, and so I could only imagine what was going through Stacy's mind.

The officers took us to their office, where they searched my wallet and her purse, and interrogated us in separate rooms. Having survived SERE and law school, and knowing that I was innocent and in America after all, I was almost enjoying the experience. That changed when they dialed the number on my business card and informed some poor government secretary that an employee named H. K. Roy had just been arrested for espionage. (I made a mental "note to self" to clean up that unfortunate mess after I got out.) I wasn't yet sure what was going on, so I told the officers I wouldn't say another word without a lawyer present. To be clear, that very American legalistic approach would not have worked so well had I been captured by the Iranians in Sarajevo, although it would have provoked a few laughs before the real fun began.

My confidence was briefly put to the test when I heard a woman sobbing from a nearby office. Was that Stacy?

A tough-looking officer then entered my room.

"Mr. Roy," she said, "I suggest you cooperate for the sake of your wife. She's not holding up well, and she *will* pay the price once she confesses. I'm talking prison time."

By now I'd convinced myself it was not Stacy's voice I'd heard coming from the adjoining room and that our arrest and interrogation were both part of the training.

"Ma'am," I replied, "after she's sent to prison, will Stacy be allowed conjugal visits?"

The officers were not nearly as amused as I was.

After a few hours of interrogation, discomfort, and intimidation, we were both released on our own recognizance. You can probably guess what kind of look Stacy shot me as we stumbled out of the office. We never returned to Hogate's for happy hour after that eventful day.

I am not going to get any further into describing the training or the methods we learned in the SE/IO course, since I consider those to be the CIA's "crown jewels" of tradecraft. Suffice it to say that by the time of my first TDY to Yugoslavia, I was 100 percent confident in my ability to detect surveillance and securely meet my sensitive agent(s) on the dark and dusty back streets of Belgrade.

* * *

Stacy and I added a second beautiful baby daughter to the mix during our eighteen months in DC. Since Stacy had been fully trained in surveillance detection and could help me operationally, she and our daughters were authorized to join me in Yugoslavia. In October 1989, the four of us made our way from Dulles International Airport to Belgrade via a tiring, circuitous, and expensive route, thanks to a US government policy requiring us to fly US-flag carriers for official travel.

In the late 1980s, Belgrade was a dismal and depressing Eastern European capital with a rather aggressive and hostile local population. Our fully furnished quarters were fine by Yugoslav standards, but it was definitely a step or two down from our wonderful Latin American home. Soon after moving in, I inadvertently confirmed our phone was being monitored when I called a family member and complained about some routine Yugoslav aggravation. The Serb SDB (Yugoslav KGB) agent listening in actually joined the conversation to argue with me. Yes, Serbs are really like this, and it partially explains why they were the common denominator in all of the Balkan wars of the 1990s. To this day I have close Serb friends, and to their credit, they would not disagree.

Since we knew our quarters and phone were both bugged, Stacy and I would have to be careful what we said inside the house. And the car. When we disagreed about something, we'd take a walk around the block so that we could talk freely. There might be an SDB car parked nearby, but the low-tech thugs inside would have no way of listening to what we were discussing.

In Belgrade, Stacy was harassed by locals on the road, in state-run stores, and on the ubiquitous streetcars. Some aggressive Serbs did not take kindly to being passed in their decrepit Ladas by a foreign woman driving a new Peugeot, and they let her know it. She was flipped off and even almost run off the road more than once by these paragons of masculinity. Walking into a state-run clothing store, Stacy would be "greeted" and then escorted back out the door by a surly, cigarette-smoking clerk, dressed in a Communist-issue smock. Salespeople had no incentive to be polite or sell her something, since they received the same paltry pay whether they made any sales or not. A common expression heard throughout the Communist world was "Government pretends to pay us and we pretend to work." Emulating the local custom of rarely buying a ticket on a Belgrade streetcar, foreigner Stacy was once rudely singled out by a city cop to pay a fine and get off the streetcar.

Other realities of daily life were annoying but harmless. Since there was almost no foreign, non-Serbian food in Belgrade, we were excited to learn of a new Mexican restaurant in town. We tried it once. Every time we hopefully asked if they had a particular menu item (taco, tostada, enchilada, etc.), we were always given the same answer: "*Da, imamo ali nema,*" meaning "Yes, we have it, but there isn't any." In one of Belgrade's finer dining establishments, the downtown Writer's Club, candlelit tables were decked out in white tablecloths and fancy silverware. Waiters wore vests and ties. American disco music blared incessantly from several speakers, so loud that you could barely hear the person seated next to you. Between courses, rather than sweeping the breadcrumbs off the table with an elegant, old-school table crumber, waiters nearly blew us out of our heavy wooden chairs with modern handheld vacuums, sucking up everything off the table with a noisy flourish.

Although it was not easy, I never ceased trying to impress my wife with my insider's knowledge of Belgrade's fine-dining scene. When the first McDonald's opened in Belgrade, the entire first batch of employees had to be fired, since they were unwilling or unable to implement the fundamental practice of being polite to customers. I learned this from the local McDonald's rep, who also told me that McDonald's hired a second crew and immediately whisked them out of the country for a few weeks of basic customer service training. Brainwashing, American-style. After that, McDonald's became our favorite restaurant, since it was the only smoke-free place in town, with friendly service to boot. You could even get ice. A waiter at another "upscale" state-run restaurant once told Stacy, after she'd asked repeatedly for some ice for her warm Coke, "*Dosta je hladna,*" meaning "Is cold enough." (For the record, Belgrade has changed drastically since our time there, and it is now a worthwhile tourist destination, as is the rest of the former Yugoslavia.)

* * *

When Stacy joined me in Belgrade, I was typically working ten- or eleven-hour days at the station. This was often followed by late-night or weekend SDRs prior to reading or marking signal sites, casing future meeting and signal sites, or conducting on-the-street agent meetings. I would return home late, reeking not of perfume but of Belgrade itself: the heavy, misty yellow air was dangerously polluted thanks to a million people burning soft coal and garbage at the same time. Belgrade's residents would toss their smoldering coal embers into large garbage dumpsters, yielding a nasty burnt garbage smell that permeated the entire city. When blended with the aforementioned soft coal smog, the results were gag inducing, especially for those of us walking the streets late at night. Meanwhile, in the winter the streets were covered with "permaslime," the name we gave to the dirty, slippery, gooey icy substance that seemed to cover all roads and sidewalks. After a few months in-country, all of our clothing turned as gray as the Belgrade sky. Our sweet second baby girl was later diagnosed with asthma, and I'm convinced it's because we subjected her to Belgrade air for the first two years of her life.

While I was out doing God's work (as we sometimes jokingly called it), Stacy was left to deal with our two daughters and this challenging way of life. A wonderful Filipina nanny helped out with our little ones, but she also hung out at the local Philippines embassy, which per a reliable source was staffed in large part by Communist New People's Army (NPA) members and sympathizers. NPA was a State Department designated terrorist organization, and at the time, they were actively targeting and killing Americans, possibly including SERE course creator Colonel Nick Rowe. Needless to say, knowing that our nanny might inadvertently facilitate our premature deaths added to Stacy's stress level, as did reported Iraqi surveillance of our older daughter's International Nursery School bus during the first Gulf War.

But not all was dark and depressing. Stacy and I and the girls would often fly, drive, or take a car train to Croatia, Slovenia, or out of Yugoslavia altogether. We enjoyed many brief but relaxing (and microphone-free) stays in Austria, Germany, Italy, and France. We even took a wonderful "special R and R" ski trip to St. Moritz, Switzerland, where we exchanged our gray "Balkan refugee" clothing for something with a little more color. Stacy and the girls also visited Dubrovnik, a magical place on the Dalmatian Coast I would not see with my own eyes until one year into the Croatian war. Oftentimes we would travel as a family from Belgrade to another European city, ostensibly on vacation. Upon arrival in Frankfurt, or wherever, I would change identities and travel on alias documentation to a third country for agent meetings, while Stacy and the girls enjoyed a respite outside of Belgrade. We also once drove nine hours through the deadly, garbage-strewn roads of Serbia and Macedonia to the Halkidiki region of Greece for a nice seaside vacation. The trip felt longer than it actually was, since we had to repeatedly listen to the only cassette tape we remembered to bring along, *Best of Raffi*.

As in Latin America, Stacy and I enjoyed a good social life with fellow American colleagues in Belgrade, although my job always seemed to impact our family fun. I recall our family spending one Christmas Eve with several other families at the home of some close US embassy friends. Everyone was having a wonderful time, including the children. It almost felt like home, until I had to leave the gathering early and without comment to run a three-hour SDR and conduct an important prewar agent meeting. My embassy friends were good about not saying anything at a time like this, since they'd been briefed in DC prior to their Belgrade assignments to not play "spot the spook" or otherwise comment on suspected CIA activity they may observe while in Belgrade. The walls had ears, and a single over-heard or monitored comment could compromise a CIA officer's identity or even a valuable operation.

✳ ✳ ✳

By now you probably won't be surprised to learn that the divorce rate for CIA officers is significantly higher than the national average. Having to endure multiple, long-term Yugoslavia TDYs was the final straw for Stacy, and we divorced upon our return to the United States. When things got too tough to handle, I made long-term TDYs back to the war zones of Croatia and Bosnia, since they provided me with welcome escapes from the stressful situation at home.

Although we divorced long ago, Stacy and I get along just fine today, but she is still paying the price for my overseas wanderlust. When our oldest daughter was in college, after I left the CIA, she asked to accompany me on a private business trip to Iraq that I had planned over her winter break. I readily agreed, since I was headed to Erbil in the generally safe Kurdistan region of northern Iraq. How many college kids get to go to Iraq for Christmas vacation? A few years earlier I took my daughters and their cousin to another country in the Middle East for spring break.

Stacy was not amused by my plan to take our first-born daughter to Iraq. While I agreed that, generally speaking, there were probably better places than Iraq for our daughter to spend her winter vacation, I assured her that Erbil was a pocket of tranquility in the otherwise insanely dangerous war zone. To further emphasize the righteousness of my position, I promised Stacy that she'd never read about this place called Erbil on the front page of the *New York Times*. (You just know where this is headed.)

About one week after our conversation, I was awakened in the middle of the night in Erbil as US Special Forces in attack helicopters and armored vehicles assaulted an Iranian "diplomatic" building a few blocks away from our hotel. My daughter's room was across the hall from mine, and she did not hear a thing. From my hotel room window, I watched a Black Hawk helicopter hover above the Iranians' building. I learned later that our troops snatched half a dozen suspected Iranian Quds Force operatives from the building. According to the *New Yorker* magazine, the raid was based on intelligence that notorious Quds Force commander Qassem Suleimani, the man responsible for Mughniyeh, the Buckley kidnapping, and recent deadly "explosively formed penetrator" attacks against US troops in Iraq, would be among those captured. Unfortunately, Suleimani had broken off from the group before they arrived at the Iranian "consulate" and was in a safe house provided by Kurdistan Regional Government (KRG) leader Masoud Barzani.[2]

I heard from my KRG contacts that the US military had not coordinated this daring operation in advance with our close (if not duplicitous) Kurdish government allies. The Kurds were furious, and the incident led to a tense armed standoff between US and Peshmerga forces later that day. Our hotel was soon swarming with US and Kurdish military officers who were frantically attempting to defuse the situation. For its part, the Iranian government predictably expressed its outrage over this blatant breach of international law, blah, blah, blah. (You can imagine my reaction to Iran's hypocritical outrage after their own blatant breach of international law nearly cost me my life in Sarajevo. The "kidnapped" Iranian operatives were not in Erbil to pass out candy, and they would not be tortured or killed as I would have been.)

Regardless, this truly was a serious international incident, and the entire story about what transpired during our daughter's winter vacation in Iraq was splashed the next morning across the front page of the *New York Times*.[3]

CHAPTER 15

SPY KIDS

Legendary CIA spymaster Burton Gerber was fond of saying that the ideal case officer had a wife and a dog but no kids. Gerber was SE Division chief in the mid-1980s, and he brilliantly managed all denied area agent operations inside the former Soviet bloc countries and Yugoslavia. His theory was that a couple on the street, perhaps walking a dog, would attract much less KGB or "nosy neighbor" scrutiny than a solitary man or woman. Together they could more securely mark and read signals, service dead drops, or meet briefly with an agent. A childless couple would also be free of the worry and responsibility that children entail, and could devote their lives 24/7 to the overriding "needs of the service."

Gerber likely knew the Cold War spy business better than anyone, and he made valid points. But, like most people, CIA officers have kids, and those kids are part of the equation. My first daughter was born during our Latin America tour, and (as Gerber could have predicted) this change in family structure did indeed affect my work schedule. After she was born and comfortable in her new crib and mosquito netting, I would try and arrange agent meetings to end at a reasonable hour so that I could be home to spend time with her in the evenings.

When our daughter was about six months old, she and Stacy and I traveled TDY to DC for psychological testing at headquarters. Picture couples counseling but without the empathy. This testing was the first hurdle for officers and spouses selected for denied area assignments. We arrived at headquarters with our daughter in tow and were told by security that babies were not allowed inside CIA headquarters. In the mid-1980s, you simply did not see children in the building. Ever.

We literally had no one to leave her with, since all of our friends were deployed overseas, but the only place where we could undergo the required psychological testing was inside the headquarters building. We were at a stand-still. We explained our dilemma to the security officers, who were sympathetic but not in a position to help. Eventually, our petition for baby access made its way up the chain of command to Burton Gerber himself, who signed off on a waiver allowing our daughter to accompany us during the psych exams. (I can just picture him shaking his head in disbelief as he processed this unusual request.) Our baby girl was then issued an "escort required" visitor's badge, which we clipped to her clothing. It was almost as big as she was.

After the three of us were badged through security, we paused for a moment at the white marble CIA Memorial Wall on the right-hand side of the main entrance. Every star etched into the wall represents a CIA life lost in the line of duty. At the time of our visit, they had just added a fifty-first star, in remembrance of former Beirut COS William Buckley, who was savagely killed by Iranian-backed Hezbollah terrorists a few years earlier. The inscription reads, "In honor of those members of the Central Intelligence Agency who gave their lives in the service of their country."[1] Every year there is a private memorial ceremony in which the names of all who lost their lives are read aloud, including the names of undercover officers whose CIA affiliation will never be made public. As of the time of this writing, there are 129 stars on the Memorial Wall. I am grateful that I am not represented there by a star and that my name is not read every year during the ceremony. I am equally and eternally thankful for the ultimate sacrifice made by my fallen colleagues and their families in service to our nation. Experiencing the wall never fails to move me.

After paying our respects at the Memorial Wall, I carried our daughter as we walked the short distance down the hall to the Office of Medical Services for our psychological evaluations. I wasn't prepared for the reception our cheerful six-month-old would receive. Her presence created quite a stir. I will never forget the way CIA employees—men and women alike—reacted upon seeing this fun-size, visitor-badged human as we made our way down the corridor. You'd think a winged unicorn was loose in the building. Most who saw her were ecstatic. A few even approached us, presumably to see for themselves if it was a real baby or maybe something Tony Mendez had cooked up in his lab for some sensitive op. I assured those few who raised an eyebrow that she'd been fully vetted, with no deception indicated during her most recent polygraph exam.

To this day, my eldest daughter relishes the fact that she was the first baby ever to set tiny little feet inside the hallowed halls of CIA headquarters. She also still treasures her first baby-faced official passport.

Things of course have changed since the days of baby prohibition, and now there are even on-site day care facilities at CIA headquarters. (Sorry, Burton, but you opened the floodgates when you agreed to let my little one in.)

My second daughter was born in Fairfax, Virginia, about six months before we began to TDY to Belgrade. She too made it inside CIA headquarters, but only in my mind. Required to pass another polygraph exam before running ops in Yugoslavia, I visualized my baby girl's serene, angelic face to keep myself calm as I sat through the always unpleasant exam. Needless to say, I passed. I could have coolly confessed to killing Abraham Lincoln with a suicide vest that day and there would have been no deception indicated.

*   *   *

Traveling overseas with small children is a universal hell experienced by many young parents, CIA and regular folks alike. You may be standing next to the Taj Mahal, but if you've got little ones, you're stuck inside what I call the "baby bubble." When inside the bubble—which is anytime baby is with you—you will be focused almost exclusively on the baby's needs: care and feeding, adjusting the stroller, changing the diaper, finding a place to dispose of the diaper, and dealing with occasional tantrums. Sure, every now and then you may poke your head outside the bubble and take a quick peek at the Grand Canyon, but otherwise you're trapped inside. It's next to impossible to take that selfie with the Eiffel Tower when you're comforting a shrieking toddler covered in vomit and rainbow sprinkles.

Some case officers cleverly use the baby bubble phenomenon to their advantage, for example, by stopping to change a diaper on top of a dead drop site, on the assumption the act will not arouse suspicion. Our good friends Scott and Amy used this ploy in Leningrad but were ambushed by the KGB. It wasn't their baby's fault, or their fault for that matter. The plan to clear the dead drop was a good one, as was their execution of the plan, but unfortunately and unbeknownst to them, their agent was under KGB control.

* * *

In Sarajevo, immediately after learning that the Iranian intelligence operative planned to kidnap me, I called my daughters on the villa's phone and involved them unwittingly in my escape plan. At the time, they were in Hawaii with Stacy, joyfully oblivious to the dire situation I was facing. After singing me a sweet rendition of "Jamaica Farewell," they asked me how I was doing. I lied and told them I had a bad stomach ache and could not leave the office. In fact, I was fine, but because of the Iranian threat, I could not leave the safety of the villa for my daily meeting at the interior ministry. My lie was for the benefit of the Bosnian spooks who were likely monitoring the office phone. I'd already phoned their boss Marko—who was collaborating in the Iranian plot against me—to say I'd come down with some sort of stomach flu and couldn't make our next meeting. This monitored call to my daughters would confirm my alibi in a natural way and would hopefully leave my enemies with their guard down, at least long enough for me to exfiltrate Sarajevo.

I will never know exactly how much that call with my unwitting spy kids contributed to my successful escape, but by answering their mom's phone that day they definitely played a role.

* * *

Halloween was always a favorite holiday of my daughters. My oldest daughter kicked off the tradition when she won "best costume" at an American embassy Halloween party for expats in Palmera when she was five months old. In the United States, she and her little sister would go trick-or-treating every year with their cousins in a neighborhood known for its over-the-top haunted houses and Halloween displays. Their uncle John turned his suburban home into one of the best attractions in the neighborhood, complete with a graveyard, rising smoke, and ghouls who appeared out of nowhere.

Growing up as spy kids, my girls heard more than they ever wished to know about Iraq and Saddam, as well as Fidel Castro and others of their ilk. As a result, they saw nothing unusual about their dad wearing a Saddam Hussein mask for Halloween. For two years in a row, I traveled home from a TDY to Croatia on Halloween day, arriving just in time to join my girls as they went trick-or-treating. They never thought to ask why I wore the same camouflage Croatian Army jacket as my costume each year. Or why I was a tad jumpy whenever some clown (or witch) set off a Halloween firecracker in my general vicinity.

✳ ✳ ✳

After I resigned from the agency, I remarried and my new wife and I had (you guessed it) a baby girl. Although I was no longer an agency employee, I continued to travel overseas and support the national security mission as needed. Because of this, my third little angel also got a taste of what it was like to grow up as a spy kid. For example, like her sisters, she too complained about the fact that the tooth fairy left her only foreign currency. None of them bought my argument that Saddam's dinars were way cooler than an ordinary American five-dollar bill.

Although my third daughter did not grow up overseas, she has traveled internationally her entire brief life. She was six weeks old (and undocumented) when she made her first road trip to Mexico, and she speaks Spanish. For as long as she can remember, I've been running a business in Iraq. Over the years, she's accumulated a nice collection of souvenirs from Iraq, Syria, Jordan, Lebanon, UAE, Oman, and the other Middle Eastern countries I've visited. She's also heard lots of exciting stories about Iraq. In one case, she and a few of her fourth-grade classmates heard an Iraqi terrorism story unfold in real-time when I was driving them to yet another field trip.

Stuck in traffic while driving to the Natural History Museum, I received a call on speakerphone from an Iraqi employee in our office in the al-Mansour neighborhood of Baghdad. He proceeded to breathlessly tell me about a massive car bomb that had just gone off across the street, killing dozens. Our guys were all accounted for. He noted that our security cameras had recorded the entire thing, and I was welcome to watch the rescue efforts unfold live as soon as I got back online. He warned me that the horrific scenes were bloody and tough to witness.

At this point I noticed that the children had quieted down. I glanced in the rearview mirror, and their eyes seemed to be open a little wider than normal. I quickly got off the phone and told them, "Sorry, kids, wrong number."

✳ ✳ ✳

I'll conclude this chapter on spy kids with the following wonderful saying about all children, translated from the original Arabic:

> A father was asked, "Which of your three children is your favorite?"
>
> He answered, "The young one until she grows up, the sick one until she is well, and the one who is away until she returns."

Baja California, Mexico, safe house.

Mt. Igman. Bosnia.

Mortar round aftermath. Sarajevo, Bosnia.

French Battalion at Mt. Igman. Bosnia.

Zemun Cemetery. Belgrade, Serbia (Yugoslavia). *Photo courtesy of SM.*

Author and Croatian colleague. Bosnia-Herzegovina.

Stari Most bridge. Mostar, Bosnia.

City park cemetery. Mostar, Bosnia.

Grand Hotel during Senator Bob Dole visit. Pristina, Kosovo.

Radovan Karadžić incognito. Belgrade, Serbia. *Photo from AP Photo.*

Stenkovec refugee camp. Macedonia.

First Lady Hillary Clinton and Ambassador Chris Hill. Stenkovec refugee camp, Macedonia.

Freedom reigns in postwar Pristina, Kosovo.

Amman, Jordan.

Saddam's arches. Iraq.

Imad's family compound. Ramadi, Iraq.

Al-Hamidiyah Souk. Damascus, Syria.

Baghdad, Iraq.

Author with Kurdistan Regional Government president Masoud Barzani. Erbil, Iraq.

DO NOT ASK FOR WATER
لا تطلب الماء من أحد
DO NOT KNOCK
ON WINDOWS
لا تطرق على الشبابيك
DO NOT PUT BADGES
IN YOUR MOUTH
لا تضع (الباج) في فمك
ONE PERSON AT A
TIME AT THE WINDOW
شخص واحد في كل مرة أمام الشباك (واحد واحد)
ALL FAKE I.D.s
WILL BE CONFISCATED
كافة الهويات المزورة سوف تتم مصادرتها

Victory Base Complex sign. Baghdad, Iraq.

Black Hawk over Baghdad, Iraq.

Syrian refugee camp. Beqaa Valley, Lebanon.

Basra, Iraq.

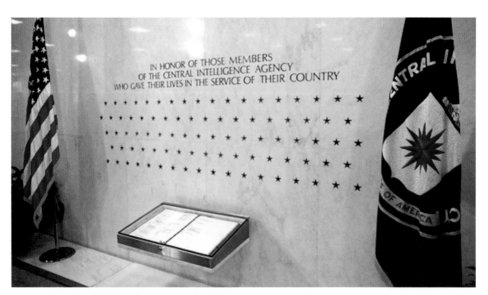

CIA Memorial Wall. *Photo from Central Intelligence Agency website.*

CHAPTER 16

CIA SAFE SEX PRACTICES

Before we begin, I should probably clarify a key point for those readers who are old enough to remember when CIA allegedly stood for Catholics in Action. The title of this chapter does not refer to the rhythm method, or even to holding garlic between your knees until after marriage. It also has nothing to do with Burton Gerber's stated preference for childless spy couples, or with "denied areas." It means, quite simply, sex on a safe. While the author has not personally engaged in this particular form of classified hanky-panky, I know that its practice on official CIA property is not all that uncommon. (Rumor has it one especially enthusiastic couple's reckless abandon shook the safe so much that the dial actually moved back and forth with just enough precision to crack it open, its classified contents spilling out onto the clothing-littered office floor. Talk about tickling the tumblers!)

Sex between CIA colleagues, both during training and overseas, is more common than one might imagine. This should not be all that surprising, however, since the CIA has strict rules governing the ins and outs of which foreigners are considered forbidden fruit. "Thou shalt not fraternize with the enemy" being the overriding principle. Certain foreigners are clearly off-limits, like North Koreans and Canadians. (Okay, not the latter, but you get the point.) For those foreigners not on the "no-fly list," CIA employees must report any relationship where the employee has developed "bonds of affection" with a foreigner. Which, naturally, raises a question: what if my relationship with Natasha is purely physical and there are no discernible bonds of affection?

Sadly, the CIA does not appreciate this kind of lawyerly nitpicking over its rules. And violation of these rules will land a CIA employee in some serious hot water (including prison, depending on how far it goes). So, CIA employees, as often as not, end up sleeping with other CIA employees. It's just easier that way. Keep it in the family, so to speak. Sure, we are allowed to sleep with State Department employees, but let's be honest: who'd want to? And technically, we can sleep with our allies. Inspiring others to follow the rules as she always did, a bombastic blond colleague of mine regularly showed up at official overseas parties, wearing a T-shirt that read, "SLEEP NATO."

During training, CTs were all stuck together in stressful conditions on remote, secret bases for months on end. Things happened. Our class's theme song was "Let's Get It On." I never passed judgment on the extracurricular activities of some of my classmates, but I always questioned their dedication to sound tradecraft practices and wondered if there shouldn't be a separate graded category for that particular skill set. If they can't pull off a simple adulterous affair on friendly soil without half of us knowing exactly what's going on, how can they expect to run clandestine operations overseas? If and when I'm ever an instructor at the Farm, you can bet your ass (so to speak) that I will grade students on their ability to keep their secret liaisons secret.

In fairness—and by now, you know I'm nothing if not fair—some of these "relationships" were no more than stormy one-night hookups, fueled by alcohol and the pheromone-like scent of recently exploded det cord. Understandably, not a lot of effort was put into keeping these kinds of flings private, and these brief encounters were often between two unmarried, consenting adults. Some just happen to be more memorable than others.

After spending two glorious weeks eating scrapple, making IEDs, yelling the phrase "Fire in the hole," and blowing things up on a secret CIA base somewhere on the Eastern Seaboard, my fellow CTs and I were treated to a farewell bash our final night. Unlimited alcohol was provided free of charge, and we were kept away from the explosives.

One of our lead instructors during the two-week demolitions program was a good-looking former surfer dude from California who prided himself on "bagging" one female trainee from each class. Fair-haired "Lance" had his eye on a lovely blond colleague of mine whom we shall call "Heather." That final evening, as we happily and loudly congregated in various groups throughout the dining and rec areas, some of us unwound by watching a *Mad Max* movie while drinking too much, and others, like Lance, remained focused on the mission while drinking too much. Lance's mission being Heather. I'll cut to the chase. Lance and Heather got drunk and began to make out right there on the floor, as people in that situation are wont to do.

At some point, being older than the rest of us, Lance excused himself to heed nature's call. In the few minutes that he was away, my classmate the Interceptor—whom you met in chapter 6—moved in to take over for Lance. Whether the Interceptor had his eye on Heather all along and struck while the iron was hot, or simply happened to sit his lucky ass down at the right place and the right time, we may never know. I'm guessing the latter, since luck seemed to follow him wherever he went. The Interceptor is the same charmed guy whose reserve chute saved his life just before he was about to "scream in" during jump school. He's the guy you want to be next to when things go sideways overseas.

Heather picked up right where she left off with Lance, and the Interceptor did an admirable job of emulating if not slightly outdoing Lance's boffo performance. In fact, Heather and the Interceptor then stumbled off to his room for a little well-deserved privacy.

When Sir Lancelot—or, as it turned out, Sir Lance-Alone, aka Sir-Not-Lancing-A-Lot-Tonight—returned from the latrine, he was understandably upset that the young Interceptor (with the more elastic bladder) had encroached on and made off with his target. Commendably, Lance did not resort to violence and resisted the undoubtedly strong urge to retrieve some of the aforementioned securely stored explosive devices. A trained professional, Lance knew that revenge is best served cold.

After disappearing again for about ten minutes, Lance returned to those of us still awake and watching the movie and told us to follow him. In his hands was a pair of NODs, very expensive night-vision goggles that were the property of the US government. Accustomed to blindly following orders, several of us struggled to our feet and followed him, like wobbly baby ducks after their mother, to the trailer that had been the cozy home to the Interceptor during the previous two weeks of demolition training.

As we approached the trailer, we could all hear the unmistakable sounds of two very drunk people loudly expressing their affection for one another. Increasingly more desperate shouts of "Harder, bitch!" flowed from Heather's sweet mouth like so many rose petals, wafting away on a midsummer's night breeze. At this point, we decided to turn around and head back to our movie, but Lance was having none of it. He cracked open the door to the Interceptor's hooch and donned his NODs, for a clear view of the action—action that was taking place about five feet in front of him, on the lower bunk, in the dark. Lance wanted to make sure all of us witnessed his successful revenge operation in the flesh (so to speak). Fortunately, neither Heather nor the Interceptor, who were both admirably focused on the task at hand, noticed that they'd attracted a small audience. I fought the urge to yell, "Fire in the hole!" one last time. We quickly left them to their own devices (and I'm not saying any were used, other than the NODs), the deafening horizontal mambo marathon continuing into the wee hours. Since the walls of our rooms were paper-thin, most of us got very little sleep that night.

* * *

Thanks to our memorable experience on that secret base somewhere on the Eastern Seaboard, I knew before heading out on my sensitive technical operation in Latin America that in CIA circles, "mounting a rear-entry penetration operation" referred to much more than merely sneaking in the back door of an enemy beach house to plant a hidden listening device.

PART VI

HOT AND COLD RUNNING WAR: YUGOSLAVIA

CHAPTER 17

DENIED AREA OPERATIONS

Quietly ascending the mossy, eighteenth-century stone steps in total darkness before slipping through the broken iron gate to the Habsburg-era cemetery, I sensed heavy male footfalls trailing me about twenty meters back. At 10:59 p.m. on a foggy, late November night, wooded Zemun Cemetery was eerily quiet and empty. Walled-in and situated on Gardoš Hill, overlooking the murky Danube River, Zemunsko Groblje was the final resting place for thousands of Yugoslavia's Orthodox, Catholic, and Jewish faithful. It was also the perfect place for a late-night clandestine agent meeting.

Or was it?

After a three-hour SDR through the grimy, dimly lit streets of Belgrade and Zemun, I confirmed my black status and was making my final approach to the meeting site Govnar, a dilapidated park bench tucked away on a narrow cemetery footpath. After months of preparation for this meeting, I was motivated and on high alert, dressed to blend in on the streets of Belgrade. To a casual observer I was just another bundled-up Serb on the street in blue jeans, leather jacket, and wool cap, on his way home.

Several months had passed since my last late-night "brief encounter" (BREN) on the back streets of Belgrade with my asset 00HITCH, a senior officer in the Yugoslav security service (SDB). I was under pressure from CIA headquarters to make this meeting, since HITCH was expected to provide another treasure trove of top secret SDB documents. We urgently needed these documents, for accurate insights into the Yugoslav government's plans and intentions as the country moved rapidly toward inevitable, bloody dissolution. HITCH's gym bag full of Cyrillic-alphabet classified documents would also clarify some critical CI concerns: what operations were the SDB running against the CIA—myself included—and other official Americans in Belgrade?

Who was behind me? It was not HITCH. I knew he would approach the meeting site from the opposite direction after conducting his own SDR. Had I somehow missed a tail, or, more likely, picked up possible "target of opportunity" surveillance that happened to be loitering in the area and glommed on to me at the last minute? Still moving, I had less than thirty seconds to decide whether or not to abort the meeting. My training and experience told me that the mystery man behind me was a ghost, a false surveillance sighting. Just bad timing and a bad coincidence, another dirty trick cooked up by the cruel espionage gods to try and spook me. If that were the case, I was indeed black and I could and should make my important agent meeting.

But what if I made the wrong call? What if I had in fact picked up SDB surveillance and led them to my meeting with the very successful, very happily married HITCH? That would spell the end of an extremely valuable, years-long agent relationship, the end of a critical intel stream to US policy makers, and the end of my agent's liberty, if not his life. I could not afford to make the wrong decision.

Without hesitation, implicitly trusting my experience and my SE/IO course training, I veered right off the main cemetery path and down the muddy, overgrown footpath toward the barely visible meeting site. Through the bone-chilling fog, I could make out HITCH silhouetted against the aging Balkan tombstones, pacing slowly toward me in the darkness.

The man behind me was a ghost. He continued on his lonely trajectory, down the main cemetery path, toward Sibinjanin Janka Street. HITCH and I stood in silence in the dark for a few moments as we waited, barely breathing, listening to confirm the man had left the area. We then spoke softly in Serbian, for just a few minutes. I quickly fired off the most pressing CIA requirements of the day, hoping for up-to-the-minute "breaking news" updates that might not be covered in the documents. He provided current, detailed answers, which I committed to memory. He then handed me the gym bag, calling my attention to several priority documents I should translate first when I got back to the station the next day. We shook hands and silently left the BREN site in different directions, both still alert to any signs of surveillance.

* * *

Approximately one hour before the BREN, I'd ditched my vehicle in the parking lot of one of the dozens of large, anonymous Stalinist "Blok" apartment complexes scattered throughout nearby Novi Beograd (New Belgrade). I'd quickly moved away on foot from my dark blue Peugeot after conducting a two-hour vehicular SDR and concluding I was black. I spent the final hour before the meeting on foot, to put distance between myself and my car and to continue to confirm my black status. Should the SDB happen to spot my vehicle after I'd parked it in that sea of cars, they'd likely assume I was inside one of the many Blok apartment buildings.

Hoofing it back to my car after the BREN via a different, more direct route, I continued to look for surveillance. Along the way I breathed a pre-liminary sigh of relief, having correctly concluded the man behind me was a ghost. But I was not yet out of the woods. I was an American CIA officer walking the back alleys and deserted side streets of Belgrade with a gym bag full of top secret SDB documents. There would be no plausible deni-ability if I was caught, no innocent explanation. Until I safely delivered the documents to the station the next day, HITCH and I were both at risk.

All seemed quiet as I approached the overflowing Blok parking lot. After visually scanning the area for any signs the SDB may have staked out my parked car, I ducked into my vehicle and headed for home. The final hurdle was to make it back across the Sava River and up through the pitch-black Košutnjak forest to our comfortable duplex without incident. My greatest fear—other than leading surveillance to an agent meeting—was becoming involved in a post-BREN traffic accident that might render me incapacitated or unconscious. The police would inevitably come across the gym bag, which would lead to my arrest and expulsion (along with my family) from the country. It would also lead the SDB to HITCH, and he would pay a much heavier price than me.

On my way home, I listened to the same SDR soundtrack I always lis-tened to after agent meetings, *Traveling Wilburys Vol. 1*. It was admittedly a silly superstition, but why take a chance by changing a successful routine? Fortunately, once again, I made it home safely and without any signs of surveillance. (Thank you, George, Tom, Bob, Roy, and Jeff, for your music and your good luck.)

I quietly entered my house, locked the front door, and went directly upstairs to our bedroom. Reeking of Belgrade, I stashed the gym bag under our bed, hoping I wouldn't wake Stacy in the process. My little girls were fast asleep in their bedroom across the hall.

Early the next morning, I brought the bag to the office, hidden inside a cardboard grocery box.

Mission accomplished.

✶ ✶ ✶

The day following a HITCH meeting always felt a lot like Christmas morning. After my experienced Vietnam vet and former US Marine COS shook my hand, as he'd also done prior to each HITCH meeting, we would carefully remove the documents from the bag and briefly marvel at the quantity and quality of the previous night's take. Faced with a stack of hundreds of top secret Serbian-language documents, all in Cyrillic, we prioritized the reports and both got to work on translating and turning the salient parts into finished intelligence reports. I also wrote up reports based on what HITCH had told me orally, either on his own initiative or in response to my specific requirements. Because of the threat of electronic eavesdropping, all of our writing was done longhand, in pencil, on legal pads and not on computers. Tracy Chapman and other songs of that era blared nonstop over cheap CIA-issue stereo speakers in our tiny, windowless office, to counter any possible audio surveillance. Once the reports were in final draft form, we would hand them to our communications specialist, who would type them up inside a secure commo "closet" and send the encrypted cable traffic via satellite to headquarters.

The entire process was slow and deliberate by design, to protect our sources and methods. To protect HITCH. We intentionally traded speed and efficiency for security, and the results were pretty damn good.

✶ ✶ ✶

My primary mission during my two years of operating in Belgrade, Yugoslavia, was to securely handle HITCH and produce intelligence reports based on oral debriefings and on the top secret documents he provided.

Every facet of my life in Belgrade was geared toward one clear objective: the secure handling of HITCH. To securely handle a sensitive penetration of a hostile security service in a denied area required a full-time commitment and focus on the mission. The first step was to follow a work and lifestyle routine to blend in and not come to the attention of the SDB. Unfortunately, I cannot describe what that entailed. Meetings with HITCH took place only once every few months, but meticulous preparation was required in advance of each meeting. All of my previous tradecraft and surveillance training and operational experience would be called upon and put to the test during this denied area assignment. This was a traditional Cold War, *Spy vs. Spy* way of life. This was why many of us joined the CIA in the first place, borrowing from the Cold War classic *Dr. Strangelove*: to go "toe-to-toe with the Russkies."[1] (Or, in my case, their cousins the Yugoslavs.)

I would typically spend from two to four months preparing for each ten-minute meeting. This was not Latin America, where I might have as many as fifteen agent meetings in one week. Generally speaking, I had to ensure I was black not only when meeting HITCH but also when performing other operational acts, such as marking signals and casing and photographing sites. It was possible to monitor signals while under surveillance. It was also possible to case and clandestinely photograph sites while under surveillance when necessary.

In the "old days," before photography and everything else was digitized, spying (to my mind anyway) was much more fun. We used old-school miniature Minox spy cameras, palmed in one hand over the steering wheel so that trailing surveillance would be unaware we were photographing something ahead of the car. We developed the tiny film strips in the station dark room. We relied on actual paper maps, which naturally were typically out of date. To ensure the accuracy of our comprehensive and operationally critical casing reports, we would laboriously case and photograph signal and meeting sites and create our own detailed, accurate maps and diagrams. We essentially created our own Google Maps and Google Street View, but instead of covering the world, we only covered routes and sites that were relevant to us as working spies. Instead of highlighting all locations of interest, the way Google does, we indicated on our maps positions of police and other threats to our SDRs and operational activities. In today's CIA, a case officer can instantly take and edit digital photos and can case sites from her/his phone or laptop, thanks to Google Earth.

The internet also plays a role in modern agent communications, and not always in a good way. Beginning in 2010, an entire CIA agent network inside China was compromised because of reliance on a "secure" internet-based communications network.[2] Old-school chalk mark signals and dead drops may be cumbersome, but they are secure, just as paper voting ballots are more secure than hackable digital voting systems.

Are denied area operations more efficient now? Without a doubt. More secure? Not likely. More fun? Hard to imagine.

Surveillance in Belgrade was generally easier to detect than what we faced during SE/IO training, since Yugoslavia had limited resources to devote to monitoring suspect American spies. Belgrade was not Moscow, where the KGB could easily blanket a foreign spy with a near-invisible surveillance network. In the land of the South Slavs, surveillance typically consisted of one or two small, white Yugos or Ladas, driven by the obligatory pair of burly thugs wearing dark leather jackets, even in summer. Both the car and its occupants smoked like grease fires, and in the winter as much smoke poured out of the car's cracked windows as from the tailpipe. In marked contrast to typically aggressive male drivers in Yugoslavia, those on a surveillance detail did not tailgate, flip off, or sideswipe their "rabbits" (those they were following). Rather, exhibiting very un-Balkan restraint, the surveillance goons would hang back a few courteous car lengths, scrupulously obey the speed limit, and in the process make themselves as conspicuous as a Boris Badenov balloon sporting an erection in the Macy's Thanksgiving Day Parade.

Good case officers will always adapt or modify traditional tradecraft practices to their particular operating environment. Prior to meeting HITCH in Belgrade, for example, I would always take my customary "black piss" toward the end of my three-hour SDR. This was my informal but dependable barometer of whether or not I was black. Taking a leak on the street is not the type of thing a (sober) guy can do if he thinks he is being watched. They didn't cover "black pisses" in CIA training, but they probably should.

One ancillary benefit of perfecting surveillance detection skills: as long as I live, I'll never *not* be aware of whether or not I am being followed. It is now instinctual and almost as involuntary as breathing.

* * *

By the end of my two years in Belgrade, I felt an exhausted but relieved sense of accomplishment. I had securely handled HITCH from start to finish with no lapses in tradecraft. The pace of HITCH meetings increased to one per week by the end of my assignment—his intelligence reporting was in great demand during the rapidly unfolding civil war scenario. After two years of running covert ops in Belgrade, I was confident I could determine almost immediately whether or not I was under SDB surveillance, but I never let my guard down, since that would be an invitation to disaster. Despite what seemed at times to be tradecraft overkill, I always ran complete, multi-hour SDRs, by the book, until the day I left the Cold War in Belgrade for the hot war in Croatia. I would not let HITCH or the CIA down on my watch.

Before executing a cold turnover of HITCH to my young replacement, I did my best to hammer home the point that his primary objective, like mine before him, was to securely handle this valuable agent. The Cold War had ended in the rest of Eastern Europe, and the operating environment in Belgrade was changing. My successor would be expected to assess and develop new sources, just as CIA officers did in more benign environments like Latin America. But that kind of developmental activity would draw the scrutiny of the increasingly nervous SDB, posing additional risks to HITCH. Like a worried parent who repeats himself unnecessarily to his children, I explained what was at stake in the starkest terms possible for my young but highly trained and professional replacement. Regardless of my lecturing, I knew I was leaving HITCH in very capable hands.

What was the point of all the methodical, high-security tradecraft, agent meetings, and intelligence reporting? Why did HITCH risk his life for the CIA? It was all for a simple but noble cause, to keep the White House and American policy makers apprised of the rapidly unfolding situation, and to forecast events, as Yugoslavia careened out of Communism and into civil war. In other words, to enhance US national security. The CIA performed admirably in Yugoslavia. Unfortunately, the same cannot be said for the White House or other US policy makers.

CHAPTER 18

I VANT A WEEZA

During one of my many long-term TDYs to the former Yugoslavia, I reconnected with an old State Department friend from Washington who was working as a visa officer in the consular section of the American embassy in Belgrade. One night over beers at a rustic, smoke-filled Yugoslav bar, "Joe" went on at length about his difficult but often entertaining job. He worked tirelessly for very long hours in the understaffed and overwhelmed visa section. As point man on the visa line, Joe had to decide who was lying and who was telling the truth, who would come back to Yugoslavia and who would not. He confessed to me that the working conditions were awful. The dilapidated embassy was continually under construction, jackhammer noise and clouds of dust sticking with employees like SDB thugs. The hordes that crammed into the visa section's muggy waiting room smelled bad. Many brought forged documents. I did not envy him in the least.

Because of my Serbian language ability and immigration law experience—and because he was desperate and overworked while his American coworker was on vacation—Joe tried to convince me to come in and help him out for a couple of days, with his hundreds of daily nonimmigrant (i.e., tourist) visa cases. I was busy doing my own thing and really had no desire to spend any time at all in a workplace he described as "a cross between the DMV at noon and the 'ward for people who constantly shout' at a Soviet-era psychiatric hospital." Joe admitted that although the work was tough, in his daily encounters with a colorful cast of Yugoslavs, he managed to find wonderful humor in their chutzpah as they matched wits with him in an effort to capture the elusive tourist visa.

Tempting as it sounded, I begged off, but Joe didn't give up. Eventually, he wore me down with his desperate pleas for help and, more importantly, with his hilarious anecdotes from the visa section. He showed me some completed visa applications to prove his point. One question on the visa form was "Distinguishing characteristics." Actual responses (in Serbian) included "Extraordinarily good-looking," "Deep voice over telephone," and "Left eye isn't mine."

Joe assured me it was just for a couple of days and it would be fun. To sweeten the deal, he said he regularly posted some of the more amusing passport photos (with captions) on the bulletproof glass between the visa section and Post One, to boost the morale of the US Marine security guards. The US Marines controlled physical access to the embassy through the front of their secure booth, and kept an eye on the unruly visa section through the back.

Joe showed me the handwritten captions under one photo, of an applicant who bore a striking resemblance to Adolf Hitler:

1. Do not salute this man.
2. Won third place in last year's Adolf Hitler lookalike contest.
3. Demands a rematch.

Joe also reminded me that it would be a good opportunity to practice my Serbian. He promised I would not regret helping him out. I said, "I'm in, but only if I can bring my boom box." He agreed. What neither of us knew at the time was that *he* would end up being the one to regret asking *me* for help.

✳ ✳ ✳

The next morning, a typically cold, polluted, and depressing Belgrade day, I showed up early at the visa section, cheap boom box in tow, to lend Joe a hand. He was happy (and I think a little surprised) to see me and gave me a crash course in how to decide whether or not an applicant should get a visa. Essentially, it all boiled down to a very simple test: if I was not convinced the applicant's family or work ties to Yugoslavia would compel his return after a brief American visit, I could not issue the tourist visa. I was already familiar with the basics of immigration law, so it did not take long for me to catch on.

Welcoming me on board, Joe solemnly issued me a used Zeleni Flo-

Master, a green felt pen with which we made notes on the applications, and captions on the funny photos. Then, he introduced me to Marija, a super-competent bilingual local employee who would make quick phone calls on our behalf to check out suspected fraud cases. Finally, he introduced me to Vesna, a sassy and foul-mouthed middle-aged receptionist who "welcomed" the hordes of visa applicants to the visa section and made sure their applications were completed properly. Just before meeting her, I overheard the woman say in Serbian to an elderly, well-dressed gentleman, "Fuck it, sir, you forgot to sign the application!"

There were two side-by-side, confessional-like interview booths, so Joe was able to do his job while keeping an eye (and ear) on me at the same time. It took less than an hour for me to conclude that I would never want Joe's job. For starters, it seemed as if most of the visa applicants lied, although I couldn't blame them. If I were from a dismal country that was going from bad to worse, from communism to civil war, I'd want out too. Making things even more interesting, deranged individuals would sometimes enter the visa section, make a scene, and have to be physically tossed out by the marines. When that happened, the consulate was transformed into a Balkan version of the *Jerry Springer Show*.

After volunteering for a couple of mornings, I had had enough. (For their part, Vesna and Marija had no doubt had enough of listening to *Freddy Fender's Greatest Hits*, which I played nonstop during my brief interlude in the visa section.) At around 11:00 a.m., I told Joe I was just too busy with my own stressful job to help him out any further, and besides, I was hungry and wanted to get lunch. I felt bad for him, but his visa section nightmare was not my problem. Joe was especially overwhelmed that day (as always) and begged me to stay another hour or two. Although I was fed up with the applicants' lies, and the generally unpleasant working environment, I reluctantly agreed to stay until noon to help reduce my friend's caseload for the afternoon.

Still hungry and eager to put this experience behind me for good, I was in no mood when the next applicant sauntered smugly up to my interview booth.

"What's your name?" I asked in English.

"Yuri Jerkov."

"And you're an asshole. Now tell me your name."

It turned out his name actually was Yuri Jerkov.

It also turned out that the bilingual Mr. Jerkov was a disturbed individual who was clearly not entitled to a tourist visa. He wrote honestly but foolishly on his application that he planned to live and work in the United States "until I dead." Mr. Jerkov did not react kindly to my obligatory rejection of his tourist visa request.

"I demand to speak to ambassador!" he barked, now in Serbian. He appeared agitated.

"I am ambassador!" I barked right back.

He pled his case again, this time to the "ambassador," who, after due consideration, also rejected his request.

"I demand to speak to Comrade President Clinton!" he yelled, eyes widening, his facial muscles beginning to twitch. The bulletproof glass prevented several tiny droplets of the angry man's spittle from making direct contact with my eyeballs.

At this point, it was clear Mr. Jerkov was the type who would not leave the visa section of his own volition. Joe had overheard our conversation and suggested I let Post One deal with the man so that I could move on to the next applicant, but I did not yet feel the need to call in close combat support in the form of willing, able, and bored young marines. I directed Mr. Jerkov to walk back around through the crowded waiting room to the receptionist area, where he had initially submitted his application. I told him he could go to the head of the line and I would meet him there.

Mr. Jerkov pushed his way to the front of the throng of applicants and arrived at the receptionist's bulletproof window at the same time I did. He was now standing opposite me and Vesna.

In a loud voice in Serbian, I asked Vesna, who brooked no crap from anyone (including me), to immediately patch me through to President Clinton at the White House. It was around 5:00 a.m. in Washington, DC. She looked at me as if I were nuttier than a shithouse rat. I discreetly indicated that she should just play along. She rolled her eyes, mumbled something vile in Serbian under her breath, punched a few numbers into the phone, and handed it to me.

When "President Clinton" came on the line, I stood at attention and said, again in Serbian, "Thank you, Comrade President, for taking my call! I'm here with Comrade Jerkov, and he would like a visa."

I pretended to listen intently for a moment, nodding, then covered the phone with one hand and addressed Mr. Jerkov: "President Clinton wants to know if you have any cows."

"*Pa, nemam, jebiga!*" was his angry, profane response. He did not.

"No, Mr. President, I'm afraid he has no cows."

Another pause, a few more nods, some more back-and-forth questions between "President Clinton" and Mr. Jerkov, then, "Thank you, Comrade President, for your time. My best to Hillary and the twins."

I handed the phone back to Vesna, who just shook her head, still mumbling.

I then broke the news to Mr. Jerkov: "Comrade President Clinton has carefully considered your case, but unfortunately, he did not approve the visa."

By this point, Mr. Jerkov had calmed down considerably and appeared reassured that his request had been given a fair hearing. He graciously accepted the visa refusal and left the consular section peacefully.

For this performance, I received a lukewarm round of applause from the dozens of other applicants, who were crammed in and standing patiently in the hot and stuffy waiting room. It also earned me a caustic comment from intrepid fraud investigator Marija. During my previous couple of visits to the visa section, she'd overheard me joking and cursing right back at many of the applicants in their own language. On one occasion she'd heard me tell an applicant who assumed I was a Yugoslav—but of a rival ethnic group—that he was not allowed to speak with an American. She saw me describe a small, plastic Chinese toy, with flashing lights emitting annoying French-ambulance sounds, as a "secret American lie detector," in order to trick applicants into admitting that they had no intention of ever returning to Yugoslavia. She watched in disbelief when I began to ask applicants if they owned cows, then issue visas to cow owners, on the eminently reasonable assumption that a Yugoslav would never abandon his or her cows to live illegally in New Jersey. She'd even witnessed me snatch an immigrant visa applicant's chest X-rays from Joe's hands as I was walking past, hold them up to the light, then say to the applicant, "I'm a doctor; you're going to be fine."

Although she clearly didn't approve of my methods, Marija grudgingly acknowledged my uncanny knack for getting at the truth. But for some reason, when I discussed Mr. Jerkov's case in Serbian with "President Clinton," that was the final straw. After Mr. Jerkov left the consulate, Marija walked up to me and in a very calm voice said, "Sir, you are *vorst* American I ever meet."

For his part, Joe decided at that point as well that perhaps my "help" was doing more harm than good. Although it was not yet noon, he asked me in a very official tone of voice to kindly turn in my Zeleni Flo-Master. Joe shook my hand, thanked me for my service, and said he would handle the remaining cases from that point forward. I was free to go.

Just my luck. I got myself fired right when I was beginning to enjoy it.

Although I find the stories amusing, I'm not necessarily proud of my behavior in the visa section. In my defense, it wasn't really my job. Moreover, many applicants lied, the conditions were awful, and we were under a lot of stress. More importantly, smartphones had not yet been invented, so I didn't run the risk of appearing on YouTube. Once again, I was spared public humiliation simply because the stars aligned just right and I was born into a low-tech world.

CHAPTER 19

KOMANDANTE GIŠKA

On September 18, 1991, just as the war in Croatia was beginning to heat up, thousands of Serb nationalists in Belgrade gave an emotional farewell to fallen Serb war "hero" Đorđe Božović, aka Komandante Giška. During my last TDY to Belgrade, I stood on the sidewalk on busy Kneza Miloša Street and watched the memorial parade as it passed by in front of me. This is the brief but unusual story of whom Božović really was, how I came to know him, and the legacy he left behind.

Born in Yugoslavia in the mid-1950s, young Božović led a troubled life. He quickly turned to the same life of crime that killed his father. In the late 1980s, Božović joined forces with fellow career mobster, future Serb warlord and indicted war criminal Željko "Arkan" Ražnatović. (Arkan, assassinated in 2001 in the lobby of Belgrade's Intercontinental Hotel, is best known as the leader of the notorious Arkan's Tigers, a bloodthirsty group of Serbian paramilitaries who wreaked havoc in Croatia, Bosnia, and Kosovo.) In addition to his life of crime, Božović was also allegedly a paid assassin for the old Yugoslav secret service (UDBA). At some point in his young adult life, Božović immigrated illegally to the United States, where, I was told, he became a car thief and small-time hood.

I came to know Božović personally in late 1991 when he returned to Yugoslavia to kill Croats.

✳ ✳ ✳

Big Đorđe Božović strode confidently into the floating Ušće restaurant, a quiet and traditional Serbian dining spot on the banks of the Sava River with excellent views of Belgrade. We shook hands, and he sat down at my table. A mutual friend had arranged the meeting so that we could discuss matters of mutual interest. Božović wanted an American visa for his underage Yugoslav girlfriend, and our mutual friend had (falsely) suggested to him that I might be able to help. Somewhat fittingly, satirical Montenegrin songwriter Rambo Amadeus's newest album, *Psychological Propaganda Set*, played in the background.

Božović was tall, a tough and physically imposing guy, but he was very friendly and personable with me. His English was excellent. He told me he'd earned the nickname Giška because he looked like a bear with the same name that used to be kept in the Belgrade Zoo. I told him truthfully that I really liked his New York–tagged Jeep CJ that was often parked in the Košutnjak forest near my house. Giška then told me what I already knew: he was the leader of a large "unofficial" militia called the Serbian Guard that trained near my Banovo Brdo residence. What he neglected to say was that he had no prior military training.

My objective was to string him along on the visa matter while extracting as much information out of him as I could about the dangerous Serbian Guard, its plans, intentions, and capabilities. After our first meeting, Božović agreed to leave his American passport with me, along with his girl-friend's Yugoslav passport, "for processing." I told him I would do my best but could make no guarantees that I could help with the visa.

We met a few more times after our initial encounter at the Ušće restaurant, and he shared some valuable information with me about the Serbian Guard. One day he told me he was headed north to take the fight to the Croats. I wished him luck. He knew I wasn't taking sides; I was just a Serbian-speaking American who wanted to understand what was happening in this complicated country.

During his first armed engagement near Gospić, Croatia, Komandante Giška stood up and was shot in the head by a Croatian sniper.

Komandante Giška's distraught Serbian Guard comrades brought his lifeless body back to Belgrade, where he was given a hero's send-off. After the parade, Božović's mother met me to retrieve her late son's passport. Sporting a respectable mustache, she kissed me three times, alternating cheeks. To this day, my Yugoslav friends who happened to witness the encounter wonder why on earth I was so tight with the mother of legendary Serb gangster and warlord Komandante Giška.

Božović's wartime exploits and the funeral parade were big news in

Belgrade, and he is remembered fondly to this day in Serbian nationalist circles. His grave is marked by a Rocky Balboa–like life-size statue of him carved into a wall, with an inscription in Cyrillic. There are also several Facebook pages in his honor.

* * *

Serbs are passionate about their history, and their wars are fueled as much by their centuries-old legends and beliefs as they are by *rakija*, traditional homemade fruit brandy. Serbs get misty-eyed when recounting the Battle of Kosovo of 1389, which they lost, and they would cite that ancient history as justification for repressing ethnic Albanians in the 1990s. It is entirely possible that Božović will go down in Serbian history as a true hero who defended his people against the Croats, and future wars and atrocities may be committed in his name.

Although Serb aggression in the 1990s is well-documented, less remembered today are true acts of heroism carried out by nationalist Serb Chetnik forces during World War II. The Chetniks fought both the Nazis and the Communists and rescued hundreds of downed American pilots in Nazi-controlled territory. The OSS (precursor of the CIA) collaborated with the Chetniks on Operation Halyard, which resulted in the rescue of between four hundred and five hundred downed American and Allied pilots. It was the largest rescue operation of its kind in American history.[1]

CHAPTER 20

FROM WAR VIRGIN TO WAR WEARY

Some of my most memorable adventures with the CIA involved operating solo in challenging environments overseas that I had never really expected to experience, and for which I had received no specialized training. The comprehensive CIA operational and paramilitary training I undertook could not cover all contingencies. This is to be expected, and it is why the CIA carefully selects applicants who demonstrate an aptitude for thinking on their feet while facing an unpredictable and ever-changing set of circumstances. The combination of training, experience, and flexibility yields a solid foundation for a CIA officer who is required to deal with new and sometimes intimidating situations, like being sent to spy in a foreign war zone, as a war virgin.

In October 1991, after operating for two years in a denied area, I was dispatched up the Sava River to Zagreb to cover the first armed conflict in the heart of Europe since World War II. My family had returned to the United States. The CIA tapped me for the job because of my previous two years of experience running covert ops in the Balkans and because I knew the country and the language as well as anyone at the time. Equally important, I was already in-theater. Sometimes just being a warm body in the right place at the right time counts for as much as anything else.

Although I was headed alone to a violent war zone, I went as a spy, not a soldier. Since 9/11, the lines between spy and soldier have oftentimes become blurred, but during the Cold War and for several years thereafter, they were still two distinct professions. Either way, I had never set foot in a war zone and did not know exactly what fate awaited me in Croatia. There were no US troops in Croatia (or in Bosnia) when I was dispatched to report on those wars. I was nervous but excited at the same time.

Since I had volunteered for this potentially hazardous solo assignment,

I was able to negotiate favorable terms. Actually, the only special treatment I requested was permission to travel first to Europe. I wanted to stop by one of our stations there to drop off my shoebox full of irreplaceable home videos of my young daughters, to ensure their safekeeping, and for onward shipment to Stacy in the United States, in the event anything happened to me in Croatia. After depositing my treasured videotapes with the station, I spent the night in the amazing capital city.

The next day, October 8, 1991, I reentered Yugoslavia by train. I was the only person left on my train car as it crossed the international border into Slovenia; all other passengers had gotten off beforehand. It was an eerie feeling. On that date in Yugoslavia's history, newly independent Slovenia issued its new currency, the tolar, and Croatia officially cut all remaining ties with Yugoslavia. I believed that these were good omens and that once again I found myself in the right place at the right time.

I spent a night in Slovenia along with a small team of American "essential personnel" who would soon enter Zagreb to reestablish an official presence in the Croatian capital. All American government employees and their dependents had previously been evacuated from Croatia, due to fears that the Serb-dominated Yugoslav People's Army (JNA) would attack and overrun Zagreb. As the only CIA officer in the group, I drove alone from Slovenia to Zagreb, Croatia, in a colleague's borrowed VW Jetta. (I loved the car so much that I later bought one for my daughter when she learned to drive; her sister learned to drive in the same reliable car. I had correctly assessed that if a Jetta could survive Croatia during the war, it could survive my daughters. Their younger sister required an even more durable 2011 Ford Ranger.)

The drive from newly liberated Slovenia to Zagreb was scenic and uneventful, since most of the fighting in Croatia was taking place in other parts of the country. I had traveled to and through Croatia several times before, but that was before civil war had broken out. Having toured civilized Europe several times, it was jarring to see bullet-riddled and pockmarked eighteenth- and nineteenth-century Austro-Hungarian buildings and storefronts in the normally peaceful and charming Croatian capital. I found it equally unsettling to be viewed with suspicion when I spoke the language of the enemy—Serbian—instead of the similar but distinct Croatian language. I once went into a small bakery and requested some bread, and out of habit I used the Serbian word (*hleb*) instead of the Croatian word (*kruh*). Everyone in the shop stopped and glared. It was understandable, since at that time the JNA and Croatian Serb paramilitary forces were laying waste throughout Croatia. I was more careful before speaking from that point on.

During my TDY to the budding war zone, I combined denied area tradecraft with war correspondent skills to cover a unique wartime situation with little recent precedent. The country was transformed almost overnight from one of the more successful components of the Socialist Federal Republic of Yugoslavia to an independent state fighting a bloody war for independence. I brought an objective outsider's perspective to the situation—those Americans covering Zagreb up until that point were beginning to "go native" and were sometimes reporting and repeating untrue Croatian propaganda and conspiracy theories. This was somewhat understandable, since the Serbs had already carried out deadly, unprovoked "self-defense" attacks in Croatia. Moreover, the "brainwashing" of neutral American officials slated for Yugoslavia began during language school in Washington, DC, where Croatian teachers attempted to indoctrinate those learning Croatian, while Serbian teachers did the same to those learning Serbian. Learning Serbo-Croatian with native-born speakers was like being stuck in the middle of someone else's tribal tug-of-war. Or an ugly divorce.

My first dispatch from Zagreb was a play on CNN's overused Bernard Shaw teaser recorded in Baghdad during the start of hostilities in Desert Storm; the two-line situation report read, "There's nothing happening outside. The skies over Zagreb have not been illuminated." The objective of this brief back-channel message was to calm official American nerves in the wake of the US consulate's previous alarmist reports that the JNA was poised to overrun Zagreb and possibly slaughter people by the thousands. Within a few days of my arrival in Zagreb, I was able to assess the situation and conclude that, despite some indicators to the contrary, this was not the case. It was true that the Yugoslav Air Force had attacked the Croatian president's residence in Zagreb just a few days before my arrival, along with several other targets in the city. (The Putin-esque Serbs immediately put out a typical and clearly false conspiracy theory, that the Croats had staged the attack by setting off an explosive in the building just as a JNA warplane flew innocently by overhead.) The JNA and Serb militias had also surrounded and were systematically destroying the old Baroque city of Vukovar, three hundred kilometers to the east, and had also begun their heinous attack on the picturesque walled city of Dubrovnik, but Zagreb was relatively secure, for the time being anyway.

Because of the recent Yugoslav Air Force attacks, the Croatian capital was on a war footing, with frequent air-raid sirens driving people into shelters. There was also a mandatory citywide blackout at night. Truckloads of Croatian Army (HV) troops regularly passed through Zagreb en route to the front lines. Late one night, I observed a Croatian troop transport vehicle driven by a soldier who was apparently not familiar with Zagreb. He stopped on the streetcar tracks. I tried to signal to him to keep driving, but he did not and the vehicle was soon hit by a streetcar. There were no injuries. While in Zagreb I also heard frequent small-arms firefights in the city, and I could hear (and feel) heavy artillery exchanges taking place in the nearby countryside.

In Zagreb I handled an existing asset and also developed new ones, including a cooperative Croatian Army colonel. I also worked with secret military operatives to identify HV antiaircraft sites that were hidden in and around Zagreb. Since I was operating solo with no commo support, I filed my daily secret reports to headquarters via a cumbersome, "portable" military secure satellite system called a TacSat. I had a ten-minute window of opportunity to connect to the satellite each night. This was no easy task for a low-tech guy like me.

At the conclusion of my first wartime TDY to Croatia, I returned to Europe to pick up my priceless "baby tapes" before flying to the United States for home leave with my family. Temperatures in Central Europe were dropping as fall turned to winter, and I was looking forward to some R and R in the warmer climate back home. After two years of denied area ops in depressing Eastern Europe, and a month of baptism under fire as Yugoslavia disintegrated into a horrific civil war, the tranquil Southwest desert would be a welcome respite.

* * *

Over the next several years, I made many more short- and long-term TDYs to the war-torn former Yugoslav republics of Croatia and Bosnia. I became more confident and comfortable operating in that stressful environment, but it was always nerve-wracking. In October 1992, I returned to Zagreb and declared myself as a CIA officer, establishing the CIA's first official relationship with the new Croatian government security service. My primary contact was the head of the service, the quiet and bookish general Ivan, whom you met in chapter 2. Admitting to a foreign government that I was a CIA officer was a new, unnatural, and unnerving experience for me. For years I had gone to great lengths and practiced sound tradecraft to ensure that no one, particularly a foreign government, learned that I was a CIA officer. That fundamental modus operandi was thrown out the window when I came out of the shadows to kick off this important relationship with the newly formed and independent Croatian government.

By this time, the war was raging in many parts of Croatia, and armed conflict had also begun to heat up in Bosnia, just as the CIA had predicted. The situation in Zagreb remained relatively stable, although it was still a tense and dangerous wartime capital. I was able to stay in the Intercontinental Hotel (now the Westin Zagreb), which made my TDY quite comfortable, at least when I was in Zagreb. The hotel "disappeared" at night, since all of the windows were covered with blackout curtains to make it invisible to JNA aircraft. The large, high-rise hotel in the center of the city was ground zero for journalists, spies, and mercenaries who needed a safe and convenient base of operations during the war. Every night the hotel's eclectic cast of characters would congregate in the hotel's raucous underground bar and restaurant for drinks and dinner, and to watch the day's events on Sky News. Cheers would break out whenever one of the hotel's journalist or mercenary guests appeared on the TV screen. I looked forward to the nightly revelry, which was reminiscent of similar scenes from *The Year of Living Dangerously*.

For those interested in more risqué entertainment, the upscale but smaller Esplanade Hotel was a short walk away. There, Ukrainian bar girls danced "ballet" every night, in the Esplanade's smoky basement nightclub, for an inebriated but appreciative audience of Croatian Army soldiers, as well as foreign fighters and reporters. I was not opposed to taking in an evening of culture at the Ukrainian cabaret, but my tastes ran more toward music. One night I paid a steep cover charge to get into a large Zagreb nightclub to hear Oliver Dragojević, a wonderful Croatian balladeer whom I used to refer to as "the Balkan Jimmy Buffett." Unfortunately, I never got to hear him perform "Vjeruj u ljubav" ("Believe in Love") or any other of his many hits live. Before the show even began, noxious Balkan cigarette smoke inside the club had become so thick that I literally could not see the stage. I felt my way back to the main entrance and burst through the exit door to the street, gasping for air.

Alcohol and AKs always seemed to go hand in hand in the Balkans. One night while talking to my daughters from inside the Intercontinental's phone booth, I was evicted by a pair of inebriated Croatian soldiers who wanted the phone. Not one to argue with a drunk with an AK, I complied with their very reasonable request. After which I retired to my room to listen to some George Strait on my portable cassette player before falling asleep.

After a week or so of official talks in Zagreb, my Croatian security service contacts took me on a "field trip" to tour the front lines in Croatia. Permanent-looking fortified trenches were dug and manned along rarely moving front lines separating JNA/Serb and Croatian forces. We also visited sandbagged frontline command centers, where officers briefed us on what was happening in their theater of operations. Military maps showing both friendly and enemy positions covered the walls and tables, and cigarette smoke was ubiquitous. The entire experience made me feel as if I'd been transported back in time to the European battlefields of World War I, which was characterized by trench warfare (although considerably more death and destruction than what I witnessed in Croatia). At the same time, many of the Croatian Army's few tanks, weapons, and military vehicles appeared to be left over from the more recent World War II.

After visiting the front lines, we drove to the divided and dangerous city of Mostar, Bosnia and Herzegovina. The fighting was fairly intense in the city that day, with mortars landing uncomfortably close to us. It turned out the previously allied Croats and Bosnian Muslims had just turned on each other, and much of the fighting that day was between the two groups, who populated and controlled most of the city. My new buddy "Colonel Markica," the head of Croatian Army counterintelligence, would shrug after every mortar hit, saying it was someone else's problem, since we were still breathing. As we made our way through the largely destroyed city to the beautiful, ancient Ottoman bridge for which the city is named, I noticed what appeared to be a couple of newlyweds inside a bombed-out Catholic church. He was in a tux, while she was in a white wedding gown, holding flowers, and the two of them were stepping over rubble. The scene was surreal, but as is often the case in these situations, people were not going to stop trying to live their normal lives simply because they were in a live fire zone. Life goes on.

Nearby, a small wooded city park had been turned into a cemetery, the entire green filled with fresh graves and makeshift markers. One grave marker simply said, "Mak, Englez"—"Mack, Englishman." Mack was undoubtedly one of the foreign fighters drawn to this Eastern European war zone to help whomever he considered to be the "good guys."

We continued walking through the rubble and shelling and made it to the Old Bridge (Stari Most), which at the time was the last bridge standing over the Neretva River. The Serbs had destroyed every other bridge in Mostar except the old stone one on which we stood. The following year, the Croats would destroy this ancient bridge during fighting with the Bosnians. The Bosnians promised to rebuild it "even better and older than before."

After visiting the Old Bridge for the first (and last) time in my life, my Croat escorts and I worked our way out of the battle zone by car and continued on our field trip. The next stop was one of Bosnia and Herzegovina's more tranquil tourist attractions, whose name I forget. At that point, ears ringing, I was still in the process of decompressing after the close calls during our Mostar city tour. After checking out the deserted tourist attraction, we went "plinking" in the Bosnian boonies with a suppressed Heckler & Koch sniper rifle. My Croat hosts wanted to see if this gringo could shoot, and seemed delighted when I kept up with them, shot for shot. I explained I'd grown up hunting in the American Southwest, although I couldn't imagine anyone *not* being able to hit a stationary target twenty meters away with a suppressed H&K rifle equipped with a massive high-powered sniper scope.

We spent that night in a serenely peaceful monastery in Medjugorje, the town in Bosnia and Herzegovina known mainly as a destination for Catholic pilgrims. During our drive back to Zagreb the next day, we talked about our personal lives. My Croatian hosts learned that I had been in Los Angeles during the riots earlier that year. These guys who lived and breathed real war on a daily basis were genuinely concerned for my safety and insisted I take a JNA "red star" 7.65 mm handgun back to the States, along with my beloved Czechoslovak Škorpion fully automatic machine pistol. Just in case. I tried to refuse their generosity, explaining the situation at home really wasn't dangerous, but they wouldn't hear of it. In the end, I gratefully accepted their well-intentioned gifts but did not tell them I would be unable to transit Frankfurt Airport—or enter the United States—so heavily armed. I left the weapons in Zagreb, where they were likely later destroyed.

* * *

Having worked with all of the factions and ethnic groups fighting one another in the former Yugoslavia—Serbs, Croats, Bosnians, and Albanians—I came to realize they share more similarities than differences. All were warm and hospitable toward me, an unbiased American, but all did their best to convince me of the righteousness of their cause. All viewed themselves as victims to one extent or another as well. They all smoked the same foul-smelling cigarettes and even told the same dark jokes.

One favorite wartime joke, told on both sides of the front lines by both Serbs and Croats about Bosnians, involved three imaginary Bosnians: Mujo (pronounced *Muyo*), his wife Fata, and Mujo's best friend, Haso. For generations of Yugoslavs, this trio symbolized the supposedly less sophisticated Bosnian people, who were often the butt of jokes. After the war started in Bosnia, the joke goes, Mujo disappeared, so Fata went looking for his corpse at the soccer stadium in Tuzla. (Unidentified or unclaimed corpses were typically brought to soccer stadiums for later identification by family members.) Haso accompanied his friend's distraught wife to the stadium. The soccer pitch was covered with the bodies of those who had been killed that day. Fata tread carefully through the bodies and lifted the sheets off several men's faces, but none of them were Mujo. Many of the corpses had no heads, or the faces were too disfigured to be identified. Haso told Fata the only way to identify Mujo would be to pull down the pants of the faceless corpses and examine their private parts. Fata was embarrassed but began to do so. After pulling down the pants of one victim, she cried, "No!" in horror and turned away. She did this several more times, saying each time, "It's not him." Approaching one final possible match, she pulled down the corpse's pants, carefully examined his private parts, then turned to Haso and said, "This guy isn't even from Tuzla."

* * *

As revealed in chapter 1, in the summer of 1995, I TDY'd to war-ravaged Sarajevo to establish the CIA's first official relationship with the Bosnian security service, much as I had done a few years earlier with the new Croatian security service. Before I was betrayed to the Iranian intelligence chief and forced to bug out in the dead of night, my commo man John and I had some free time with which to seek answers to some of the less sensitive questions put to us by UN ambassador Madeleine Albright and by agency analysts. One requirement was to provide an assessment of the availability of consumer goods in Sarajevo. Interpreting this guidance as broadly as possible, John and I searched and found several pizza restaurants in the general vicinity of our villa. With flour from relief agencies ingeniously combined with homemade cheese and Slovenian ketchup, the wood-burning oven pizzas tasted great. Keeping in mind "hunger is the best gravy." One war zone pizzeria even delivered. Their motto, loosely translated, was "Guaranteed delivery within fifteen minutes unless hit by sniper."

We also found a tiny, private dive bar called Kućica (Little House), which was frequented by Bosnian soldiers, as well as foreign spies and mercenaries. I felt right at home. A car battery powered a small FM radio for music, tables were candlelit by necessity, and Sarajevsko Pivo flowed freely if warmly. It was inadvisable to use or get anywhere near the bar's tiny Turkish hole-in-the-floor toilet, since it had not experienced running water in years.

One night, we were down at the Kućica, drinking warm beer and listening to oldies on Bosnian Serb radio from nearby Pale. Pale, of course, was the stronghold of sadistic war criminals Radovan Karadžić and Ratko Mladić. That night, as the radio played "Imagine," John Lennon's plea for world peace and understanding, we could barely hear the song over the roar of nearby Serb tank fire against the city's civilian targets. Who says Bosnian Serbs have no sense of humor?

Later that same night, in a bit of a Sarajevsko Pivo–induced haze, John and I discovered that we were both huge fans of *Beavis and Butthead*. During times of great stress, comrades in arms tend to share some of their innermost secrets. Thus, with the sound of artillery shells landing in the distance, John learned that I favored Butthead, while he considered Beavis to be the bigger moron. As we made our way back to the station through the darkened, cobblestone streets of Sarajevo, we also concluded that we should probably not give up our day jobs in order to do voices for MTV cartoons. Nonetheless, our spot-on renditions of "Snipers suck!" and "Serbs rule!" did serve to amuse, at least until the next shell landed.

Another night, during an especially intense firefight between the Bosnian Muslims and the Serbs right outside our villa, John was busy watching a

Vietnam War movie, *Full Metal Jacket*. As the real battle raged around us and grew more deafening, John had trouble hearing his movie. He'd inch closer to the generator-powered TV and turn up the volume so he wouldn't miss any of the action, all the while oblivious to the shooting going on outside. I yelled at John that he *might want to pause the movie for a while and come out and see the real thing*, but he was glued to the set and didn't hear a word I said.

✴ ✴ ✴

On Halloween day of 1992, on a flight from Zagreb to Frankfurt, I was seated next to a pretty Croatian war widow with big, sad brown eyes. Milana appeared to be about my age. In a barely audible voice, she told me her husband had been a banker and he was killed during the recent fighting in Zadar. She was devastated. When she told me her story, in addition to sympathy, I felt guilt. As always, I was able to leave this war behind and return to my family and life in America. She and many others like her could not so easily escape this reality. As we both looked out her window in silence, I thought about the previous week's adventure with my Croatian security service colleagues. One minute, we were on the front lines in Mostar, dodging bullets and shelling, death and destruction all around us. The next, we were enjoying the idyllic Bosnian countryside and a good meal. It was all in a day's work for General Ivan, Colonel Markica, and the other Croat officials who joined us that day. I marveled at how they dealt with this stressful way of life. It had become normal for them. I was pretty sure I could never become accustomed to living life with my family in a war zone. Like Markica had said after the mortars landed uncomfortably close to us, war was always someone else's problem. This Balkan civil war, like the war in Iraq, was wicked, but it wasn't mine to own. I was merely an outside observer. I wasn't a soldier, whose job it was to seek out the enemy and who was targeted for annihilation by that same enemy. I was a spy who had much more control over my destiny than did the average soldier. And, unlike the poor people who have no choice but to try and survive in war zones, I knew I could always return home.

That night, about sixteen hours later, I arrived home just in time to go trick-or-treating with my little girls. When I knelt down and hugged them for the first time in months, I did not want to ever let them go.

CHAPTER 21

LIFE IMITATES ART IMITATES LIFE– HUNTING BOSNIAN WAR CRIMINALS

Within two years of my final Balkans TDY to Sarajevo, I resigned from the CIA and settled in California with my daughters. After resigning, I formed a private business intelligence firm, which I operated like an overseas station. The CIA way of life was in my blood and was all I knew. Contrary to what the CIA recruiter had told me during law school, offering my services to the Mafia was *not* my only fallback option. I continued to recruit and run foreign agents and provide secret intelligence reports in response to specific requirements, but now the requirements came from private instead of US government clients. As a private citizen, I also continued to support the US government's overseas mission on an as-needed basis. The geographic focus of my private intelligence network was the Balkans, Central and Eastern Europe, and the former Soviet Union. As a corporate spy who no longer enjoyed the many benefits of traveling the world as a government spy on an official passport under Cold War rules, I adopted and adhered to a very clear company policy: I'd agree to take on a new case only if odds were I'd spend less than a week in jail if caught, and would suffer no more than a light to moderate beating.

In 2001, I began to write a realistic historical fiction book entitled "Balkan Justice," based in part on my own wartime CIA experience in Sarajevo. Chapter 3 of *American Spy* was initially written as a prologue to "Balkan Justice." The opening line of the novel's synopsis read, "Vowing to avenge the horrific death of his lover and agent, a former CIA officer returns to his Bosnian nightmare in pursuit of the real 'Butcher of the Balkans,' Bosnian Serb general Ratko Mladić." The US government was in fact offering five million dollars in reward money for either Mladić or his partner in evil, Bosnian Serb politician and psychiatrist Radovan Karadžić. Much of the rest of the prospective novel was purely fictional, since I had never been directly involved in the hunt for war criminals. Moreover, my real-life Sarajevo adventure did not actually involve a secret lover/agent (and if it had, I would not admit it here, because it was a clear violation of CIA rules to fall in love with one's agent).

My novel-writing effort got off to a solid start. By August 2001 I had completed the synopsis and the first nine chapters. I brought copies to the Maui Writer's Conference, where I pitched the novel and learned more about the (unclassified) writing business. I also shared the synopsis with several people in the entertainment industry in Los Angeles.

Then 9/11 happened. I immediately stopped work on the novel. I could not dwell on the past, no matter how compelling, when each of us needed to deal with our new reality. I also assumed there would be little public interest in the hunt for Bosnian War criminals now that we were dealing with the likes of bin Laden. Plus, writing novels wasn't going to pay the bills, at least not anytime soon.

✶ ✶ ✶

Two years later, like most people in my profession, my mind and much of my work was preoccupied with America's almost obsessive "war on terror." I initially explored kicking off a project in Afghanistan but instead decided to gamble on a start-up in Iraq, since it was becoming increasingly clear the Bush administration was hell-bent on overthrowing Saddam. Despite my almost single-minded post-9/11 focus on the Middle East, I would never get the Balkans completely out of my system (and that remains true to this day).

Although there were advantages to running my own business, one downside compared to my CIA career was I could not count on a regular salary. You eat what you kill when you operate solo. Steady income became a real concern with my one-person firm; there were limits to how many cases I could handle at one time.

Then one day it dawned on me. *Instead of writing about the hunt for Bosnian War criminals, why not do exactly what the protagonist of my novel was doing?* To collect the reward money, I would have to provide intelligence that led to the capture of either Mladić or Karadžić. How hard could it be?

The more I thought about it, the more convinced I became I should give the "Balkan war crimes lottery" a whirl. I understood better than most the nature of the crimes against humanity committed by Bosnia's top two war criminals, I still had solid in-country contacts, and I wanted nothing more than to help put those two sadistic bastards behind bars for the rest of their miserable lives, assuming they weren't killed in the process, which was of course another acceptable outcome. Either way, justice would be served. My share of the five million dollars in reward money would be icing on the cake. With it I could afford to slow the pace of my career and finish writing "Balkan Justice," although in that case I'd be pitching a nonfiction book instead of a novel.

By late 2003, I was winding down my private intelligence work to focus on my nascent and potentially more rewarding Iraqi venture, but I still couldn't let go of my desire to take care of unfinished Bosnia business. I quietly discussed my idea to track down Mladić and/or Karadžić with "Jovan," a trusted source in the former Yugoslavia, whom I frequently hired to investigate counterfeit tobacco and other illicit activity in the Balkans on behalf of my Fortune 500 corporate clientele. Since the Serb organized crime groups who ran the counterfeit trade were closely linked to Serb war criminals like Željko "Arkan" Ražnatović, we came up with a game plan to track down priority target Radovan Karadžić, using Jovan's existing network. As the Serbs would say about the difference between the war criminals and the organized crime groups, "*Isto sranje, drugo pakovanje.*" ("Same shit, different packaging.") Always trying to one-up their Serb rivals, the Croats would have characterized the differences as follows: "*Isti drek, druga frizura.*" ("Same shit, different hairdo.")

I had assessed, developed, and recruited Jovan after resigning from the CIA and forming my own firm. I always thought of jovial, mustachioed Jovan as a Slavic Barney Miller. Built like a fire plug, he was a serious professional, with an impressive stable of vetted police, intelligence, and organized crime sources, in all regions of the former Yugoslavia. He worked equally well with Serbs, Croats, Slovenes, Albanians, Macedonians, and Bosnians. Jovan had grown up under Tito as a true Yugoslav, and he lamented the ethnic hatreds and civil wars that had engulfed his country in recent years. When Jovan was a youth, his Communist curriculum taught him to despise and fear Americans, but after school he'd secretly play cowboys and Indians. Like many who grew up in the Communist world, he always had a wary fascination for all things American.

When I first cold contacted him, the personable but very astute Jovan assumed I was a CIA "agent." I told him truthfully that I'd left my government career and was working privately, but I don't know if he ever completely believed me. (To this day, my oldest daughter also remains dubious that I ever really left the service.) Over time, Jovan and I developed a solid working and personal relationship. I met his wonderful family and spent many hours as a nervous passenger in his little white Yugo, while he enthusiastically sped us around the dangerous roads of the former Yugoslavia.

Sitting at a tiny table in a ritzy Balkan restaurant,[1] feasting on crusty bread, Dalmatian prosciutto, kajmak cheese, and marinated Montenegrin olives, Jovan and I reviewed every detail of our plan to locate Karadžić and collect the reward money. Jovan would be responsible for handling his agent network in Bosnia and securely relaying the intelligence to me, and I'd take care of the more difficult part: dealing with the US government and coalition forces—coalition forces that were responsible for finding and arresting Karadžić and other indicted war criminals in Bosnia and Herzegovina.

Relying on Jovan's existing agent network, we made rapid progress and soon had a source inside the fugitive Karadžić's personal security detail. We were able to track the movements of Karadžić—who slept in a different location each night—on an almost real-time basis. There were now five of us in the information "chain"—myself, Jovan, Jovan's immediate contact, the intermediary between Jovan's immediate contact and Karadžić's trusted aide, and, key to the entire operation, Karadžić's aide. Success would net us each one million dollars. This chain also ensured the source next to Karadžić would not and could not know of my identity, a factor that would yield very practical benefits in the event he were suspected of being a mole and subjected to torture.

Sweet justice for the victims of Srebrenica and a million bucks in my pocket. What's not to like?

In late December 2003, I reported and coordinated my game plan with relevant US officials, and they in turn coordinated with their coalition forces counterparts in Bosnia. Because Karadžić and his small entourage were constantly on the move, and communication with our source inside his security detail was sporadic and indirect, the key to successfully apprehending Karadžić depended on the military doing things our way. We would have no more than a few hours' notice to react once we'd pinpointed Karadžić's exact location. I had no illusions about how difficult this would be to pull off. Even if I were still an inside officer, where I'd have more control over influencing both government and military bureaucracies to do things my way, it would be an uphill battle. Now I was on the outside, and all I could do was my best to convince all involved that my approach would actually work.

Coalition forces in Bosnia were interested but demanded to know the identities of our sources and other related operational details. They would not agree to act unless we shared more information. They'd been on the receiving end of several false tips, so their position was understandable. Initially I balked at their request and tried to convince them to do things the way we recommended. I knew that once I ceded control, the odds of success would decrease exponentially. I had considerable Balkan experience with the CIA, and in my judgment, this was our best chance to capture Karadžić. The military refused to accept my recommended approach, and so I reluctantly shared sourcing and other information with them. I had no other choice if I wished to move forward.

We knew generally where Karadžić was and which way he was headed, but our intelligence was often one day old. Our source then reported one crucial fact: Karadžić had an injury to his leg that would require him at some point to stop for two days for surgery and preliminary recuperation before moving on. That would be our window of opportunity, and we would only have a few hours' notice. I made my case as clearly and as strongly as possible that coalition forces must hold off on doing anything until we gave the green light. If they tried to corroborate my information by going to my sources, or if they jumped the gun before I gave the go-ahead, they'd spook Karadžić and he'd likely slip away once again.

Everything was teed up on our end, and the military was reportedly ready to launch. I was in constant, 24/7 communication with both Jovan and my government contacts. All we could do at that point was await confirmation from Jovan's source that Karadžić was temporarily immobile and vulnerable in a specific location. As soon as we got that word, I would immediately alert my government contacts, and coalition forces could move in for the capture/kill.

✱ ✱ ✱

While we were anxiously standing by, news outlets in Bosnia reported that around midnight on January 10, 2004, coalition forces raided and searched Radovan Karadžić's home near Pale, Bosnia. Karadžić was not there.

WTF?

A very pissed-off Jovan told me that a coalition spokesman held a press conference after the raid to explain why the units moved in when they did. The coalition representative also revealed some of the intelligence that we had provided, including the key bit about Karadžić's leg. Aside from bungling the entire operation because they made their move before we gave the green light, the coalition inexplicably revealed information to the public (and to Karadžić) that could have only come from someone inside Karadžić's inner circle. It would be impossible to un-fuck this situation.

Shortly thereafter, Jovan heard that Karadžić conducted a frantic mole search within his own ranks because of the leaked coalition information, but thankfully he never identified our source as the spy. I also learned from Jovan that during the noisy, telegraphed military raid on his house, Karadžić stayed put for three full days at a nearby abandoned building with a clear view of the main road leading to his house. Karadžić had no food for those three days while he hid out in the cold, empty building, waiting for the all clear. But he succeeded in avoiding capture. He returned briefly to his home near Pale afterward, knowing troops would not raid it a second time so soon after the first.

Needless to say, I was disappointed but hardly surprised coalition forces had botched the operation. What did catch me off guard was the coalition press conference in which they discussed the intelligence I had provided. That was inexcusable. My US government contacts never did explain to me why they jumped the gun or failed to follow my recommended plan. Not that they owed me anything. But clearly, some coalition forces genius had decided that he knew best and was probably promoted as a result, even though he failed to apprehend Karadžić.

Several months later, I learned that US intelligence and/or coalition forces had made direct contact with two of Jovan's sources whom I had reluctantly identified to them in January. Those same sources told Jovan they would never work with him again, because we had failed to follow their instructions and Karadžić evaded capture because of it. Just as importantly, they missed out on collecting their richly deserved reward money that would have set them and their families up for life. They were not the first, and would not be the last, to learn the hard way about misplacing trust in the US government.

✱ ✱ ✱

Radovan Karadžić was arrested about four years later in Belgrade, where he was hiding in plain sight under an assumed identity as a spiritual healer (I am not making this up).[2] He had also changed his appearance, by growing a long, bushy white beard and mustache. Picture Santa Claus, if Santa were a psychotic mass murderer wearing huge 1980s-style plastic rim glasses. His long, snowy-white hair was pulled up into some sort of shamanic man bun. I'm somewhat surprised his fellow macho Serbs hadn't already beaten him to death on general principle before his eventual unmasking and apprehension.

It took thirteen years, but Karadžić would finally face justice for the July 1995 mass murder of eight thousand innocent compatriots in Srebrenica. On March 24, 2016, Karadžić was convicted of genocide, war crimes, and crimes against humanity.[3] The UN tribunal in The Hague sentenced the seventy-year-old mass murderer to forty years of imprisonment.

Not long after his conviction, Karadžić complained that his prison conditions were "19th century, like some Communist or Turkish prison."[4] Keep in mind, Karadžić was the political leader responsible for setting up a network of concentration camps across Bosnia to imprison, starve, and kill innocent Bosnian Muslims, less than fifty years after the end of World War II. Karadžić and other Bosnian Serbs would often scornfully refer to their despised Bosnian Muslim victims as "Turks" to dehumanize and delegitimize them and to justify their rape, torture, abuse, and murder. Karadžić will deservedly spend the remainder of his rotten life in a prison cell. If only it were Turkish.

* * *

As an interesting aside, while recently watching the 2007 Bosnian War movie *The Hunting Party* starring Richard Gere,[5] I was gobsmacked by the numerous uncanny similarities between the movie and the synopsis of my novel "Balkan Justice." The movie was loosely based on a 2000 *Esquire* magazine article by Scott Anderson, but it bears more resemblance to my novel's synopsis than to the *Esquire* article. It may be just an amazing coincidence, but there are many striking similarities between my book's synopsis and the movie's unique characters, story lines, and plot twists. Even the unexpected surprise ending is eerily similar.

Looking back, I realize that my assumption that, after 9/11, there would be no interest in the hunt for Bosnian War criminals may have been misguided. In an endnote, I spell out the startling similarities between my novel and the movie in a dozen side-by-side synopsis/movie comparisons.[6]

PART VII

IRAQ:
IT SEEMED LIKE
A GOOD IDEA AT THE TIME

CHAPTER 22

THE ROAD TO BABYLON

On St. Patrick's Day of 2003, following a long day of meetings, I was relaxing over a pint of Guinness with a British colleague at a quiet waterfront pub outside of London. His private security firm often hired me to conduct due diligence investigations in Eastern Europe and the former Soviet Union on behalf of large corporate and banking clients. I wanted to thank him with a beer and enjoy one last English sunset before heading back to the United States. Uncle Kracker's version of the timeless Dobie Gray hit "Drift Away" was playing in the background, and, despite my initial negative reaction to this sacrilege, the song was beginning to grow on me. But I wasn't there just to toast the past. I also briefed my buddy on my plans to launch a risky business venture in Iraq just as soon as the irrational but inevitable invasion of Iraq was deemed a success. Some of his firm's clients would undoubtedly set up operations in postwar Iraq and might require the services of my new start-up, "Babylon Inc." (Not the actual name.) We agreed to touch base once we were both operational inside Iraq. *Cheers!*

Three days later, on March 20, 2003, the United States and its allies invaded Iraq. Forty days after that, President George W. Bush all but declared victory.

"Mission Accomplished." So read the huge banner serving as a backdrop to President Bush as he gave his televised May 1, 2003, speech on board the USS *Abraham Lincoln*, announcing the end of hostilities in Iraq. Bush's speech was the green light I'd been waiting for. A few weeks later, as I raced *Mad Max*-style across the Iraqi desert in the back seat of a Chevy Suburban, my fate rested in the hands of a grief-stricken Sunni tribal chief whose entire family had just been wiped out by the US military. Inside the speeding vehicle, I was beginning to have second thoughts about my audacious business plan, but at that point it was too late to turn back.

Looking back, I am grateful I stuck with my plan, even though the venture required me to survive more obstacles, challenges, and close calls than ever before. Babylon Inc.'s performance has exceeded everyone's expectations (including mine) both in terms of business success and tactical intelligence collection.

Hindsight is of course twenty-twenty, so it's no surprise I harbor no regrets over taking the chance when I did. But what on earth possessed me to borrow money to finance a speculative business venture in war-torn Iraq when all of my experience to date had been in the Balkans and Latin America? For starters, I needed to bring in more income, and my marketable skills were somewhat narrowly focused. I decided to make the most of the talents I had, which boiled down to knowing how to develop and lead a team of trusted agents to get results in foreign lands. What follows is the first part of the story of how and why I thought it was a good idea to infiltrate Iraq in the back seat of a Sunni tribal chief's American-made SUV.

* * *

Before Iraq, there was Kosovo. Until the late 1990s, the odd, little Yugoslav autonomous province of Kosovo was reminiscent of South Africa during apartheid; in this case, the minority were the Serbs who persecuted the majority ethnic Albanians. A similar thing occurred in Iraq, where the minority Sunnis, led by Saddam Hussein, oppressed the Shi'ite majority. In both Kosovo and Iraq, it was just a matter of time before the natural balance was restored, with the help of American firepower, for better or worse.

During my many long-term TDYs to the former Yugoslavia, I often traveled to the disputed region of Kosovo, since it was one of the former Yugoslavia's most volatile hot spots. (As you have probably deduced by now, CIA officers have a soft spot for hot spots.) One of my last and most memorable TDYs to Pristina, Kosovo's dreary capital, began on August 29, 1990. On that pivotal day in Kosovo's history, Senator Bob Dole and six other US senators arrived in Kosovo to meet with Albanian democratic opposition leaders and the future first president of Kosovo, Ibrahim Rugova. Because of my Serbian language ability and experience in Kosovo, I was sent down to the restive province to help coordinate the historic meeting between the Dole congressional delegation and Rugova. Another American and I left Belgrade early and arrived midmorning at Pristina's Grand Hotel, where we met with Rugova to review the day's schedule. Like many post–Berlin Wall leaders, Rugova was an interesting character, an intellectual, a journalist, and the former chairman of the Kosovo Writers Union. He wore almost stylish glasses and unkempt, longish brown hair. Rugova always donned his trademark neck scarf, even in the summer. He looked as if he could have been a Latin professor from Harvard.

While we were going over the day's agenda with Rugova in the hotel's ground-floor car rental office, overlooking Pristina's cozy town square, our Serb driver took the official limo out to be washed, since he would use it later in the day to ferry Dole to the hotel for the meetings. Mistakenly believing Dole must have been in the oversized dark American sedan, a crowd of around ten thousand ethnic Albanians immediately converged on the square, chanting, "USA! USA!" I asked Rugova if he had organized this "spontaneous" demonstration. He just shrugged. After we agreed on the game plan for the day, Rugova promised to return later that afternoon to meet Senator Dole. Rugova's driver then transported him back to his office across town.

The Serbs were not pleased by this grassroots outpouring of pro-American sentiment by the freedom-craving ethnic Albanian Kosovars, and they soon surrounded the growing crowd (and our hotel) with armored personnel carriers and big, well-trained, and well-armed Serb special police known as *specialci*. Outside of town, the Serbs also tried to prevent Dole's plane from landing, in order to keep him from meeting with Rugova. Predictably, they did not succeed in keeping this decorated World War II hero out of Kosovo. By the time Senator Dole arrived later that day under police escort at the Grand Hotel, demonstrations had broken out across Pristina and the feared specialci had teargassed, beaten with clubs, and arrested many of the ethnic Albanian demonstrators.

Understandably fearing he might be arrested and possibly killed at one of the many specialci checkpoints set up across the city by the now very angry Serbs, Rugova sent a messenger to say he could not make the meeting with Dole.

Dole and his Senate colleagues had not traveled all this way to a very uncomfortable corner of the earth to be stood up, and so they dispatched me to personally escort Rugova back to the Grand Hotel. The assumption was the Serbs would be less likely to arrest or harm Rugova if he was accompanied by an American officer.

I took a taxi across town to Rugova's secret lair, a smoke-filled, underground conference room known as the "Writers' Club." Rugova and a dozen or so of his Democratic League of Kosovo colleagues warmly welcomed me to their hideout. I sat next to Rugova at the head of the large conference table while hot tea was served. After putting a spoonful of sugar in his mouth, Rugova returned the spoon to the sugar bowl before passing it on to me. I normally put sugar in my hot tea, but in this instance, I politely declined.

After a brief discussion of the game plan and securing Rugova's agreement to venture out again, we went upstairs and walked toward a small Soviet Lada, in which we would ride across town to the Grand Hotel. The driver opened the door for future president Rugova, who got in and sat in the back seat of his beat-up Communist limo. I rode shotgun and would deal with any police checkpoints we might encounter. We then drove off through chaotic streets of Pristina, weaving our way through running battles between ethnic Albanian demonstrators and Serb specialci. Tear gas hung in the air and made breathing difficult.

As expected, we were soon stopped at a specialci roadblock. A big Serb specialist in full riot gear approached my side of the car. I rolled down the window, and he immediately put his AK to my head. His specialci brethren surrounded the car and could see that the instantly recognizable Rugova was in the back seat. Rugova remained motionless and said nothing. It was make or break time for me, a genetically calm person and, at the time, a fluent speaker of Serbian. If I failed to talk us through this situation, the Serbs would arrest, beat, and possibly kill the future president of Kosovo. Doing my best to ignore the barrel of the assault rifle that was aimed directly at my forehead, I explained to the officer who we were and where we were headed. I lied and told him we had been assured safe passage by senior Serb police officials.

The big *specialac* looked at me as if I were from another planet. After what seemed like an eternity, he lowered his gun and signaled for us to proceed. His colleagues made a hole and allowed us to drive through the makeshift checkpoint. We all breathed a sigh of relief. My two traveling companions each lit up a vile Balkan cigarette.

After my heart stopped racing, about the same time we were safely pulling up to the bustling entrance to the Grand Hotel, I replayed the entire conversation with the specialac in my head. What exactly had I said, and how exactly did the cop respond? Things obviously went well, we had survived, but still, something didn't add up. Mentally re-creating the conversation, I realized that although I had indeed coolly and calmly explained the situation to the Serb specialac, every word I uttered was not in Serbian but in perfect Spanish.

Funny what a gun to the temple will do to a guy. It was no wonder the cop looked at me as if somewhere a village must be missing an idiot.

✷ ✷ ✷

Fast-forward almost nine years. In the spring of 1999, after the launch of the NATO air campaign against Yugoslavia, Serbs began the barbaric and systematic "ethnic cleansing" of the Kosovo region. Reminiscent of Nazi Germany, hundreds of thousands of ethnic Albanians were rounded up by the Serbs, packed onto trains, or hounded through the countryside to neighboring Macedonia, where survivors were eventually housed in sprawling refugee camps. After having their asses handed to them in Slovenia, Croatia, and Bosnia, this was the Serbs' last chance to rid mythical Kosovo of the despised *Shiptars* and create a rump "Greater Serbia." Their campaign was characteristically savage. A Catholic Albanian village called Meja was the site of the war's worst, Srebrenica-like massacre. Serb specialci pulled nearly four hundred men and boys from refugee columns and shot them to death. Their missing bodies were discovered years later in a mass grave on a specialci training camp near Belgrade.[1]

By this time, I had resigned from the CIA and was working privately. A wealthy American client of mine was growing anxious watching nightly news reports from Kosovo. His ancestors had fled Nazi Germany, and he was understandably disturbed by the unimaginable horror taking place, once again, in Europe. He knew I was an old "Yugoslav hand" and asked if there was anything he could do to help. I thought about it and then convinced him to finance a one-year donation of his company's goods and services, which would provide much-needed short-term relief to the refugees. I told him I would travel to Macedonia to manage the project. All I needed was financing. He agreed.

I immediately traveled across the world to Stenkovec, the largest of the refugee camps in Macedonia, to make it happen. Shortly after my arrival in the hot, dusty camp, still jet-lagged, I was invited to spend an hour inside a UN Refugee Agency tent with First Lady Hillary Clinton.

I'll explain. She had just arrived by military helicopter to check on conditions inside the teeming camp and to give a talk to assembled government, military, and nongovernmental representatives. CNN's Christiane Amanpour, a veteran war correspondent, was there to cover the event. Clinton immediately grasped the historic gravity of the situation and commented that the scenes reminded her of Nazi war movies like *Schindler's List* or *Sophie's Choice*.[2]

As hungry, thirsty refugees continued to stream into the camp, I visited a displaced family inside their suffocating tent. I spoke in Serbian with an ethnic Albanian mother and her children who had fled Kosovo on foot, spending several days fleeing through the woods, without food or water. The children were safe now, but they did not know where their father was or if he was still alive. Barely subsisting in dirty, prisonlike conditions, all were distraught and uncertain of their future. There was not much I could do for them, other than wish them luck and move forward with my project. Once the project was up and running, in coordination with the International Organization of Migration (IOM), I returned to my easy life in the United States.

Fortunately for those who survived, the ethnic Albanian exodus was relatively short-lived. At war's end, hundreds of thousands of desperate refugees returned to their homes (or what was left of them) in Kosovo. By then, an estimated eleven thousand ethnic Albanians from Kosovo had been killed or went missing.[3] I returned once again to the still-volatile war zone, ignoring the US embassy-in-exile's demand that I not enter Kosovo before they had received country clearance to go in themselves. Transferring the donation from IOM control to the International Rescue Committee (IRC), we moved the humanitarian project from Macedonia to Kosovo's capital of Pristina, where it became an integral part of Kosovo's reconstruction. (Neither the IOM nor IRC was aware of my CIA background, and the CIA had nothing to do with this purely private humanitarian project.)

Getting into and out of war-ravaged Kosovo via Skopje, Macedonia's then backward and overwhelmed capital, was like navigating a postapocalyptic obstacle course. The border crossing was a hellish scene of chaos, with thousands of people vying for a visa or exit stamp from one of the few surly, overworked Macedonian border guards. I managed to fight my way through the mob, got my passport stamped, and hitched a ride to Pristina with some French Kosovo Force soldiers who were part of a NATO convoy entering Kosovo. While the miles-long convoy was delayed for half an hour or so, two of the French soldiers in my vehicle hopped out to conduct business with some desperate but enterprising young roadside prostitutes. *Vive la France!*

After several hours we finally reached our destination. I made my way to the Grand Hotel—a misnomer if ever there was one—in the heart of Pristina. I was already familiar with the hotel, since I had always stayed there during my many TDYs in the past. The Balkan breakfasts were wonderful, but the number of neon stars on top of the hotel seemed to increase in direct proportion to the building's growing cockroach population.[4] Walking the familiar, filthy streets of my old stomping ground, I surveyed the damage done during the brief but violent war. I also couldn't help but notice the absence of smothering Serb surveillance, which I had always attracted during earlier trips to Kosovo. The freedom was actually a bit disconcerting. (During one earlier official trip to Kosovo, our US government car broke down on a snow-bound highway outside of Pristina, but my mind was at ease, knowing our chain-smoking secret police escorts were parked right behind us.)

As I strolled around postwar Pristina, refreshingly free of Serb surveillance, it was evident that NATO planes had done an excellent job of precision bombing only key targets, pancaking several Serb regime buildings. Otherwise, Pristina was left largely intact, in dramatic contrast to the towns and cities the Serbs had completely trashed and destroyed many years earlier in Croatia and Bosnia—places like Čilipi, Mostar, and Sarajevo, all of which I visited during the war and saw with my own eyes. Not to mention Dubrovnik's airport, where I observed that the Serbs had mined the runway, trashed the tower along with every window, sign, and fixture in the airport, and stolen all valuable radar and other equipment, along with several nearby dairy cows. (The Croats did their fair share of destruction in Mostar and other places once they and the Bosnian Muslims turned on each other.)

The ethnic Albanian manager of the Grand Hotel, who remembered me from my official TDYs in the early 1990s, dragged me down to the hotel's basement to show me a recently abandoned Serb communications, interrogation, and torture center. Navigating the stairway down was tricky as we had to step over and around a dozen or so temporary Serb communications cables the size of garden hoses that ran up the stairway. The grimy walls of the dimly lit basement were stained with bloody handprints, and victims' sandals were scattered across the garbage-strewn floor. The filth reminded me of the mindless devastation the Serbs had left behind in other parts of the country.

But not all was grim during this trip: besides enjoying the sense of freedom that permeated Kosovo for the first time in recent memory, I was also able to roam for free on the Serbs' still-functioning cellular network, the appropriately named MobTel.

* * *

My "temporary" war zone humanitarian project evolved over the next few years into a successful for-profit business, not for me but for my client and for others on the ground in Kosovo who developed and grew the venture. One of the project's key local employees went on to become Kosovo's ambassador to the United States. It turned out this particular business was ideally suited to conflict zones that experienced bloody transitions from authoritarian rule to freedom and independence—an unusual niche, but a niche nonetheless. Although the idea for the initial wartime project was mine, the postwar business in Kosovo was managed by and belonged to others.

In addition to doing the good it was intended to do, this successful Kosovo project served as a model for my Iraqi start-up four years later. The key difference being in Iraq I would own and operate the business myself. I expected to enjoy a "first-in" competitive advantage in Iraq, since other, more risk-averse companies in that industry would not likely enter the Iraqi market until after the situation had stabilized. I was hoping for a three-to-six-month head start before the competition felt safe enough to enter the huge and promising Iraqi market. Because of the deadly insurgency, my competitive advantage ended up lasting for many years. This unusual business model is not likely to be discussed at Harvard Business School, but I believed at the time it could be successfully replicated in other post-9/11 hot spots like Afghanistan or Yemen. The slogan for my unorthodox business plan may not have been Harvard-worthy, but it did accurately describe my vision: "One man's axis of evil is another man's blueprint for growth."

CHAPTER 23

MISSION: IMPROBABLE

As any CIA officer will tell you, the key to securely achieving solid results in a foreign land, whether in benign or hostile environments, is recruiting trusted local agents who do most of the "heavy lifting." Whether the objective is to influence events or simply to report on what's actually happening on the ground, rarely if ever can a CIA officer accomplish much of value overseas on his or her own. The same held true for me in my post-CIA life. I knew I could not just show up in Baghdad, where I did not even speak the language, and expect to survive, much less succeed with a new business venture. I needed a vetted Iraqi partner with the right access, background, and connections.

With almost zero Iraq experience under my belt, how would I go about finding such a partner? I immediately turned to my informal network of fellow former CIA officers. Between us we covered the world. More importantly, we were connected by unspoken bonds of trust, based on years of shared training and overseas experience. If anyone needed anything done in the Balkans, for example, they reached out to me for help. Other CIA alumni covered Asia, Africa, and Latin America, some specializing in a single difficult country, like China or Russia. For Iraq, I called on my old friend and colleague "Dan," a Middle East expert who had successfully run Iraqi agents inside Saddam's regime. Among other things, Dan was an Arabist who continued to enjoy unparalleled access, influence, and respect in Iraq and throughout the Middle East. He readily and graciously agreed to assist.

After giving it some thought, Dan recommended I partner with a wealthy and important Sunni tribal sheik from Ramadi, the capital of Anbar province. "Imad" was a prominent leader of the Dulaimi tribe, the largest in Iraq. The Dulaimi had been in the region for centuries, long before present-day borders were drawn and long before the dawn of Saddam Hussein's reign of terror. The Dulaimi would be there long after Saddam as well. Imad and his extended Sunni family had close ties to Saddam, but in order to survive under Saddam, one had to play Saddam's game. Imad's family was heavily invested in a number of industries in Iraq and would likely welcome the opportunity to introduce a much-needed and previously outlawed American business into post-Saddam Iraq.

Imad agreed to meet me in Amman, the beautiful and ancient capital of the Hashemite Kingdom of Jordan. Once we were both satisfied with the partnership agreement, Imad would personally ensure that both my team and our equipment made it across the lawless Jordan-Iraq border and into Baghdad. He would also house and feed us and assist with other start-up preliminaries. Handling security and logistics had long been a routine and necessary part of Imad's life in Iraq. If there were complications entering Iraq through official border crossings, we'd detour via traditional smuggling routes across the desert that his tribe had been using for centuries. As Dan put it, "Imad could move an aircraft carrier from Amman to Baghdad without anyone knowing about it."

Before traveling to the Middle East, I offered to discuss my Iraq business plans with relevant US government authorities, as I had done prior to traveling to Kosovo. I thought they might find some benefit in at least knowing what I was doing. Once again, they expressed zero interest in my plan, and they also tried to talk me out of it. One US official even told me it was illegal for me to enter Iraq. In the Balkans, after trying to prevent me from traveling to Pristina, the US government eventually became my customer. I planned to make my move into Iraq, with or without their official blessing, and I suspected the same sequence of events would play out as it had in Kosovo. I wasn't wrong.

After arriving at Amman's Queen Alia Airport late one night in May 2003, two American volunteers and I took a taxi into the city and checked into the modern Sheraton Amman al-Nabil Hotel. The Sheraton Amman would become a welcome layover spot during my many future trips into and out of Iraq. Because of the war in neighboring Iraq and the very real possibility of terror spilling over into Jordan, security was tight in Amman. Gaining access to the hotel was not unlike entering any major airport. After driving through a maze of heavy concrete barriers, guests and their luggage were required to pass through metal detectors and physical searches by courteous guards who controlled access to the hotel.

The next morning, while my colleagues went shopping for supplies that might be difficult to find in Iraq, I met with Dan at his hotel to review our game plan prior to my first meeting with Imad later that night. It was during our morning meeting that Dan shared some somber news. A few weeks earlier, US forces killed over a dozen of Imad's family members, including his four young daughters and his only son. American warplanes dropped six JDAMs (Joint Direct Attack Munitions) on his large family compound in Ramadi, in the Sunni triangle west of Baghdad. The American bombing of Imad's huge main house was based on intelligence reports that Saddam Hussein and his sons, Uday and Qusay, were holed up there. Over twenty people, mainly women and children, were killed in the attack. All were members of Imad's immediate or extended family, or were beloved household staff.

My first question for Dan was whether Saddam and his two sadistic sons really were hiding out at Imad's family compound. Dan said initial after-action reports concluded the so-called intelligence was false, and the bombing had been a tragic mistake. Imad believed that his cousin, a rival for power within the tribe, intentionally passed the false report to the US military in order to prompt this deadly strike. *Murder by military*. If this were in fact true, Imad's cousin would not be long for this world. The tribe would dispense swift justice as it had for centuries.

A year or two later, I heard a different version of events. According to this new information, Saddam and his two sons were indeed holed up at Imad's compound when it was bombed, but they (along with Imad) all survived the attack, since they were in adjacent buildings or standing outside the main house, using their Thuraya satellite phones. Also allegedly present during the attack was Barzan Ibrahim al-Tikriti, Saddam's half brother and head of the feared Mukhabarat, the Iraqi intelligence service. This version of events has Saddam weeping at the site of the carnage and his son Uday pulling a child's body out of the rubble in the aftermath of the bombing.

Either way, the attack on Imad's family compound in Ramadi produced outrage in Iraq's Sunni heartland and jump-started the deadly Sunni insurgency that continues to this day, spreading as far as Syria and beyond, in the form of ISIS.

* * *

After learning the shocking details of what Imad had just survived, I was a bit nervous about meeting him later that night. For starters, I could not begin to imagine how he could even function, after having lost most of his family in such a horrific event. I honestly don't know how I would handle something so devastating. Under the circumstances, it was also difficult to understand how Imad could be willing to help me, an American whom he knew had ties to the CIA. But my trust in Dan was unwavering, and so I arrived on time at an inviting open-air Lebanese restaurant on the outskirts of Amman to meet with Dan and my future Iraqi business partner. As the infectious Arabic dance tune "Nour El Ain" by Egyptian pop star Amr Diab played softly over the restaurant's sound system, I took in the spectacular view of the blood-orange, dust-enhanced sunset from the hilltop restaurant.

After shaking Imad's hand, I briefly pressed my open right hand to my heart, as did Imad, a traditional Iraqi greeting indicating respect and sincerity. He was wearing sandals and a traditional white dishdasha, or tunic. For the next couple of hours, his fingers never stopped manipulating the well-worn wooden prayer beads that dangled off his left hand. Grief was etched on Imad's face like a permanent mask. Sitting next to him was almost physically painful. He spoke in a soft voice, and only enough to deal with the matter at hand. His dark eyes were barely able to contain his unbearable sadness. The one and only time Imad smiled was when, recalling my hunger-filled days in food-scarce Sarajevo, I asked if we should stock up on food supplies to bring with us to Baghdad. Imad and Dan just looked at each other and laughed.

After briefly reviewing our partnership agreement, we agreed to meet up two days later at 4:00 a.m. to begin our dangerous overland trek to Baghdad. We said goodbye, and Imad left the restaurant without eating, accompanied by his driver and bodyguard.

After confirming the details of our plan one last time, I also bid farewell to Dan, who would return to the United States the next day. I'll never forget his parting words of advice, meant to keep me safe inside Iraq: "Keep your mouth shut and follow Imad's lead."

* * *

Originally built on seven hills, the city of Amman is now spread out over almost twenty hills and as many *wadis*, or valleys. Most of Amman's residential buildings are of the same sand color and are limited to four stories. The low, undulating skyline is occasionally punctuated by exotic domes and minarets of the city's many mosques. I never tire of the grand views of the sprawling, hilly city from my hotel room balcony. Unlike "artificial" Dubai, an admittedly fun and easy city to visit, Amman is an authentic Arab city and, along with Damascus and Muscat, one of my favorites in the Middle East.

During the final two days prior to our late May departure for Baghdad, the skies around Amman began to slowly fill up with dust. Winds were not especially high, and it did not yet amount to a blinding dust storm, at least not the kind I had grown up with back home. But I felt something ominous was slowly and steadily developing.

At 4:00 a.m. on the designated morning, we met Imad and several of his AK-armed Iraqi colleagues on a quiet side street outside the Sheraton Amman. We loaded up several white Chevrolet Suburbans with our gear and other supplies, then wound our way out of the darkened city of Amman, heading northeast for the Iraqi border. It was now getting harder to breathe as dust continued to pour into the city and the winds were picking up. What I did not realize then was that a monster sandstorm had been building up near Amman, it was headed east, and it would make getting to Baghdad later that day next to impossible.

The drive on the two-lane highway from Amman to the Iraqi border crossing at Tureibil was largely uneventful. We stopped for shawarma at the last small town on the Jordanian side of the border before crossing into Iraq. A miles-long line of parked trucks waiting to enter Iraq reminded me of similar scenes during the Balkan wars.

By late May 2003, military hostilities may have temporarily ended, but chaos had broken out across Iraq. In its rush to overthrow Saddam, the Bush administration ignored military and intelligence experts who had warned about the need to be prepared for the postwar scenario. Scenes of Iraqis looting while US soldiers stood helplessly by were commonplace. American soldiers were trained to fight a war, not secure and run the country afterward. The insurgency had not yet gotten underway on the day we entered Iraq, but armed bandits roamed the desert along our route from Jordan to Baghdad. Our four-vehicle convoy would drive at high speed across the desert until we reached Baghdad. Like just about every other Iraqi, civilian or military, our escorts were armed with AK-47s, sometimes concealed under their dishdashas.

Our favorite armed escort was Abdul, a tall, athletic Iraqi who had previously worked as a bodyguard for Saddam's psychotic son Uday. (Rumor has it he also served as a body double.) Years earlier, Uday had sentenced Abdul and other members of the Iraqi Olympic basketball team to serve time in jail after they lost a game to another country. Abdul was lucky. Uday was known to abuse, torture, and kill other Iraqi athletes who failed to live up to his expectations, including an Iraqi table tennis player.[1]

Our plans to race to Baghdad were rudely interrupted by the shamal sandstorm that was beginning to hit its stride just as we crossed the border into Iraq. On the Iraqi side of the border, all visitors were greeted by two giant, dramatic Islamic arches and a portrait of Saddam that had not yet been taken down. The ugly Iraqi border-crossing building on the north side of the highway was crowded and chaotic, reminding me of Macedonia, but much to my surprise it was more or less functioning. A solitary, dazed-looking American soldier sheltered against the storm as best he could outside the building, but he did not have a border control role. Imad's colleagues took care of getting us processed through the border, and we got back into the vehicles for the drive to Baghdad. A small refugee camp set up just inside Iraq was reminiscent of the scene in Kosovo. It occurred to me that besides the indiscriminate destruction and killing, all wars seem to share lots of other, more mundane characteristics as well.

By the time we left the border area, visibility was greatly reduced to about a hundred meters; this was not ideal, but it was still good enough to drive relatively safely. A half an hour later, the storm had worsened and had completely enveloped the entire region, turning day into night. Visibility dropped to zero with occasional gaps of ten feet or so. Winds were howling, and we were engulfed in total darkness, the only light an eerie dark orange glow. It was how I imagined a Martian landscape. The time of day was around noon, but because of the total darkness, it looked like midnight. I felt as though we were skiing above the timberline during a snowstorm; it was impossible to gauge how fast we were moving, or if we were even moving at all. On several occasions our sandstorm-experienced Iraqi drivers narrowly avoided crashing into disabled vehicles, which appeared like a flash out of nowhere as we swerved past, our headlights briefly illuminating the hopeless wreckage.

I later heard there were over fifty pileups on the road to Baghdad during that day's fierce sandstorm. There would have been many more accidents and fatalities had traffic not been traveling on Saddam's well-paved, well-marked, straight-as-an-arrow divided highway. Two of our escort vehicles were involved in accidents shortly after entering Iraq. Imad insisted we leave them behind and press on, since to pause even momentarily would invite the risk of being robbed or killed by the bandits lurking in the desert. A few times we had to stop the vehicles completely because it was impossible to see. I stepped out of the SUV once and was nearly blown off my feet by the force of the winds. After a brief but intense sandblasting, I returned to the relative safety, comfort, and quiet of the air-conditioned, American-made Suburban.

The entire experience was surreal and nothing like the dust storms I'd experienced growing up. There was a real chance we would be involved in an accident and be attacked by armed bandits. I knew our remaining armed escorts would do their best to protect us, but I was hoping to make it to Baghdad without experiencing my first desert firefight. Being trapped in the sandstorm on the lawless highway was nerve-wracking, much more so than operating under "normal" wartime conditions, where at least a person has some control over his environment. To their credit, my two American war virgin colleagues were not as nervous as I was about the perils we were facing that day on Saddam's highway. The experience confirmed my belief, formed over the years in the former Yugoslavia, that one of the most dangerous aspects of being in a war zone—as a civilian—is driving through it.

Somehow, miraculously, after spending about fourteen hours on the road, we made it as far as Ramadi before sunset. We would not make it to Baghdad, another hour and a half away. By the time we pulled off Saddam's highway and turned south toward the welcoming date palms of Ramadi, the storm had subsided considerably and visibility was decent. Since Imad's family compound had been recently destroyed, he put us up in the large, comfortable home of his uncle "Omar," an even more prominent tribal sheik. Mine was not a sentiment to be shared by the many American troops who would soon find themselves there, but I was thankful to be in Ramadi.

After we were shown to our rooms and had a chance to catch our breaths, my two American colleagues and I were treated to a phenomenal Arabic feast in the formal dining room of the large Iraqi house. Since we were unexpected guests, I could not fathom how, on short notice, they could pull together such huge platters of rice, lamb, and chicken that literally took two men to carry to the table. We never saw any women, but we knew they were in the next room, preparing the feast. I was beginning to understand why Dan and Imad had laughed when I asked if we should bring in food supplies.

After dinner, I took a few things out of my backpack. My Toshiba laptop had made the entire trip in a zippered sleeve, inside my backpack, which remained inside the closed, air-conditioned Suburban. When I pulled it out, the laptop was covered with dust as fine as baby powder that had somehow penetrated the several layers of "security." After confirming the laptop still worked, I walked outside to call my daughters on my satellite phone before passing out for the best night's sleep I'd experienced in a week.

The next morning, before leaving Ramadi, we stopped to see the damage done by the bombing of Imad's nearby family compound. The large concrete structure had been flattened by the precision bombs. The sight of the collapsed three-story home reminded me of the Serb government buildings in Pristina that had been similarly targeted during the war in Kosovo. It was not difficult to understand why no one inside the house had survived.

We then drove on in silence, heading east on Saddam's highway, through Fallujah and into chaotic Baghdad. There was no discernible police presence in Iraq's hot and noisy capital. Traffic was out of control, and overwhelmed young American troops tried their best to provide security in the city's jammed traffic circles. I felt bad for our troops; they were sitting ducks, surrounded by thousands of vehicles and unable to scan them all for threats. Not that it was easy to distinguish between a threat and an innocent Iraqi. Because of the traffic jam, we drove the wrong way down a one-way street to our final destination, a villa owned by Imad in the al-Mansour district of Baghdad.

Imad had turned one of the villa's offices into our bedroom, complete with three comfortable twin beds. Our meals were prepared outside and brought in daily. Food was always plentiful, and it was, without fail, delicious. One of my two American colleagues had planned to lose weight during his month-long stay in Baghdad. I'd told him about the weight I'd lost during my wartime "Sarajevo diet" and cautioned him the situation in Baghdad could be similar. I could not have been more wrong. Instead of losing weight, my colleague put on fifteen pounds during his stay in Baghdad.

Just as I had done after surviving the deadly trek into Sarajevo, I slept like a baby once we reached Baghdad. Arriving safely at ground zero is a welcome relief; it's the anticipation and the risky trip in or out that produces the adrenaline rush. Before hitting the rack, I would position my flip-flops next to my bed to avoid stepping on a cockroach with my bare feet in case I had to get up during the night. On my first night, I got up in the dark and stepped into my sandals, squishing a giant cockroach that was resting comfortably on top of the left one. *Welcome to Baghdad.*

While in Baghdad, we checked out potential office buildings and even made some preliminary sales calls on prospective customers. We also interviewed our first potential employees, including one named Osama. Abdul happily drove us around Baghdad in a little white car, seemingly tempting fate at every turn. During one trip along the banks of the Tigris River to the Babylon Hotel, he got into a one-sided road rage argument with some unseen Iraqis inside a BMW with blacked-out windows and no tags—not the kind of people you want to mess with at that particular time in Iraq's history. Another time, he failed to slow down as we approached the Palestine Hotel, ignoring the commands of US troops who were understandably nervous about potential suicide car bombers. We were fortunate the troops did not light us up as we approached. Abdul also failed to declare his hidden gun and was lucky the troops did not discover that as well. Back at our villa, wild man Abdul kept us entertained with his antics and even provided wake-up service in the mornings with a couple of pokes to the chest with his AK. He spoke no English, and we spoke almost no Arabic, but we still managed to communicate. Whenever we'd hit the deck after hearing small-arms fire outside, Abdul would point toward the sound of the gunfire and say, knowingly, "Ali Baba."

* * *

After spending a week on the ground in Baghdad, I left my two colleagues behind and returned to Amman via the same desert route. They courageously remained in Baghdad for another month to deal with the myriad business start-up issues.

During the drive from Baghdad to Amman, I stopped off again in Ramadi to meet with Imad's uncle, Sheik Omar. Chapter 29 reveals the details of our brief but historic conversation.

As we sped west across Anbar Province, I was able to experience things I had not seen on my way in, due to the blinding sandstorm. The western Iraqi desert is not unlike parts of the American Southwest and northern Baja California, Mexico. A couple of fundamental differences included the large herds of camels roaming freely in the desert, and having to detour around modern freeway overpasses and bridges that had been recently destroyed by US forces.

The trip out of Iraq and into Jordan was smooth compared to the trip in. After checking into my room at the Sheraton Amman, I opened up my dusty duffel bag and watched a huge Iraqi cockroach crawl out. It looked as though it could've been related to the one I flattened in Baghdad. I shooed the cockroach onto the balcony and bid it a fond farewell. At that point the pest was someone else's problem. Little did I know at that moment that my border-crossing Mesopotamian cockroach was a fitting metaphor for the evil genie that had been let out of its bottle when the United States carried out its ill-advised invasion of Iraq.

CHAPTER 24

TRIBALISM

Although Babylon Inc. is registered in Iraq and is staffed almost exclusively by Iraqis, from day one I have tried to instill in our workforce American values and business practices. Our first office manager, "Ali Baba," was a former sergeant in Saddam's army, so his reflexive response when an employee showed up late for work was to beat him senseless. This was apparently the only motivational tool at this former Iraqi soldier's disposal. We counseled him that corporal punishment of tardy employees was no longer acceptable, since he was now working for an American-run company. Ali Baba viewed Americans as weak, but so did Saddam, and we all know where he ended up: cowering in a filthy spider hole until he and his flea-infested beard were captured by US forces.

My approach to Iraq was informed in large part by my decade of experience in the former Yugoslavia, a similarly cobbled-together mosaic of a state where ancient ethnic hatreds were stoked by modern-day demagogues until civil war literally destroyed the country. For better or worse, I viewed Iraq through the Yugoslavia prism because of the centuries-old bad blood and rivalries between the Sunnis, Shi'ites, and Kurds, in a country whose borders were drawn by the British. With openly sectarian post-Saddam leadership and demonization of "the other," Iraq could easily go the way of Yugoslavia, breaking up into two or three separate countries. That was my assumption anyway, and so we immediately set up shop in all three regions of Iraq. Beyond that, I had no control over what happened in Iraq. What I *could* control was how we hired and treated employees.

Simply stated, we hire Iraqi employees based on their qualifications, attitude, integrity, and skills, without regard for their ethnic or religious background. As a result, from the day we opened for business in May 2003, my company has employed Sunnis, Shi'ites, Kurds, Turkmen, and Iraqi

Christians, based solely on merit. Neither management nor employees ever discuss politics, religion, or ethnicity. It ceases to be an issue. Our employees work together beautifully (for the most part) for the sake of the company and the customers. Issues and conflicts between employees certainly arise but not because of religion or ethnicity. All of our employees bring something special to the table, and they work together as a team. We consider ourselves a family. The younger Iraqi employees especially seem to thrive in this "new" American-style environment. This phenomenon gives me hope that over time, life will improve for the average Iraqi.

Outside our corporate environment, the employees continue to face risks and unfair treatment at the hands of other, less-enlightened Iraqis. For example, after our Arab employees from Baghdad completed a huge project on behalf of the Kurdistan Regional Government (KRG) in Erbil, the KRG expelled them from the Kurdistan region under threat of arrest. Why? Because they were Arabs and not Kurds. We would have happily hired Kurds to work on the project, but at that moment in history they did not have the training or skills needed to do the job. Our Iraqi Arab employees were dedicated and did a beautiful job on behalf of our xenophobic Kurdish customer, but in the end, they were treated badly by those they had faithfully served because of ethnicity and paranoia.

After we trained the Kurds and taught the KRG how to do what we do, they also gave our company the boot, breaching a huge contract and nearly destroying our business in the process. For years after the costly 2003 invasion, which gave the Kurds considerable freedom and autonomy, the KRG also cheated many other foreign companies that invested in ostensibly more advanced Kurdistan. The KRG has its hands in every business in Kurdistan. The most succinct way to describe KRG leadership in Erbil is, "Like *The Sopranos*, but with bad food."

The ethnic and religious differences of our employees impacted them outside the office in humorous and deadly ways, sometimes simultaneously. Our Shi'ite employees faced increased risks in Sunni sections of Iraq, and vice versa. Baghdad itself is broken down into a multitude of Sunni and Shi'ite areas. It is almost as difficult to be in a mixed marriage in Iraq today as it was in Yugoslavia in the early 1990s. These realities and the never-ending insurgency did not prevent our dedicated and courageous employees from venturing out to all parts of Iraq in order to take care of our customers, Iraqi and foreign alike, who depended very much on Babylon Inc. and its true 24/7, 365-days-per-year philosophy.

To the average American, Iraq's Sunnis and Shi'ites appear and behave remarkably alike and would seem to have more in common than not. Serbs and Croats also strike outsiders as having more in common with each other than with anyone else on the planet, but that did not prevent them from hating and slaughtering one another. There are books devoted to explaining the differences between Sunnis and Shi'ites and are worth reading for those interested in understanding the history behind today's conflicts. I will very briefly explain the differences between Shi'ites and Sunnis, since knowing that saga even in very basic terms is key to understanding what's happening today in the Middle East (and beyond). It will also help to explain what happened to three of my employees—and why—when they were captured by dangerous Islamic extremists in Mosul.

When the founder of Islam, the Prophet Muhammad, died in 632, a violent dispute arose among the growing religion's faithful over who should succeed him. Those who believed Muhammad wanted his title passed to his cousin and son-in-law, Ali, went on to form the Shia branch of the religion. The word Shi'ite derives from the term Shiat-Ali, meaning "partisans of Ali."[1] Shi'ites have generally been an oppressed minority in the Muslim world. Those who believed the Prophet Muhammad died without appointing a successor regard themselves as the true adherents to the Sunnah, or the Prophet's tradition. Sunnis make up about 85 percent of the world's 1.5 billion Muslims and are led by Saudi Arabia.[2] Saudi Arabia has historically promoted an extreme form of Sunni Islam called Wahhabism, which underpins beliefs and actions by extremists like al-Qaeda and ISIS. Iran is the dominant Shi'ite country, and there are also Shi'ite majorities in Iraq and Bahrain. Iran extends its often malign influence across the Middle East through its Shi'ite allies and proxies in Iraq, Syria (Bashar al-Assad's Alawite Shi'ite regime), and Lebanon (Hezbollah). Understanding the Shi'ite-Sunni schism also helps explain why the United States found itself on the same side as (Shi'ite) Iran and Syria—two regimes it otherwise opposes—in the effort to eradicate (Sunni) ISIS. Our enemy's enemy is sometimes, at least temporarily, our ally.

✱ ✱ ✱

Mosul is one of Iraq's largest cities, and historically it has been home not only to Sunni Arabs but also Kurds, Assyrians, Turkmen, Armenians, Yazidis, and other minority groups. Despite its diversity, in recent history Mosul has become known as a bastion of Sunni extremism. Al-Qaeda took root in Mosul and other Sunni areas after the 2003 invasion of Iraq. Daesh/ISIS easily took over the entire city of Mosul in the summer of 2014, with the cooperation of many of the city's Sunnis. ISIS's task was made easier because the US-backed Shi'ite government of Nouri al-Maliki had a track record of blatantly mistreating Iraq's Sunnis, in part because Saddam and his Sunni minority regime had a history of mistreating Iraq's majority Shi'ites. When it comes to ethnic and religious grudges, the circular blame and revenge game is never-ending, and all sides can legitimately cite grievances against each other.

In 2007, Babylon Inc. won a contract with a large corporate customer located not far from the US military forward operating bases (FOBs) Diamondback and Marez, established at Mosul International Airport. The dining facility (DFAC) on FOB Marez was the site of the 2004 suicide bombing by Ansar al-Sunna, which killed fourteen American soldiers, eight others, and injured dozens more. One day in early July 2007, after completing a job for the new customer in Mosul, three of our Iraqi employees were returning by car to the safety of Erbil, some fifty miles to the east, when they found themselves face-to-face with a gang of (Sunni) Islamic extremists likely connected to those who committed the Marez DFAC atrocity. "Hassan" and "Sadiq" were Shi'ite, and "Omar" was Sunni.

Hassan was our "superman" employee, a tough but soft-spoken Shi'ite from Baghdad who operated on our behalf night and day in all parts of Iraq, regardless of the threat from insurgents. Babylon Inc. quickly developed a reputation for performing under fire in Iraq's lawless "red zones," thanks in large part to employees like Hassan. US Marines once raided Hassan's apartment building in Baghdad, searching for insurgents. After they were satisfied he was not a threat, several young US Marines removed their helmets and sat with Hassan on the couch, where together they all played *Call of Duty*. Another time, Hassan was arrested by MPs when he showed up at a base, carrying what they deemed suspicious equipment. We had been invited to send Hassan and the equipment to the base by an officer, but unfortunately, he neglected to coordinate Hassan's visit with the MPs at the gate. Hassan was arrested and interrogated, but he told us, despite that, he was treated well and spent most of the night playing cards with his American jailers.

When Hassan made it back to the office, we paid him a bonus for his troubles. Word got out, and we were afraid other employees might intentionally seek out arrest at the hands of friendly Americans in order to enhance their incomes. In response, we put up a fake, Occupational Safety and Health Administration–like poster listing how much an employee would be paid if arrested ($75), tortured ($150), or forced to "sample the kebab" ($250) while in captivity. (Old nonconsensual-anal-sex-humor-habits die hard.)

These experiences, and many others like them, did not in any way deter ever-positive Hassan from doing his job. We always instructed our employees to remain home or in the office during intense insurgent activity, but Hassan usually refused to heed our warnings.

After I asked Hassan to stay home one especially bloody day, he said, "Sir, Allah has a plan for me. My fate is in Allah's hands."

"Hassan," I responded, "I do not disagree at all, but could you at least not make Allah's job any easier?"

Hassan has survived more close calls than anyone I know, and yet he still walks among us. Who's to say that his approach to life isn't the wisest?

Sadiq, also Shi'ite, was the polar opposite of Hassan in almost every respect, but he treated Hassan like a little brother. Sadiq was a large, roly-poly mountain of a man who was endlessly upbeat and happy. A natural-born fast-talking salesman, he would sing, dance, and joke with practically everyone he met. Sadiq also fancied himself an amateur race car driver, proudly wheeling around Iraq in his used BMW 3 Series while singing along to Arabic pop hits by Tamer Hosny. When the KRG once refused to pay us, in violation of our contract, Sadiq sat reading a magazine in the KRG finance minister's office for days on end, often leaving his family in the car outside the office. Eventually the Kurds realized Sadiq was not going away, and they reluctantly made payment.

On more than one occasion, thanks to Sadiq's perseverance, the KRG paid us over a million dollars in one fell swoop—in cash and in Iraqi dinars. Since the exchange rate was around 1,100 Iraqi dinars to each US dollar, the cash payments were made in large packages that resembled bales of hay. Sadiq would then patiently count each dinar and, after a day or two, typically report a shortfall of a few hundred dollars. If he were dishonest, he could have easily disappeared with the million bucks and been set for life. But like most of our other Iraqi employees, Sadiq was loyal and trustworthy.

Omar, a Sunni in his forties, was the "old man" of the three, with a family at home in Baghdad. Omar was quiet and unassuming and worked as our driver. He had not planned to drive Hassan and Sadiq from Erbil to Mosul, because he was unfamiliar with the route, but our Kurdish driver Rebaz refused to go to Mosul because of the danger. So Omar agreed to drive the three of them to Mosul in our beat-up white Russian Volga with Baghdad tags. They would not take our nicer and more reliable truck, because it had Kurdish tags, which could invite trouble in Mosul.

Hassan, Sadiq, and Omar made the trip from Erbil to Mosul in the morning, completed their tasks near the American base, and set out for what should have been an easy return drive to Erbil by early evening. Unfortunately, none of them could remember the exact route they had taken coming in. At the time there were very few secure routes into and out of Mosul, which was increasingly infested by Sunni insurgents. Mosul was a city that gave no mercy for a wrong turn. The trio became disoriented and got off the main road and onto a neighborhood side street.

Ever-trusting Sadiq suggested they pull over and ask directions of a man with a long black beard who was standing on the side of the street, holding an AK. The man approached their vehicle and asked who they were and where they were headed. Initially Omar said they were workers from Kirkuk, a relatively safe answer, but then Sadiq made the mistake of mentioning Erbil. The bearded man became angry, accused them of working for the enemy Kurdish Peshmerga, pointed his AK at them, and called on his cell phone for backup. He was al-Qaeda in Iraq (AQI). More armed insurgents appeared in several vehicles. They searched our three employees, discovering an ID card on one that had been issued in Erbil.

At this point our guys were forced to admit that they worked in Kurdistan, but they said they were just simple workers. At no time did they acknowledge working for an American company, nor did they reveal they had just come from performing a job near an American military base, whose mission included killing as many of these bearded assholes as possible. Unfortunately for our guys, in AQI's eyes, the Kurds were just as bad if not worse than the Americans. Although they admitted to working in Kurdistan, they did not reveal they were working on a Babylon Inc. contract for the KRG that would, in part, help the KRG to defend against AQI.

The terrorists quickly ascertained that Sadiq (because of his first name) and Hassan (because of his last name) were Shi'ites, and they put guns to their heads. The armed terrorists roughly pulled all three employees out of the vehicle and confiscated their wallets, cell phones, laptops, and documents.

Sadiq's immediate response when faced with this obvious threat was to exclaim, "Don't hit me! I'll tell you everything I know!"

As Shi'ites, Hassan and Sadiq knew they were in imminent danger of literally having their heads cut off by their mujahedin captors. The bad guys shoved Omar into the trunk of one of their vehicles. They tried to forcefully stuff Sadiq into the trunk of our little Volga, but he was so fat that they were unable to close the lid of the trunk with Sadiq in it. After some animated discussion, the terrorists yanked Sadiq back out of the trunk and put him in the driver's seat. After putting Hassan in the front passenger seat, and a jihadi in the back, they ordered Sadiq to drive our Volga and follow their lead vehicle to wherever it was they were going to take them next. Most likely to their execution spot on the banks of the Tigris River, which ran through the middle of the divided city of Mosul. Sadiq did as he was told and began to follow the lead car of the terrorists; about four other AQI vehicles, one of which held Omar, brought up the rear of the motley convoy.

The terrorist in the back seat of Sadiq's car placed his pistol on the seat next to his crotch and began to look through the confiscated cell phones. Hassan knew he and Sadiq were likely being led to their deaths, and this was his last and only chance to act. Fearless Hassan turned around and snatched the bad guy's gun and began to beat him with it. The startled and weaker bad guy bit Hassan on the arm. Hassan refrained from killing the jihadi with the gun and ordered him out of the moving vehicle. The jihadi complied. Sadiq immediately veered down a side street, speeding. The al-Qaeda douchebags in the vehicles behind Sadiq saw what happened, gave chase, and wildly fired their weapons in typical, undisciplined "spray and pray" fashion. Several bullets hit the Volga, but fortunately none hit the tires, Sadiq, or Hassan. At least three AQI vehicles were in hot pursuit of Sadiq and Hassan. Literally fleeing for his life, Sadiq put his superior driving skills to good use, trying to shake his pursuers as he sped down unfamiliar alleyways and side streets.

Allah was with Sadiq that day. Within minutes he happened upon a well-armed Kurdish checkpoint in Nineveh, eastern Mosul. Fearful of the more professional and deadly accurate Kurds, the AQI terrorists backed off like scared jackals. Hassan and Sadiq escaped with their heads. Unfortunately, AQI still had family man Omar in the trunk of a car.

✱ ✱ ✱

Badly shaken and bruised, but grateful to be alive, Sadiq and Hassan drove as far as the Kurdistan border crossing. Since they had been relieved of their IDs and documents, they were unable to reenter Kurdistan. The Kurdish guards allowed them to use a cell phone to call coworkers in Erbil, who drove out to the checkpoint to vouch for them. They eventually made it back to Erbil, still in possession of the "cool," modified AQI pistol that Hassan had taken from his captor. An Arab from Baghdad, Hassan did not want to be caught with a weapon in Kurdistan, so he gave the gun to our Kurdish driver Rebaz for safekeeping.

Upon learning of what had happened, I immediately alerted my former CIA colleague "Mac," a long-time Iraq hand who had recently retired and was working privately with the Kurdish security services in Erbil. He enlisted the support of the Kurdish service, which conducted its own investigation. I also reported the details of what had happened to US authorities. I provided our guys' cell phone numbers and the MAC (media access control) addresses of the confiscated laptops, along with our best guess as to where they were abducted. The US government told me there was nothing they could do since the kidnapped employee was Iraqi. (I should mention here that besides knowingly risking their lives by providing support to American troops, our Iraqi employees were also unwittingly supporting the US counterterrorism mission in Iraq. Babylon Inc.'s work with the US government in Iraq is the subject of chapter 30.)

When I relayed the government's discouraging response to Mac, he emailed me back: "I was hoping that would not be their answer. It's not true, that is a chicken shit answer. They CAN do something if they choose to do the right thing. While I was there [in Iraq] in '04 we rescued a number of Iraqis who had been snatched, and killed a lot of kidnappers in the process, but the default 'We can't' is the answer of choice today. The Kurds will turn up something."

Unfortunately, the Kurds never did turn up anything. Our Baghdad manager Ali Baba, the former Iraqi Army sergeant who was fond of beating tardy employees, was originally from Mosul. He called his cousin Hatem, also a Sunni who still lived in Mosul, and asked him to look into what had happened. Hatem carefully wandered into the neighborhood where the kidnapping had taken place. He discreetly asked around and made contact with some "intermediaries," quickly ascertaining that Omar was kidnapped by AQI and not by organized criminals (although both groups ran a lucrative kidnap and ransom business). Trying to reduce both the risk to Omar and the expected ransom demand, Hatem told the AQI intermediaries that Omar was a Sunni and nothing but a poor worker. Hatem left his neighborhood recon mission with the impression that Omar was probably still alive. Hatem was not snatched himself since he was a Sunni from Mosul, he had no connection to Kurdistan, and the bad guys would need someone to handle the expected ransom payment.

Four days after the kidnapping, Omar's family in Baghdad received a phone call from the terrorists. They asked angrily why Omar collaborated with Kurds and Shi'ites, then demanded $50,000 to be paid immediately. If we did not come up with the money, they said they would cut off Omar's head the next day. In Iraq, this was not an idle threat.

We knew that AQI kidnappers typically adhered to a "rate card" when demanding ransom. A taxi driver was worth $5,000, a teacher $10,000, and so on. Asking $50,000 for a driver indicated they had some reason to believe he could come up with that much money. It turned out that Omar's family, extremely upset and (not unfairly) blaming Babylon Inc. for his kidnapping, told the bad guys we would pay whatever they demanded if they would just release Omar alive. Our manager Ali Baba was able to speak to the terrorists, and he played the Sunni card: "I am from Mosul too. If you want to kill Shi'ites, come to Baghdad where we need you. Omar is a poor Sunni, so let him go." Their hostile response was the same they gave to Omar's family: why would a Sunni company in Baghdad hire Shi'ites (Hassan and Sadiq) and collaborate with the Kurds? They also accused "the fat one" (Sadiq) of being a spy for the Kurds. Ali Baba asked them how we could be certain they would release Omar, and they hung up on him.

Although the ransom was exorbitant, we were willing to pay it in order to secure Omar's release. His wife and daughter were extremely distraught. After the terrorists threatened to decapitate Omar, his wife shrieked and wailed so much in front of the young daughter that days later the daughter actually began to grow hair on her face, apparently from the emotional trauma of seeing her mother react that way and fearing for her father's safety.

Just because we were willing to pay the ransom did not mean we would ever see Omar alive again. For starters, the captors were furious that Omar worked with Shi'ites and Kurds. What's more, AQI and others of their ilk in Iraq had a nasty habit of forcing victims' families to sell everything they owned, borrow more, and pay it all as ransom in exchange for their loved one, after which the kidnappers would sometimes kill the hostage anyway. A Shi'ite partner of ours in Baghdad did just that, paying everything he had for the release of his fourteen-year-old younger brother. The terrorists told him he could find his brother in a car parked in a specific location in Baghdad. When our partner approached the vehicle, he found no one inside. He then broke into the trunk, which contained his young brother's severed head. Not long after, our grieving partner was killed by a car bomb that went off in front of his house in a Shi'ite neighborhood of Baghdad.

Omar's captors agreed to our proof of life request, allowing him to speak briefly with his family. He did not sound good, but he was at least alive. For the next several days, Ali Baba and his cousin Hatem worked out the details of the payment. Each phone call was to a different number; the terrorists never used the same number twice. They would use "burner phones" that they had taken from their victims. I instructed Ali Baba and his cousin to do their best to reach an agreement without angering the terrorists further, since our objective was to get Omar back to his family.

We ended up "wiring" the cash from Baghdad to AQI in Mosul, using an informal *hawala* money transfer network as instructed by Omar's captors. *Hawala* is a common Islamic nonbanking method for transferring funds without actually moving money.[3] We delivered the cash to the AQI-designated *hawala* rep in Baghdad, and the Mosul *hawala* rep gave the same amount to the kidnappers. The system is based on trust and works remarkably well.

After AQI received the funds, one of Omar's captors gave him five thousand Iraqi dinars (about five dollars) and drove him to a prominent Mosul mosque, where he was transferred to the custody of an "honest broker" sheik. After depositing Omar at the mosque, the captor who had given him the money told Omar to give it back, as payment for the ride. A former Iraqi military officer, who had been kidnapped and ransomed himself in the past in Baghdad and whom Omar had driven home, demonstrated his gratitude by risking his life again by retrieving Omar from the mosque and driving him back to Baghdad.

After holding him for eight days, the terrorists kept their word and released Omar. The entire Babylon Inc. family breathed a collective sigh of relief.

✷ ✷ ✷

During a recent trip to Baghdad, I sat down with Omar for several hours over dinner and asked if he would not mind recounting his ordeal with me one more time. I wanted to make sure I had all of the facts straight in my mind. He agreed to submit to my gentle interview, although even twelve years after the fact, it was clear Omar was still suffering the effects of the terrifying experience. He stopped talking and teared up many times while relating to me the details of his capture and detention.

Omar said that after he was caught on the street, he was brought in the trunk of a car to a "normal" house, occupied by a family. He was blindfolded and hog-tied, his hands and feet chained to each other and to the wall, underneath a stairway. The chains were too tight, and his hands swelled up. A hot light bulb shone directly above him, heating up the chains, which then burned his skin. When after three days his captors finally brought him some water, he used most of it to cool his skin. Omar had no food for the first four days, and one small meal per day after that. He was held with three other hostages at a time. Omar said that over the course of a week, his AQI captors would routinely take two hostages out and bring two new ones in. They appeared to be running a very successful kidnap and ransom business with high "inventory" turnover. Omar was able to speak at length with one hostage, a successful Christian car dealer from Mosul who had been held over forty days.

Immediately after Omar arrived at the first house, the jihadi whom tough guy Hassan had humiliated in the car burst into the house, extremely angry. He wanted to kill Omar, but the other captors prevented him from doing so, since they said Omar was worth more alive than dead. The furious jihadi fired several rounds near Omar's head and stormed out of the house. Note that had Hassan killed the jihadi when they were in the car, AQI would have killed Omar in retaliation.

Omar said his captors moved him from house to house in Mosul. Dying of thirst, he asked a child who lived in one house to bring him water. The child refused.

Barefoot, Omar discovered that the floor was sticky, with the still-moist bloodstains left by previous hostages. The entire time he was in captivity, his thoughts were only of his children, since he assumed that AQI would kill him. He knew nothing about the ongoing negotiations between AQI and Babylon Inc. One day, the terrorists put Omar into a vehicle and took him to a remote spot along the banks of the Tigris River. They made him kneel down and put a gun to his head. Omar began to pray. The terrorist pulled the trigger, but it just clicked. There were no rounds in the chamber. They were just "toying" with him, inflicting emotional abuse because they could.

Another day, a filthy, smelly, scraggly-bearded terrorist came into the house where fellow Sunni Omar was being held and sat down to talk with him, apparently eager for conversation. The jihadi told Omar that he was an AQI sniper and that he was filthy because he posed as a beggar on the streets (beggars are a sad and common sight to this day in Iraq, and they are typically women and children). He told Omar that because people tend to avoid looking at beggars, this made it easy for him to hide in plain view anywhere he wanted in the city. He told Omar that he had just recently begun to work as a sniper for AQI. Omar asked him how many people he had killed, and he replied that so far he had killed six military and police targets. The sniper said AQI paid him twenty-five thousand Iraqi dinars— just under twenty-five dollars—per kill. Omar later heard that the man went on to become known as "the Sniper of Mosul."

Omar never told his captors that he worked for an American company. He told them Babylon Inc. was owned by a Sunni who lived outside Iraq, and they seemed to believe him. From day one I had intentionally kept my company off the radar, with a very low and very Iraqi profile, with precisely this scenario in mind. Only US government and American corporate customers knew we were American. A higher profile might have cost Omar his life. A few years earlier I had to part ways with one of my two American "volunteers" who accompanied me to Baghdad in May 2003 because he insisted against my wishes on talking with a reporter from *Newsweek* about our business. I reached out to the reporter prior to publication, and she graciously agreed not to mention my company's name in the article.

The terrorists had gone through our guys' pockets and found several business cards of high-ranking KRG officials inside Sadiq's wallet, including that of powerful KRG interior (and Peshmerga) minister Karim Sinjari. They forcefully questioned Omar about each and every business card. When Omar told them he knew nothing of Sadiq's contacts, they beat him. One beating per business card.

Omar eventually came back to work. He had no idea we had paid so much money for his release, and he was appreciative. We were grateful that he was alive. At the time, there were no doctors in Baghdad who could treat the kinds of PTSD suffered by both Omar and his daughter. Even if there were, the doctors would have been overwhelmed with patients. I cannot begin to imagine how mental health professionals will deal with the women, children, and men who were subjected to unspeakable forms of abuse, rape, and torture, first by AQI and later by ISIS during their three-year occupation of Mosul. Omar's daughter went to Syria for treatment for her PTSD-caused condition, and today, years later, she is happily married.

Omar is now as "back to normal" as can be expected. During my most recent trip to Baghdad, he cheerfully drove me around the congested city night and day and helped me out in numerous other ways as well.

I was impressed with the bravery and initiative shown by Ali Baba's cousin Hatem in Mosul and suggested we hire him to open Babylon Inc.'s first office in the city of Mosul. He agreed and went on to run one of our more profitable offices in Iraq. Babylon Inc. remained in business before, during, and after ISIS's brutal occupation of the city. ISIS briefly shut us down but then gave us written permission to continue to operate. Our local employees in Mosul had no idea they were working for an American company. It was better for them, and for us, to keep that fact secret.

* * *

Once Omar was back in Baghdad, I casually asked Ali Baba for the receipt from al-Qaeda for the ransom payment. My request was made almost reflexively, based on my years of CIA experience. Ali Baba thought I was serious and explained to me why that was probably a bad idea. Reacting like a CIA bean counter, I instructed him to send Hatem back to the muja-hedin neighborhood to get a receipt, or he'd have to eat the expense per-sonally. He finally figured out I was joking.

The ransom payment was not the most unusual item I ever encoun-tered in expense reports from Baghdad. One employee actually submitted a seventy-five-dollar claim for a sheep. He corroborated his claim by sub-mitting a photo of the hog-tied sheep in the trunk of his car, which was parked in front of our office in the al-Mansour neighborhood of Baghdad. My only question was whether the sheep was to be categorized as meals, or entertainment, or both. (It turned out our office gave the sheep to the family of an employee whose mother had just died.)

* * *

As for the handgun Hassan took from his would-be al-Qaeda murderer, years after the incident, we asked our Kurdish driver Rebaz to return it to us. Rebaz went inside his house and came out with a pellet gun that more or less resembled the al-Qaeda gun. He no longer had our gun and was apparently hoping we had forgotten what it looked like. He eventually admitted he sold our prized possession without telling us. We fired him. It was long overdue.

* * *

A bit of advice for wannabe terrorists: don't be distracted by cell phones! Hassan and Sadiq were able to escape with their heads in part because the bearded fuck-stick in the back seat was staring intently at a cell phone. Boston Marathon bombers Tamerlan and Dzhokhar Tsarnaev were caught in part because they were distracted and tracked by a cell phone and a GPS device.[4]

To my former CIA colleagues and other naturally skeptical readers who may be wondering whether this entire incident might not have been staged as a creative way to extort money from the company: I considered that from the start, investigated the possibility from all angles, and was able to rule it out. Omar's demeanor while recounting the ordeal twelve years after the fact was further evidence that it really happened.

To this day, Sadiq swears he will never go on a diet again, because being fat saved his life.

CHAPTER 25

TRAVELS IN ARABIA

I had never traveled to the Middle East until after I resigned from the CIA. Since then, I've made dozens of trips to multiple Arab countries, as well as Turkey and Iraqi Kurdistan. Two countries I have never visited are mortal enemies Israel and Iran, although I'm always a little nervous when my sixteen-hour, globe-spanning Emirates flight overflies Iran, en route to Dubai. *If we are forced to make an emergency landing*, I think to myself, *let it be anywhere other than Iran.* I shudder at the thought of how the MOIS would deal with me now, on their turf, years after I miraculously managed to slip through their murderous fingers in Sarajevo. I envision myself shackled to the wall in some dank Persian dungeon, spending my final moments hallucinating about the sweet freedom I enjoyed only days earlier inside my first-class Emirates cabin. I am always cognizant of the fact that my past can catch up with me at any time and that life can change in an instant.

Thoughts of an agonizing death on Iranian soil aside, at least once or twice a year, Arabia beckons, and I come up with a suitable excuse to travel there. Most of my Middle East trips are ostensibly for work, but oftentimes they are equally motivated by a simple desire to escape the routine at home and take off on another Arabian adventure. Just as I felt in the past with the Balkans, I seem to get the itch to visit that part of the world on a regular basis. I've also found that you can learn a lot about your own country—for better or for worse—by experiencing life in others.

My travels in Arabia rank among the most enjoyable and enriching experiences of my life. I find the Arab world to be enchanting, a never-ending kaleidoscope of exotic foods, eye-pleasing sights, and warm, welcoming people. The first sound I hear in the predawn hours—the ethereal call to prayer (*adhan*) being broadcast over loudspeakers from neighborhood mosques—instantly reminds me I am no longer in modern-day America. The pleasing, calming scents of hibiscus, jasmine, and frankincense seem to permeate every aspect of life in the Middle East, from the bustling souks to quiet corners inside private homes and hotels. To my mind, scalding hot, sugar-laden black teas, infused with hints of cardamom or mint, are always better sipped in the Arab world. Although popular Arabic music can be found at all hours on MTV Lebanon and Rotana Music, I never travel to the Middle East without my *Sublime Ailleurs* album (on iPod), just in case. It's the perfect soundtrack for unwinding at day's end while gazing up at the stars, red wine and a Cuban cigar at the ready. The last sound I may hear before going to sleep at night, particularly in a place like Damascus, is equally evocative of *A Thousand and One Nights*: old men noisily talking and laughing while smoking sweet-scented hookahs and playing yet another game of backgammon. It's a fitting end to a busy day in Arabia; backgammon is the world's oldest board game and was likely invented somewhere in Mesopotamia.

During one road trip in the not-too-distant past, my good friend and colleague "Tarek" and I took a taxi from the sometimes war-torn but always fun-loving Mediterranean city of Beirut to the ancient city of Damascus for meetings with our Iraqi manager, Ali Baba. At the time, it was safer for all of us to meet in Syria instead of Iraq. As we left behind the cacophony of car horns in Beirut and headed south toward the fertile Beqaa Valley, it occurred to me I was likely retracing the same route taken by former Beirut CIA station chief William Buckley when he was moved by his Hezbollah captors from the Shi'ite slums of southern Beirut to the Iranian-controlled Sheik Abdullah military barracks in Baalbeck. Buckley's final, anguished moments were spent in brutal Iranian and Hezbollah captivity.

Naturally, Tarek's and my taxi broke down in the Beqaa Valley just as I was reflecting on Buckley's horrific fate. While we waited for the car to be repaired, it struck me that if we were forced to show our documents to roving Hezbollah security forces, it would not take them long to run my name and learn from their Iranian masters that they should hang on to me and await further instructions. I had escaped Iranian "justice" once in Sarajevo years earlier, but this time there would be no second chances. Fortunately, our car was soon fixed and we were on our way to Damascus before coming to the attention of any local Hezbollah supporters. The popular Netflix series *Al Hayba* provides a glamorized window into the organized crime lifestyle in the lawless Lebanon-Syria border region.

I loved traveling to prewar Syria, a country many consider to be the true heart of Arabia and the Middle East. Prior to entering Syria, foreigners are required to apply for and obtain a visa from the embassy of Syria located in their home country. I dutifully complied with this cumbersome process for my first trip, but on my second trip I neglected to obtain a visa before setting off for Syria. I did not realize my blunder until I was on board the flight to Damascus. I was actually watching the Syrian torture scene from the movie *Body of Lies* when it hit me. There was nothing I could do at that point other than try and talk my way through the situation. Upon my arrival at Damascus International Airport, the immigration official was not amused. I explained the situation as best I could (keeping in mind I had no good excuse for showing up without a visa) and also enlisted the support of the Four Seasons Damascus. Since the Syrian regime was also close to Hezbollah and Iran, I was hoping they'd deport me to Beirut on the next flight rather than detain and interrogate me. After about four hours of negotiation (and a dinner of some decent airport shawarma), the Syrian officials agreed to let me pay a "penalty," and I was given a visa and allowed entry into the country.

Sitting in the back seat of a Syrian taxi on the way to my hotel, reviving myself with a blast of fresh night air through the open window, it occurred to me that a Syrian showing up at Dulles airport without an American visa would probably not have the same good fortune I had.

✻ ✻ ✻

One advantage to living life under a secular dictator like Bashar al-Assad—at least until the Syrian war broke out—was that anyone could safely walk the streets at any time of day or night. As long as you didn't challenge the ruling family, average Syrians, as well as foreign visitors, were free to experience all that Syria had to offer. Syria is home to an endless array of awe-inspiring historic sites that even the well traveled among us generally know little about. Unfortunately, many of these world treasures were destroyed during the war. For example, in 2015, ISIS destroyed many temples, columns, and works of art in the ancient city of Palmyra.

During my first trip to Damascus, I visited the simple tomb of Salah al-Din and the nearby, breathtakingly beautiful Umayyad Mosque. Along with thousands of other pilgrims and tourists, I then wandered through the bustling al-Hamidiyah Souk, the largest and oldest in Syria. Gazing up at the souk's blocks-long black iron ceiling, shot full of holes by French warplanes in 1925, was like looking up at a night sky filled with twinkling stars. Sunlight poked through the holes punctured in the roof. During a day trip to the ancient city of Bosra in southern Syria, Tarek, Ali Baba, and I took a horse-drawn buggy tour of the town's ancient Roman ruins, including a Roman theater that still hosts concerts. (It would have been romantic but for the presence of Tarek and Ali Baba.) Accustomed to having to contend with hordes of visitors to the Colosseum in Rome, I found it was a nice change of pace to encounter almost no other tourists taking in the historic sites in Bosra. Unlike Damascus, there is not much in the way of shopping in Bosra, but it is possible to find some genuine Syrian handicrafts. Oil paintings of typical Syrian scenes I purchased from a local Bosra artist now adorn my office wall.

During one crazy half-hour ride from downtown Damascus to the international airport southeast of the city, my taxi was involved in not one but two separate fender benders. The first occurred when my driver cut someone off, and we were rear-ended by another taxi. The drivers cursed and gestured furiously at each other, but neither stopped nor got out to assess the damage. The second accident occurred about three minutes later when someone cut us off, and we rear-ended them. Again, neither car stopped, and my driver delivered me, slightly shaken but on time, for my flight to London. Before my flight departed, I purchased a Hassan Nasrallah key fob in the airport souvenir shop, in silent tribute to the fact that I had avoided capture by Hezbollah in the Beqaa Valley one week earlier. Nasrallah is the popular bearded leader of Syrian- and Iranian-backed Hezbollah.

Unfortunately, Syria is no longer a safe destination for intrepid travelers. Assad chose to mercilessly destroy his own country rather than relinquish power. It's more complicated than that, but explaining all facets of the Syrian war is beyond the scope of this book. The war has killed hundreds of thousands of innocent people, pushed nearly six million Syrian refugees out of their country, and displaced millions more, most of whom are in desperate need of humanitarian assistance.[1]

* * *

A few years before my bumper car send-off from Damascus, I made my first trip to Sulaymaniyah ("Suly") in the mountainous Kurdish region of northern Iraq. In the fall of 2003, I was summoned to meet with the prime minister of the Kurdistan Regional Government (KRG), Barham Salih, at his parents' home in Suly. Until recently, Salih was affiliated with the Suly-based Patriotic Union of Kurdistan political party. At the time of this writing, Barham Salih is president of Iraq. Dr. Salih, a dignified and globally respected Iraqi Kurd leader, wished to discuss a project that he hoped would help to bring Suly into the twenty-first century. Babylon Inc. had been operational in Iraq for a few months, and we were ready to help with his visionary project. There were no commercial flights connecting Iraq to the rest of the world in October 2003, so I embarked upon a difficult and at times dangerous journey to Kurdistan's ancient intellectual center.

I flew from Istanbul to Diyarbakir in southeastern Turkey, where in my hotel restaurant I attended a lively and colorful Kurdish wedding reception for two young newlyweds I had never met before. Copious amounts of red wine helped to erode the cultural and language barriers. At least for me. The next morning, I found a taxi that would take me from Diyarbakir to the Ibrahim Khalil border crossing, near Zakho, Iraq. The taxi broke down halfway between Diyarbakir and the Iraqi border, and the hours-long delay resulted in my having to make a dangerous, high-speed nighttime sprint through Mosul later that night. ("Trouble with taxis" is a recurring theme in the Middle East and would be a fitting title for this chapter.) I made the risky overland trip to Suly because it was key to landing an important initial contract for Babylon Inc. Thanks to the broken-down Turkish taxi, I almost didn't make it.

The plan was for Prime Minister Salih's highly trained bodyguards to meet me on the Iraqi side of the border for the onward trek to Suly. Time was of the essence, since the bodyguards wanted to make it through the dangerous city of Mosul before dark. Five of their colleagues had been killed by extremists one year earlier during an assassination attempt on Salih, so their security concerns were legitimate. I was instructed to arrive at the border by noon. Unfortunately, because my taxi broke down in the middle of nowhere, my arrival at the border crossing was delayed by a few hours.

At the border crossing, Turkish border police detained and interrogated me for two hours. Even though my project was in no way detrimental to Turkey, the paranoid Turks were suspicious of this American with stated plans to assist the Iraqi Kurds. By the time I was allowed to cross the border into Iraq, it was late afternoon with only an hour or so of daylight left. I was relieved to be out of Turkey and in Iraq. Prime Minister Salih's nervous Kurdish bodyguards put me in the back seat of one of their convoy's Toyota Land Cruisers and took off at high speed. After winding through Dohuk, we headed straight for the deadly city of Mosul. Our average speed on the narrow, chaotic Iraqi highway was 100 mph. We somehow made it through Mosul and Kirkuk without incident. The bodyguards did not breathe a sigh of relief until they safely delivered me to the old Palace Hotel in downtown Suly later that night.

A few days later, my meetings with Salih concluded, the same bodyguards returned me to the Turkish border via the same bare-knuckle route. We were briefly delayed in Mosul while explosives were cleared off the road and detonated, but otherwise the return trip was uneventful. After we arrived at the border crossing, I took a group photo with my seven guardian angels and bid them a grateful farewell.

The Suly project was a resounding success, and Salih labeled it "an example for the Middle East."

Two years later, I traveled on a 3:00 a.m. flight from Amman to the Kurdish capital city of Erbil to meet with President Masoud Barzani of the KRG. The Barzani clan controls Iraqi Kurdistan's other major political party, the Erbil-based Kurdistan Democratic Party. Royal Jordanian Airlines initially bumped me off the very popular and typically overbooked flight, but KRG interior minister Karim Sinjari, who was on the same flight, made a call and arranged for someone else to be bumped so that I could make the flight. The KRG treated me and my colleagues royally during our Erbil visit. They put us up in a huge, modern presidential guest mansion in Sari Rash, the KRG leadership community a short drive up the mountain from Erbil. President Barzani paid us a visit one day to discuss a possible contract with Babylon Inc. During his visit, the genial and legendary Barzani displayed typical Kurdish hospitality, breaking off a piece of cooked chicken for me with his bare hands. We also met with his son Masrour Barzani, then head of the Kurdish intelligence service, and with his nephew, then KRG prime minister Nechirvan Barzani, at the opulent Kurdish "White House." The trip was both comfortable and memorable, and led to the signing of Babylon Inc.'s largest contract to date. (A contract the KRG would later breach.)

* * *

Five years after my unforgettable first foray into Iraq, life had become calmer and more predictable. By then I had bought out Imad's half of the company and was managing the surprisingly successful Babylon Inc. from our very cool, industrial-style office in Los Angeles. Work was never-ending, averaging twelve-hour (or more) workdays, seven days a week, year in and year out. But it was exciting, and I enjoyed it, as did my hard-working colleagues. This high-paced work routine in Los Angeles was sup-plemented by occasional trips to Iraq, Syria, Lebanon, Dubai, and Jordan to meet with key employees and customers or to attend trade shows. About 90 percent of the employees (almost all Iraqis) staffed our various offices in all regions of Iraq, and 10 percent of us were in the United States. It was not an ideal way to run a business, but it worked. It also allowed me to raise my rapidly growing up daughters at home.

Although things were going well, my routine left something to be desired. I still traveled to the Middle East, but I missed the risky, exciting start-up phase of the business. That period was much more fun than man-aging an established company, even though creating a profitable business was the whole point of the exercise. Plus, I wasn't getting any younger. The thought of turning fifty was a sobering reminder that life will pass you by whether you're paying attention or not.

Not one who normally celebrates birthdays, I decided I would do something memorable for my fiftieth to make me feel alive again. I briefly considered enrolling in an introductory twerking class at the local YMCA, but in the end, I spent my birthday strapped inside a heavily armed Black Hawk helicopter over Baghdad.

By the time of my fiftieth birthday escape to Iraq, one could fly to Baghdad commercially on board an unmarked Royal Jordanian flight from Amman. Iraqi Airways also provided regular service. This means of transport was much safer and faster than traveling overland, although the civilian aircraft was still forced to make the traditionally military cork-screw landing into Baghdad International Airport (BIAP) in order to avoid being targeted by insurgents. Pilots were required to take this precaution after a DHL cargo plane was hit by a surface-to-air missile when taking off from BIAP a few years earlier. Because the pilots severely bank the aircraft during the spiral maneuver, the plane I was on was practically on its side as it rapidly wound its way down to the airport. I recall looking straight down out of the plane's window, at the barren Iraqi ground quickly approaching below us.

The stated reason for my trip was to visit my employees in Baghdad. Rather than stay in the dangerous city, I'd been invited by a civilian friend to spend time with him on sprawling Victory Base Complex (VBC), home of al-Faw Palace and headquarters of US forces—Iraq. Although my trip was not related to the US military, my friend was able to get me access to the Black Hawk helicopter "taxi service" for a few flights around Baghdad. Picture Uber, but in the air and heavily armed. I had to go through a lengthy bureaucratic process to take a helicopter from point A to point B, but it was safer than driving. It was also a lot of fun. After buckling up—no easy task when wearing body armor with steel plate inserts—I enjoyed my fast and noisy Black Hawk flights around Baghdad. Black Hawks typically flew in pairs for security reasons, and I could see our escort helicopter off to our left. Door gunners manned machine guns, pointed menacingly out each side, although I wondered how they could identify a threat in the congested city we were rapidly passing by from above.

After spending a couple of nights in one part of Baghdad, I wanted to return to the VBC, but the helicopter "dispatcher" told me there was no space available on a Black Hawk that day. I told him that was no problem, since my Iraqi colleague Hassan could pick me up in his little white car and drive me across Baghdad to the VBC. Apparently nervous that something might happen to me, the dispatcher became Radar O'Reilly from *M*A*S*H* and found space available on a helo later that day.

During my stay on the VBC, I was able to observe what day-to-day life was like for our troops there. Compared to the relatively civilized life most of us enjoy in the United States, they willingly sacrificed a lot by living and working on a base in Iraq. For starters, they were in a war zone, some engaged in combat operations, and all equally exposed to the risks of war simply by being present. The base itself was like a small but very busy, very dusty city, and everything was the color of the Iraqi desert. Streets and roads were overrun with a wide variety of military vehicles, from Humvees to MRAPs. There was no escaping the dust or the vehicle noise, and loud helicopters flew low and fast over the base at all hours of the day and night. Meals in the DFAC were better than they were in previous wars, but the routine and food options quickly became tiresome. There were a couple of fast-food outlets for a change of pace. Like soldiers in wars everywhere, our troops in Iraq were away from family for extended periods of time, serving their country and for relatively low salaries.

Despite conditions that were harsh compared to life at home, I could not help but notice that soldiers and civilians on the VBC generally treated each other with respect. Traffic laws on the sprawling base were followed and enforced. Everyone had a positive attitude, and I don't recall ever hearing anyone complain. When I finally made it back to my comfortable enclave in the United States, it really struck me that the troops who sacrifice so much for the rest of us, while living in such uncomfortable and dangerous conditions, treat each other with more respect and decency than do the often self-centered "privileged people behaving badly" whom I encountered daily on the west side of LA. There is little to no thought given by most Americans to those who serve our country in war zones and foreign lands. As of the time of this writing, there are American troops fighting and dying in Afghanistan, Iraq, and Syria, and yet we hear next to nothing about it on the news. Domestic politics trumps everything else.

I believe one reason for the stark contrast between life on a spartan war zone military base and life in the United States is the military demands its members to treat each other fairly and with respect. To quote the superintendent of the US Air Force Academy in the wake of finding racist graffiti on campus, "If you can't treat someone with dignity and respect . . . get out."[2] Our citizens would do well to emulate this simple rule the US military has preached and practiced for decades. Until that day comes, I will continue to fantasize about getting around nasty, congested Los Angeles in a Black Hawk helicopter. With two door gunners, just in case.

PART VIII

BRUSHES WITH CELEBRITY

CHAPTER 26

DID I INSPIRE AN *SNL* SKIT?

In the late 1980s, after returning to DC for specialized training prior to my onward CIA assignment in the Balkans, I took my eighteen-month-old daughter on the Amtrak from Union Station to New York for a long weekend. Stacy flew up ahead of us to spend time with her family. When my daughter and I got off the train at Penn Station, we were met by her uncle John and his childhood friend Jon Lovitz. Lovitz was a popular *Saturday Night Live (SNL)* cast member at the time, famous for his role as Tommy Flanagan, the Pathological Liar. (Since I had been out of the country for the preceding three years, I was only peripherally aware of this particular bit of American pop culture.) Afterward I handed off my daughter to Stacy before John, Jon, and I spent a laugh-filled afternoon over lunch and walking aimlessly around midtown Manhattan.

During our few hours together, Lovitz was relentless in asking me probing questions about my real work overseas, while I was hoping to learn more about the *SNL* cast and upcoming skits before Saturday's live performance, to which Lovitz graciously provided tickets.

"What exactly do you do for the government?" Lovitz began. "Are you a spy?"

"Do I look like a spy?" I replied, a change from my usual "If I am, no one told me!" response. "Will Dana Carvey do Church Lady this weekend?" I was hoping to change the subject, and I really was looking forward to a live performance of the Church Lady.

"Tell the truth, do you kill people?" Lovitz continued, ignoring my question. "How many people have you killed?"

"If I told you, I'd have to blind you. Is Phil Hartman ever *not* funny?" I queried. Bear in mind, this was *before* Phil Hartman evolved into Unfrozen Caveman Lawyer.

Displeased by my vague and evasive answers, Lovitz mercilessly turned up the heat.

"Did you fart?" he asked me, for the first of several times.

"No."

Lovitz then turned to my brother-in-law and asked, "John, did you fart?"

"No."

"Huh. Must have been me," was his response. Every time.

Despite Lovitz's ruthless use of these comedy-enhanced interrogation techniques, I never broke cover or admitted to working for the CIA. I was caught off guard by his aggressive line of questioning, but I thought I handled things pretty well, under the circumstances. My secret would remain safe, for now.

The next day, Stacy, my daughter, and I arrived early for *SNL*'s Friday rehearsal at Rockefeller Center. Before the rehearsal began, Lovitz introduced us to some of his fellow cast members. Dana Carvey was smitten with our little angel, and he did a hilarious Popeye impression for her. My daughter was nonplussed, but I loved it. I also fought the urge to say, "What she really wants to see is Church Lady."

On Saturday night, Stacy and I attended an unforgettable live taping of *SNL*. Musical guests were the inimitable Randy Newman, and Mark Knopfler of Dire Straits fame, and together they performed "It's Money That Matters" and "Dixie Flyer." On Sunday, Stacy, baby girl, and I returned to our decidedly unglamorous routines in Washington.

✻ ✻ ✻

Months later, I was trying not to fall asleep while watching *SNL* at home one Saturday night. I sprang back to full consciousness when a skit came on about a CIA Christmas party. All of the guests were asking probing questions of each other and receiving vague answers in response. The skit was about a lot of cocktail party conversation that went nowhere. The audience seemed to appreciate the humor, but it was making me a little uncomfortable. Then it struck me: *Was that skit Jon Lovitz's idea? Was it inspired by our afternoon of spy talk and fart jokes?*

I never did find out the answer to that question, but I don't believe in coincidences.

CHAPTER 27

BREAKING BAD IN TIJUANA

My former CIA colleague Bob Baer is now a celebrity author, journalist, and intelligence analyst for CNN. Bob appears on CNN when the network requires his expert analysis of fast-breaking events involving the Middle East, counterterrorism, or counterintelligence issues.

Actor George Clooney was cast to portray CIA man Bob Baer in *Syriana*, a 2005 movie that was loosely based on Bob's book *See No Evil: The True Story of a Ground Soldier in the CIA's War against Terrorism*. Like most former CIA officers, Bob is much better looking than George Clooney. That minor divergence from the truth should surprise no one, however, since much of the movie is completely detached from reality. Spoiler alert: Bob is still very much alive, while George Clooney's character was not so lucky in the movie. Or in the making of the movie, for that matter. Clooney was seriously injured while filming the movie's infamous torture scene.[1]

Bob Baer is a busy guy who turns down exciting Hollywood requests the way most of us politely pass on another serving of Brussels sprouts. One day several years ago, Bob called me to ask if I would be interested in helping out a friend of his, a very successful writer/producer of *Breaking Bad*, since Bob did not have the time. Although he was busy with *Breaking Bad*, "Walt" was also considering creating a new show, about the exploits of an LA-based CIA officer who mixes business with pleasure south of the border. Walt was a seasoned Hollywood professional, but he knew little about Mexico or the world of spies. Since Mexico and espionage happen to be two of my favorite pursuits, Bob introduced us so that I might give Walt a crash course in both.

My plan was to take Walt on a "ride-along" in Tijuana to demonstrate how good guys and bad guys would operate against each other on the dusty streets and back alleys of one of Mexico's more dangerous cities. I would provide insights into the tradecraft of the good guys, and I enlisted my friend "Don Chuy" to illustrate the bad guy side of the equation. Discretion and the fact that relevant statutes of limitations have yet to expire prevent me from revealing too many additional details about Don Chuy.

Walt, Don Chuy, and I met up for lunch at cash-only Gilbert's El Indio restaurant in Santa Monica for chicken enchiladas and to review the game plan. Walt was initially unsure of what to make of this "odd couple" seated across from him, but by the time the lunch had ended, he seemed eager to move forward. A few days later, Don Chuy and I were showing our celebrity writer friend the ropes in some of Tijuana's more colorful neighborhoods. I demonstrated for Walt how a CIA officer might operate and watch for surveillance in a place like Tijuana, while Don Chuy took us on a cook's tour of seedy bars and brothels. If only *Breaking Bad*'s brilliant narcocorrido, "Negro y Azul: The Ballad of Heisenberg," had been playing over Don Chuy's car radio, everything would have been perfect.

Later that evening, the three of us met up for dinner, along with several of my local friends, at Cien Años, a phenomenal Mexican restaurant a few miles south of the border. The memorable, hours-long dinner involved mariachis, *molcajete* salsa, raucous laughter, and multiple rounds of smooth *reposado* tequila. About the only other thing I remember from that night was Don Chuy's masterful recounting of a scene from a *Jackass*-like movie, where two guys dressed up like a zebra and stood in front of a lion's den to see what would happen.

After dinner, we all bade each other a tipsy farewell and somehow made our way back to our hotels.

* * *

Several months later, I was curious about the status of the new show. I called Walt and learned that, unfortunately, the studio heads had decided not to move forward with the idea.

The Tijuana excursion was not a total waste of time, however. Don Chuy remained in contact with Walt, eventually convincing him to incorporate his family name into *Breaking Bad*. If you've ever wondered why the German parent company of Los Pollos Hermanos is called a very Spanish-sounding Madrigal Electromotive GmbH, wonder no more.

CHAPTER 28

SITTING NEXT TO A ROCK STAR

'm guessing that most people, if asked who they'd most like to sit next to in an airplane, would name their favorite actor, athlete, or Kardashian. I always thought I'd like to sit next to Paul McCartney—as if he'd fly commercial—so that I could ask him about his inspiration for "Let It Be." Although I've never bumped into any of the former Beatles, I was fortunate enough to sit next to someone else I consider a bona fide rock star, on a flight from DC to California: General Stanley McChrystal, legendary American warrior and former commander of the Joint Special Operations Command (JSOC).

Over the years, on the many flights I've taken, I've had several "celebrity sightings" and even had the opportunity to meet one or two of them in the process. I sat in front of a beret-wearing Samuel L. Jackson on a night flight to London, and across the aisle from late, great US Marine and *Full Metal Jacket* actor R. Lee Ermey on a flight to DC. American treasure Stevie Wonder wrote a touching message on my youngest daughter's boarding pass after we gave up our seats for the kind-hearted musical genius and his assistant on a post–Fourth of July flight from DC. While all of these brushes with celebrity were exciting, none of them compared with my encounter with the man many of us in my line of work consider to be an unsung American hero.

I first noticed McChrystal, whom I'd never met in person, waiting at the hectic departure gate at Dulles International Airport before our flight to California. Recently retired, he was attired in civilian clothing. I'd been in DC the previous several days to attend my old friend R. J.'s retirement ceremony at CIA headquarters. I was wearing an OSS baseball cap that I'd purchased at the CIA gift shop after the ceremony. (The CIA gift shop has evolved from a tiny space hidden somewhere in the warren of dark, unmarked hallways in the headquarters basement to a ground-floor, Pentagon-worthy smorgasbord of CIA souvenirs and memorabilia. CIA golf balls, anyone?)

When they called our flight, I boarded and took my window seat. I generally prefer the aisle seat, but it was a full flight and this was the last seat available. Even though I was in the first-class cabin, I was not looking forward to spending the next five hours stuck in a window seat.

Much to my very pleasant surprise, General McChrystal had the aisle seat next to me.

As the general was stowing his bag in the overhead compartment, the flight attendant asked me about my OSS hat, with its distinctive spear insignia. It was clear she did not recognize McChrystal, or she would have made conversation with him instead of me.

"Is that a Batman hat?" she queried, almost hopefully.

"Sadly, no," I responded.

I then addressed the general, who had just sat down: "Sir, I'm guessing you're the only other person on this plane who knows what this hat represents."

With a smile, he said he did.

After takeoff, I introduced myself and (for once) was able to share with someone the classified truth about my CIA career and past work with the US military, from the Balkans to Iraq. I told him briefly about my work with the special operators during the wars in Croatia and Bosnia, before he became JSOC commander. General McChrystal was especially pleased to learn that I had recently provided the government with sensitive, actionable intelligence.

Not surprisingly, it turned out we had a number of friends and colleagues in common, some of whom worked side by side with him in his Joint Base Balad command center in Iraq. The genius of McChrystal's approach, and one of the reasons for his unprecedented success, was his insistence on bringing together all key players (the CIA, FBI, NSA, and JSOC, among others) in one room, where they were forced to share intelligence and focus on the mission. Coincidentally, I ran our Babylon Inc. US headquarters much the same way: all of us sat around one massive, Persian stone conference table, and together we hashed out problems and came up with decisions that took everyone's input into account. No one at Babylon

Inc., me included, would segregate himself from his colleagues inside an office or cubicle.

Had the CIA and FBI cooperated McChrystal-style, for the sake of the mission and of the nation, we might have been able to prevent 9/11 from ever happening.

* * *

Aware of General McChrystal's reputation as a "soldier's soldier" who slept only a few hours each night, ran PT, and ate only one meal per day, I refrained from touching my airline lunch until I saw that he had started his own. The last thing I wanted was for him to witness just how weak and ordinary I really was.

We had a memorable conversation during the flight, and when I shook his hand to bid him farewell, he sincerely thanked me for my service. I was nearly speechless.

We don't join the CIA for the money, or for public recognition. We rarely if ever expect to receive thanks for our service. Being thanked by this true American hero, who has risked it all serving his country in ways most of us cannot begin to imagine, is a memory I will cherish for the rest of my life.

General McChrystal repeated his appreciation for my service a few weeks later, in a handwritten note to me inside a copy of his memoir, *My Share of the Task*. His book now occupies a place of honor on my bookshelf at home.

PART IX

THE SPY WHO
CAME DOWN WITH A COLD

CHAPTER 29

IGNORE MY INTELLIGENCE AT YOUR PERIL (I AM NOT AS STUPID AS I LOOK)

A former Bulgarian friend of mine, when trying to convince me of the righteousness of some absurd argument, was fond of saying, in his very heavy Bulgarian accent, "But, H. K., you don't understand. I am not as stupid as I look."

To clarify, he's a former friend, but he's still Bulgarian.

After resigning from the CIA, and even after launching my Iraqi start-up, Babylon Inc., I have continued to support the US government national security mission with the same dedication as when I was a staff officer. Unfortunately, I have been repeatedly reminded that American officials and policy makers routinely ignore potentially valuable intelligence, possibly to the detriment of America's national security.

I often felt like my former friend from Bulgaria when it became clear my efforts to report important intelligence to relevant US government authorities were in vain. To cite but one example, I'm still convinced that had the government done things my way in Bosnia, we could have captured notorious Serb war criminal Radovan Karadžić at that time, and my team and I could have collected the icing-on-the-cake five million dollars in reward money. What follows are several more examples of this maddening phenomenon and compelling evidence, I hope, that I am not nearly as stupid as I look.

During the three years leading up to the 9/11 attacks, I was working with the wealthy client mentioned in chapter 22, who financed the humanitarian project in Macedonia and Kosovo. Unrelated to me or the Kosovo project, my client found himself in some legal hot water of the white-collar-crime variety. The federal government investigated his company's accounting practices, and the US Attorney's Office successfully prosecuted him for insider trading. Before sentencing, as in any criminal case, the judge would assess my former client's lifetime behavioral "balance sheet" and take his positive contributions to society into account when deciding his fate.

While my client was dealing with his legal problems, I continued to work with his company, which operated as usual in all parts of the world. The company happened to have direct access inside the Taliban's only foreign "diplomatic mission" in Pakistan, a country that recognized the Taliban as the legitimate government of Afghanistan. With my client's permission, I proposed to my US government contacts that they exploit this unique access to the Taliban, which at the time was providing safe haven to Usama bin Laden (UBL) and al-Qaeda inside Afghanistan. My assumption was that the Taliban's support for UBL might be discussed inside their Pakistan mission, and we might be able to gain access to those discussions and documents. In my proposal to the government, I spelled out in detail the kinds of critical intelligence they might expect to collect if they were to take advantage of this unique window of opportunity. At the top of my printed list of possible intelligence targets and topics was UBL, followed by al-Qaeda and their terrorist-related activities inside Pakistan and Afghanistan.

Keep in mind, this was an opportunity to collect intelligence on al-Qaeda *before* the 9/11 attacks. The US intelligence community was already well aware of the threat posed by UBL and al-Qaeda, who were responsible for the August 7, 1998, US embassy bombings in Dar es Salaam, Tanzania, and in Nairobi, Kenya, killing over two hundred people.[1] Al-Qaeda also carried out the October 12, 2000, attack on the USS *Cole* in Yemen's Aden harbor, killing seventeen American sailors.[2] Terrorists tied to and trained by al-Qaeda in Afghanistan also carried out the 1993 bombing of the World Trade Center.

Although the government was interested in principle, the agent in charge of investigating my client was vehemently opposed to the US government taking advantage of my—and in effect my client's—offer. He suspected my client would then use proof of that cooperation in an effort to reduce his sentence. My argument was, "Who cares? If gaining access to intel on UBL means a white-collar criminal might get a reduced sentence, so be it!" To me it was a no-brainer.

Unfortunately, the agent stubbornly blocked this effort, and the US intelligence community never exploited this very unique opportunity to gather intelligence on the Taliban and possibly UBL and al-Qaeda just prior to 9/11.

Rarely is a single source of intelligence responsible for a monumental military or intelligence success, such as the killing of bin Laden in Pakistan. The ultimately successful post-9/11 hunt for bin Laden was built on a giant tapestry of intelligence bits and pieces, meticulously collected, collated, and analyzed over many years. Remove one thread, one source or report, and the entire effort could unravel.

Had the government put national security interests ahead of one agent's personal obsession with sticking it to my client, would it have yielded a piece of the intelligence puzzle that could have led to the prevention of the 9/11 attacks? We will never know. But as I watched the news coverage of al-Qaeda-hijacked American commercial jet airplanes slamming into the World Trade Center towers on September 11, 2001, I could not help but wonder.

I am not first to butt heads with law enforcement officials who put criminal justice objectives ahead of intelligence, counterintelligence, or national security interests. Having worked with passion for two different prosecutors' offices, I fully support prosecuting criminals. I get it. But sometimes we need to look at the bigger picture and put longer-term intelligence needs ahead of short-term law enforcement objectives. Even mobsters get it. To quote Donald Trump associate Felix Sater, an alleged mobster who several years before 9/11 was providing information about al-Qaeda to the CIA, "So I'm giving the CIA bin Laden's sat phone numbers, and this guy [Assistant US Attorney Sack] is more concerned with going after 'Vinny Boom Botz.'"[3]

✱ ✱ ✱

After the 9/11 attacks, the FBI requested the public's assistance in identifying dozens of suspected al-Qaeda support assets in the United States, some of whom they believed may have fled to Mexico. The number of al-

Qaeda operatives in the United States leading up to the 9/11 attacks was much greater than the nineteen hijackers killed during the attacks. Like any organized criminal or terrorist organization, al-Qaeda relied on a human network of coconspirators who could rent vehicles and apartments; case airports and aircraft, including crew procedures and responses to behaviors during specific flights; conduct targeting research; handle finances; and conduct a host of other logistical support tasks. Following the wildly successful 9/11 attacks, these al-Qaeda support personnel inside the United States went to ground, and many of them undoubtedly left the country.

The day after the FBI's televised plea for the public's assistance, an American friend of mine, who was living in the small, remote Mexican town where I also live, emailed me to say that a "suspicious" person had just arrived in our quiet fishing village. My friend "Bob," who had lived in the town for twenty years at that point, knew I was somehow connected to the US government and thought he should pass along the tip.

Baja is my safe zone. I live there because there's no better place to get away from my work and the madness of the world in which we live. In Baja, nobody cares who you are, where you're from, or what you do, which probably explains why so many Americans flee the law, their enemies, or former spouses, and hide out in Baja. For me, this concept is captured beautifully by George Strait's music video "The Seashores of Old Mexico." Baja is a thousand miles of inhospitable, uninhabited desert, mountains, and beach. It's anonymous. It's also the perfect place for an al-Qaeda operative to lay low for a while. Unless he picks the wrong place. In which case he'll stick out like, well, an Islamic terrorist in a gossipy small town in Baja.

I asked Bob, who ran the town's local internet café, why he considered this out-of-town visitor to be suspicious. A regular guy, imbued with a healthy dose of common sense, Bob said that the man did not fit the profile of our town's typical visitors: Americans and Mexicans who come to fish, participate in the off-road races, eat shrimp and drink tequila, or just enjoy a low-cost relaxing vacation. The visitor was a young, Middle Eastern–looking man in his middle to late twenties. "Amin" arrived a day or two after 9/11 in an expensive vehicle with California tags and was living in it on the street, rather than rent one of the small town's many cheap hotel rooms. He frequented Bob's internet café every day and visited Islamic extremist websites. (Bob helpfully provided me with Amin's browsing history.) Bob would chat with Amin and developed a bit of a rapport with him, although Amin would never give his full name. Amin came across as very well educated and well traveled and said he had spent considerable time in the United States, as well as in many Muslim countries of Asia, such as Indonesia. Amin generally appeared nervous and revealed very few details about himself.

Amin did tell Bob that he planned to stay in Baja for a few more days and then would return to California. For reasons he never explained, Amin said he wanted to buy a different vehicle for the return drive north.

I ran the tags from Amin's vehicle with a former federal law enforcement friend of mine, and it came back as a reported stolen vehicle. I prepared a report with all details and passed it to my US government contacts. Although most leads like this turn out to be nothing, in light of the recent 9/11 attacks and active search for al-Qaeda support assets (some of whom were possibly in Mexico), I recommended that our government at the very least task their Mexican security service counterparts to pick up Amin to find out who he was and why he was in Baja. They should do this immediately, since Amin said he planned to return soon to California in a different vehicle, and I may not be able to get the second tag number. I also was unable to come up with Amin's full name or other bio data. It was imperative that police locate and question Amin ASAP while he was still in Baja.

The US government did nothing in response to my urgent report. Bob told me he had called in this same information to the FBI Counterterrorism Squad in San Diego and to the FBI field office in Palm Springs; both FBI offices told him it was probably nothing and to not worry about it.

Frustrated, I then faxed the same information to the US ambassador to Mexico, with whom I'd worked in Latin America many years earlier. The ambassador was a brilliant and highly respected foreign service officer with the rank of career ambassador. He immediately grasped the significance of the report and arranged for an agent to knock on Amin's (car) door. Unfortunately, by the time the agent arrived at the remote Baja village, Amin had found another vehicle and had presumably reentered the United States. He had vanished.

Was Amin an al-Qaeda support asset who facilitated the 9/11 attacks and who remains active inside the United States to this day? Because two different branches of the US government failed to act, we will likely never know the answer to that question.

* * *

One of the many justifications given by the Bush administration for the invasion of Iraq after 9/11 was purported ties between Saddam Hussein's regime and al-Qaeda. To provide evidence of these alleged ties, the administration cited a dubious Czech intelligence service report that an Iraqi secret agent met with 9/11 bomber Mohammed Atta in Prague, prior to the 9/11 attacks.[4] If true, this would have established a link between Saddam, al-Qaeda, and possibly the 9/11 attacks.

Both before and after 9/11, I was conducting private business investigations in the Czech Republic, using my unilateral sources. My trusted and reliable "agents" worked privately for me and had no axe to grind in terms of influencing official policy one way or the other. Our clients were typically private companies, not governments, and they would only pay for solid, reliable intelligence. My agents had an exceptional five-year reporting track record with my firm.

Because I had proven unilateral sources in Prague, US government authorities reached out to me to investigate whether or not Mohammed Atta had ever met with an Iraqi intelligence agent in Prague, as alleged. The US government presumably also directly asked their Czech counterparts this same question, but it's always good to have multiple sources, particularly when a requirement is so critical that deploying American troops to wage war abroad may hinge on the answer.

My agents conducted a thorough investigation and reported confidently and conclusively that no such meeting between Iraqi intelligence and al-Qaeda ever took place in Prague. I passed the report on to my US government contacts. In light of my Czech sources' stellar intelligence reporting history, my belief is their intel was accurate. My Czech contacts could not speculate as to why the head of the Czech intelligence service had allegedly reported otherwise. Their position was that no one inside the Czech service believed the al-Qaeda meeting had taken place. My own speculation is that perhaps an American official in Prague, wishing to tell the Bush administration what it wanted to hear, passed along this false report.

Although my report was just one small piece of the puzzle, shortly after I submitted it, the Bush administration began to downplay the alleged link between Saddam and al-Qaeda, although "dead enders" Donald Rumsfeld and Dick Cheney continued to suggest that the ties existed, in order to justify their inevitable invasion of Iraq.[5]

Bush and his neocon advisers were intent on overthrowing Saddam following 9/11, and nothing was going to stop them. Their other justification for going to war—Saddam's alleged weapons of mass destruction—also turned out to be false.

✷ ✷ ✷

In early June 2003, after kicking off Babylon Inc. operations in Baghdad with the able assistance of my Iraqi partner Imad, I traveled overland from Baghdad back to Amman, Jordan. An hour after leaving Baghdad, I stopped off again in Ramadi to pay a courtesy call on Imad's uncle Omar, one of Iraq's most respected and influential Sunni tribal sheiks. Omar was an Iraqi first and foremost, but over the years, he and his family had also been friends of the US government.

Apparently assuming I was still connected to the CIA, Sheik Omar asked me over tea to relay an important message to the Bush administration. First, he wanted to thank the administration for getting rid of the curse of Saddam. Second, he said, you need to understand that removing Saddam was primarily of benefit to our mutual enemy, the Shia of Iran. Islamic Iran was never able to get rid of secular Saddam on its own, and now Iran's malignant influence in Iraq would increase dramatically thanks to the US invasion. Third, he cautioned that Iraqis were proud people and would not long tolerate an American occupation, particularly when so many mistakes were being made. He referenced the very recent (May 23, 2003) disbanding of Iraq's entire military by Coalition Provisional Authority administrator Paul Bremer, a strategically idiotic move that ignored the advice given to Bremer by my former CIA colleagues, including Mac, among others. Finally, Sheik Omar said bluntly that if the United States did not change course and pull out of Iraq, Sunnis from Anbar province would begin to attack American troops. This was a clear and stark warning about the deadly insurgency that was indeed soon targeting and killing Americans.

I thanked Sheik Omar for his hospitality and his advice and promised I would relay his concerns to Washington. As my Iraqi escorts and I headed out across the Iraqi desert for Amman, my thoughts kept turning to the significance of Sheik Omar's words and how they would be received by those in power. It was clear to me that if the US government did not immediately alter course and implement some intelligent, commonsense policies along the lines of what Sheik Omar had suggested, the situation would become irreversibly FUBAR in Anbar.

A few days later, I relayed his important messages and warnings to Washington via my US government contacts. Given the Bush administration's serial bungling of events in Iraq, I did not expect anyone in DC to pay much heed to my report. As history has since shown, my expectations were met if not exceeded.

The Anbar-based, anti-American insurgency began almost immediately after Sheik Omar's explicit warning. Ramadi and Fallujah formed the heart of Iraq's Sunni insurgency, which soon became known as al-Qaeda in Iraq (AQI). Until the US invasion of Iraq, there was neither a foreign nor a home-grown al-Qaeda presence in the country. Afterward, both existed, in large part because Bremer's dismantling of the Iraqi Army and the Ba'ath Party resulted in tens of thousands of angry, well-armed Iraqis with nothing but time on their hands.

There was also no link between Saddam and the 9/11 attacks. Much as the Serbs had done in Bosnia when they cynically claimed they were defending the West against Muslim extremism (which was minimal in Bosnia until the Serbs started the war), the United States created a self-fulfilling prophecy in Iraq. Previously nonexistent AQI was formed precisely because of the invasion, and it later morphed into ISIS (Daesh). Foreign fighters poured into Iraq to join AQI and ISIS and to kill American troops who had invaded a Middle Eastern country without justification. There is no question that Saddam was a despicable, murderous thug, but he did not pose a threat to America's national security.

There is a clear, "proximate cause" link between the US invasion and removal of Saddam, Bremer's disbanding of the Iraqi military (and other bad decisions), and the evolution of the scourge of AQI and ISIS. The Bush administration was willfully blind to the dangerous reality that Sheik Omar could see and articulated so clearly. The entire world suffers the consequences of this willful blindness to this day.

✱ ✱ ✱

A common expression, misattributed to Albert Einstein, claims insanity is doing the same thing over and over again and expecting different results. After all these years, I know there's a good chance the US government will ignore my intelligence, so why will I continue to do my part as long as I'm able? I think it's because I believe so much in the ideals of the CIA and America that I'll never stop trying, the same way a devoted parent will never, ever give up on his child. America's ideals are sound, even when individual government employees willfully or ignorantly mishandle intelligence. Politicians do it all the time, but the CIA and those of us who privately support the US mission must never lose focus or stop doing our jobs. Devotion to duty by apolitical intelligence, military, and law enforcement professionals is key to the survival of our republic.

CHAPTER 30

IRAQ INTELLIGENCE FAILURE

This story could have been included in the previous chapter, but as you will read, this premeditated intelligence failure in Iraq is so mind-boggling in nature that it deserves a chapter all its own. Technically it was not an intelligence failure; it was a spectacular tactical intelligence success story, followed by an unconscionable bureaucratic failure to properly manage an invaluable ongoing counterterrorism intelligence operation. This breakdown in leadership may have inadvertently facilitated the rise of ISIS. The purpose of this story is not to spill secrets or share sources and methods, which I will not do, but rather to shed light on how the US government's careerist management culture sometimes results in truly unbelievable intelligence failures for the most mundane of reasons. As far as I can tell, there is zero accountability when this happens. To echo my former military colleagues' advice as we crossed over Mount Igman into deadly "Indian territory" en route to war-ravaged Sarajevo, "Hang on to your butts because here we go!"

The US government had no interest in hearing about my business start-up in Iraq in May 2003. In fact, they advised me against the venture, since I was a somewhat known former CIA officer, and that (in their considered opinion) would only lead to disaster.

Fair enough. They had zero obligation to be interested, and I may have reacted the same way if I'd been in their shoes.

By 2005, my Iraqi gamble was paying off. Although we operated across all regions of Iraq, we intentionally maintained a very low profile, with a very Iraqi business "face." Babylon Inc. was not publicly perceived as an American company. It was much safer that way, and it was also smart business. For example, we would not pay for heavily armed private military company convoys to get ourselves around the country. They were expensive and unnecessary, and they often made a target of those they were designed to protect. Our employees traveled around the country in non-descript Iraqi cars and trucks, blending in beautifully. (Although once in Basra, diligent police at a checkpoint stopped and questioned us because they wanted to make sure I wasn't being kidnapped; they were not used to seeing an American cruising around Basra with Iraqis inside a typical Iraqi vehicle.) Because of our responsiveness and our modus operandi, we were not confined to the relative safety of military bases and "green zones"; we covered 100 percent of the country.

US government authorities in Iraq got wind of my company's success and solicited my cooperation. As always, I was happy to cooperate in any and every way possible. Two years after the invasion, confronting the very insurgency Sheik Omar warned about, the US government had begun to appreciate the value of my Iraqi entity with its country-wide "red zone" access. Babylon Inc. was held back by none of the constraints faced by the government. Risky and dangerous activities, which happened to be a routine part of Babylon Inc.'s business, would prove to be valuable to the government's counterterrorism mission.

Despite their initial concerns, my CIA background remained hidden and a nonissue while I was running Babylon Inc. That said, the fact that I was a former CIA officer running an Iraqi company tailor-made for their requirements made it very easy for the US government to work with me. We spoke the same language. In the process, we both learned that I could do more for the US government mission from the outside—where I was free to run things my own way—than from the inside. The arrangement was good for them and good for me. The results of this unique collaboration were also decidedly good for force protection and America's national security.

Although the government officials with whom I was dealing clearly understood the potential payoff (as well as the risks) of collaborating with Babylon Inc., something did not add up for some of them, who were almost instinctively opposed. How could a former CIA officer possibly run a business in Iraq? (Answer: it's not easy, but it can be done.) Unfortunately, the reality is that no situation is ever perfect. If you wait to find the perfect, risk-free environment before acting, you'll never act. You give it your best shot, try not to do anything stupid, and move forward, with the implicit awareness that no scenario is perfect and there is always some risk that things will go south. If the risks or consequences of not acting outweigh the risks of acting in an imperfect situation, you do the best you can, but you proceed. In the end, since I was willing to risk my company's future in order to support the US security mission in Iraq, the government was too.

Babylon Inc. was not tied to the military or US government going in, and it would not be so encumbered going out. But our collaboration provided lots of bang for the buck. Both literally and figuratively.

By now it is no doubt aggravatingly clear that I cannot get into much detail, but through Babylon's collaboration I was returning the favor of life-saving benefits I'd received in the past, by saving the lives of other Americans (and Iraqis), whether they realized it or not. (And for the most part, they did not.) I was paying it forward in a meaningful and anonymous way, and it felt good. I ran Babylon Inc. based on my own unique experience, accomplishing things inside Iraq the US government could not possibly do on their own.

As the United States wound down its military operations in Iraq in late 2011, my government contacts informed me they no longer required my company's services in Iraq. My arguments—and those of several inside the government—fell on deaf ears. The bad guys were not going away. My business in Iraq continued as usual. President Obama had made good on his promise to get the United States out of Iraq, consequences be damned.

✳ ✳ ✳

Fast-forward to June 2014. ISIS appeared "out of nowhere" and took over Mosul.

They didn't really appear out of nowhere. After American troops left Iraq, a crippled but not yet defeated AQI continued to rebuild, as predicted, and eventually morphed into what is now known as ISIS or Daesh. By early 2014, ISIS had taken over Ramadi and Fallujah, after which the terror group formally split from al-Qaeda Central (UBL's old shop). By mid-June, Mosul was under ISIS control. A handful of scraggly, bearded ISIS terrorists spooked thousands of Iraqi troops, who dropped their American-provided weapons before retreating. President Obama, whose White House had been ignoring Iraq (and CIA warnings about Iraq), said the intelligence community had missed warning signs about the rise of ISIS.[1]

I contacted my old friends in the US government and reminded them that since my business in ISIS-controlled Mosul was still up and running, they might like to collaborate once again. We routinely continued to send money, equipment, and personnel into and out of Mosul, and we had communication with our people inside Mosul (a rarity at the time). According to press reports, the intelligence community had little to no insights into what was happening inside Mosul, so I assumed it would be a no-brainer to gain valuable intelligence. I know I should not have been surprised, but I was when the US government expressed no interest.

I shook the US government tree a few more times, but still with no luck. Despite having experienced everything you read in the previous chapter, I was still flabbergasted. This was ISIS after all. Although Babylon Inc. was now losing money in Mosul, I decided to subsidize the business there rather than shut it down, on the assumption that eventually the US government would come to their senses. How could they not?

Since there was literally no conceivable reason *not* to resume the collaboration, I had to ask the obvious question: how is it possible that the government has no interest? For me it was like attempting to decipher the nonsensical "Aserejé," aka "The Ketchup Song"; try as I might, it made no sense. Unfortunately, I cannot share with you the details of their response, but the bottom line is this costly and mind-numbingly idiotic fiasco may have been due to the career concerns of a single, feckless US government employee. I cannot confirm that this is what actually happened. In fact, I hope this is not what actually happened, but I suspect it is. Because nothing else makes sense.

✳ ✳ ✳

Fast-forward to 2017. Predictably, US troops returned to Iraq to help the Iraqi Army take back ISIS-controlled territory. Together they pushed ISIS out of Mosul, destroying the historic city in the process. The price of the operation to retake Mosul, in Iraqi blood and American treasure, was steep. After Mosul's liberation, Babylon Inc.'s manager there (Hatem) was briefly arrested by the Iraqi government, until they ascertained he was not a member of ISIS. The government's suspicions were understandable.

Had the US government not stopped their collaboration with Babylon Inc., would the Obama administration have had advance warning about

ISIS and its designs on Mosul? Could we have prevented the ISIS takeover of Mosul? If the US government had agreed to renew their collaboration with Babylon Inc. in June 2014, would the ISIS occupation of Mosul have lasted three years, or much less? Would the price paid by the United States and Iraq to remove ISIS have been as high?

Once again, we will never know the answers to these important questions. At the very least, we *do* know the situation could not have been any worse. As discussed in the previous chapter, a single intelligence source is rarely dispositive of the outcome in complex situations like Iraq. The Babylon Inc. collaboration was only one of many pieces of the overall intelligence puzzle on Iraq and AQI. But I believe it was an important piece.

Will anyone in the US government ever be held accountable for this colossal blunder? If history is any indication, probably not.

CHAPTER 31

THE SPY WHO
CAME DOWN WITH A COLD

You wouldn't know it from watching James Bond movies, but spies are vulnerable to coming down with a bug (and not just the electronic kind). Worse, CIA officers have been poisoned by Russians and recently subjected to mysterious acoustic attacks in China and Cuba.[1] Much like a devoted single parent, however, a spy can't take a sick day. Wars aren't put on hold while you recover, and agent meetings planned months in advance can't be postponed just because a case officer has the sniffles.

Prior to my first overseas assignment to Latin America, I was required to get a series of two typhoid shots. After the first shot, I contracted typhoid fever. I recovered, but I skipped the second shot because I didn't want to risk postponing my PCS move to Latin America, where agent turnover meetings had already been scheduled. In Belgrade, I contracted Lyme disease while skulking around the Balkan woods. Mine was the first recorded case in Yugoslavia and was detected thanks to the dedication of our regional American doctor. I hate to think what might have happened had he not been there to make the very tough diagnosis. During the war in Sarajevo, I feigned illness to explain a canceled meeting with the Bosnian security service, in order to avoid being kidnapped and tortured by Iranian agents. Years later, the night before I set off from Amman for my first overland journey to Baghdad through *Mad Max*–like chaos and an unforgettable sandstorm, I had a severe allergic reaction to a bee sting that took place a week earlier while I was jogging in the Santa Monica Mountains. Thanks to the late-night intervention of the Sheraton Amman's on-call Jordanian doctor, the swelling and itching subsided enough for me to make the trek to Iraq the next day.

Sickness—real and feigned—is a fact of life for spies, but it rarely slows us down.

What *does* slow spies down are the myriad nonmedical, bureaucratic, and other maladies that plague us throughout our careers: risk-averse CIA bureaucrats whose "Just say no" mind-set frequently undermines the CIA's raison d'être; subjecting ourselves and our families to difficult and some-times dangerous ways of life; the CIA's sky-high divorce rate; dealing with lies and betrayals on a daily basis; having to obey operational decisions based not on the merits of an operation but on administrative consider-ations of lawyers, bean counters, or ambitious, career-conscious managers; and so on. A spy who manages to survive all of that, and still successfully produces solid intelligence, may then face presidents and policy makers who ignore or politicize the CIA's intelligence.

Spies are also slowed down by countless Bohica moments. As I men-tioned in chapter 6, Bohica in CIA and military circles means "Bend over, here it comes again." It typically refers to the phenomenon of getting screwed by your own bureaucracy, and often in the context of personnel matters. (The nonconsensual buggery humor just never seems to end, does it?) Being drafted to learn French and serve in Africa after being promised that would not happen was one of my earliest Bohica moments. Over the years, several more followed.

One of my final Bohica moments took place when I resigned from the agency. Technically it was a classic case of sleeper-cell Bohica, since it related to my prior TDY to Sarajevo. During the Bosnian War, the "offi-cial" currency in the country was the German deutsche mark (DM). When I first met them in Split, Croatia, the US military operatives who drove down from Zagreb passed me an envelope containing 500 DM to advance to me in case I needed it while in Sarajevo. Since I bugged out of Sarajevo early, I never spent any of the advance. When I stopped off in Washington to brief the congressional intelligence committee, I also paid a visit to CIA headquarters, where I attempted to return the 500 DM. I was told that per regulations, they could not take the cash back at headquarters, since it was advanced in the field. I'd have to turn it in where I received it.

I explained I left Sarajevo under somewhat hasty circumstances and did not have a chance to return it in the field. Headquarters bean coun-ters mulled it over and decided they'd make an exception and allow me to turn the advance in to admin people in another admin office across town. I drove across town and attempted to turn the foreign currency in to the admin officer there. She informed me government regulations prevented her from accepting foreign currency, and I would have to exchange the DM for US dollars at a bank before returning the money. I dutifully complied, handed over the dollars, and assumed this annoying and time-consuming admin matter was finally closed. (Admittedly, I'm a slow learner.)

About one year later, I received a cable from headquarters saying I owed about $150 because the value of the DM had fluctuated between the time I was advanced the DM in Bosnia and the time I turned them in to the cross-town admin person months later in US dollars. Plus, the bank's commission ate up some of the value. I explained that I'd never requested or touched the advance, which I returned in full, so I should not owe anything. Moreover, the unsolicited advance was made so that I could perform official duties—namely, volunteering to risk my life in Sarajevo to report critical intelligence. This wasn't a car loan from the CIA's credit union.

"Surely," I concluded in the cable to headquarters in which I pled my case, "under these circumstances, CIA should assume responsibility and absorb the $150 loss."

"Request denied," was the curt reply. "And stop calling me Shirley." (If only they'd added that last sentence, since a bit of humor might have induced me to pay up and settle the matter once and for all.)

As a fair-minded Libra, I ignored this clearly unjust order to pay $150 to the CIA and was hoping they'd forget about it. I'd almost forgotten about it myself.

* * *

When I resigned from the CIA, I learned I had the option of leaving my retirement money in the CIA retirement fund, or taking a cash payout. I opted for the cash payout. After I made my official request, headquarters informed me that they would not release my retirement funds until I paid the $150 I owed from my Sarajevo TDY. The CIA's memory is long, whether tracking a Hezbollah terrorist for years after his kidnapping and murder of a CIA officer, or keeping a watchful eye on a dubious debt owed to headquarters by a staff operations officer. The CIA was holding my retirement fund hostage until I paid "ransom" for a problem I did not create.

Just as I would do years later when our employee Omar was kidnapped by AQI in Mosul, I caved in to the demands of these merciless bean counters. I had no choice if I wanted my retirement money. I was not pleased.

On my final drive home from the CIA, I got my head back together by listening to "The Cowboy Rides Away." Repeatedly.

We've now established that as much as I've loved working with and for the CIA, a spy's life has its downsides. For starters, there's a never-ending string of Bohica moments, from the day you join until the day you resign or retire. They really do get you coming and going, but the CIA is a bureaucracy, and so that's to be expected. Having hard-earned intelligence ignored or politicized is a tougher pill to swallow. In fact, it's downright demoralizing, whether you're on the inside or the outside. Despite these downsides to a life of espionage, which I have experienced firsthand for decades, I'll never turn down a request or an opportunity to support the US government national security mission.

Because of my seemingly irrational tendency to never give up on the government mission, even when others have, my former CIA colleagues now refer to me as "the Last of the Bohicans."

"And ye shall know the truth, and the truth shall make you free."[2] This biblical verse is carved into the wall at CIA headquarters and stands as the agency's motto. I joined the CIA in part because of my own deeply held convictions about truth, fairness, and justice. The title of this chapter, aside from being a playful twist on John le Carré's Cold War classic, is a metaphor for my own growing disillusionment with the system after many years of service.

Intelligence is essential to our national security and to our very survival as a nation. American spies sacrifice in the shadows to report the truth to power. If US presidents and policy makers continue to ignore or politicize the CIA, the "American empire" may be very short-lived. American presidents from both political parties ignore sound intelligence and thus make disastrous foreign policy decisions. Disasters that adversely affect millions of people around the world.

The current president has pushed matters to dangerous extremes never before experienced with leaders of either party. It's one thing to ignore solid intelligence and forge ahead with risky policies; presidents have every right to do so. It's another thing entirely to take the word of Vladimir Putin over your own intelligence services on the issue of the risk of North Korean missiles to the United States. Or to publicly and personally denigrate the leadership of the American intelligence community, as Trump did in January 2019,[3] because their objective intelligence assessments happen to contradict almost every false belief he spouted, from Syria to Russia to North Korea. Trump is apparently personally offended if the intelligence community fails to modify the truth to conform with his own twisted views of reality. Publicly referring to apolitical intelligence professionals (whom Trump handpicked for their jobs) as "naïve," "wrong," and saying they should "go back to school" is spectacularly reckless and dangerous behavior by a willfully ignorant American president.

Even more troubling is Trump's penchant for tribalism. In Yugoslavia I witnessed firsthand how a shameless demagogue's incitement of fear and hatred in otherwise "normal people" led to a bloody civil war and the literal destruction and breakup of an entire country. I was not surprised by the savagery later committed in Iraq, also in the name of tribalism. What I never expected to experience was the threat from tribalism in my own country, much less at the direction of the president of the United States.

If there's a merciful God, the expression *President Trump* will be preceded by the word *former* by the time this book is published. By then, there's a good chance he will have resigned, been impeached, or been forcibly removed from office as unfit to lead pursuant to a Twenty-Fifth Amendment "Constitutional mutiny" (my personal favorite). Because Trump's malignant upside-down reality is completely antithetical to the sacred American notions of truth and freedom, many more of America's spies will likely decide it is time for them as well to come in from the cold. His destructive, narcissistic, and juvenile approach to foreign policy makes it more difficult today for our spies and diplomats to represent America and pursue American interests abroad than when we truly lived and breathed American exceptionalism.

Trump's disgraceful display in front of the CIA's Memorial Wall the day after his inauguration was the final straw for many.[4] In the days following his shameful performance at headquarters, where he rambled on about himself and exaggerated the size of his inauguration crowd, many CIA employees left flowers at the Memorial Wall in silent protest. He disgraced the CIA's sacrosanct ground the same way he went on to disgrace the office of the White House. In my view, Trump's words and actions seriously undermine America's moral authority and our national security, and thus represent an existential threat to our nation.

Every cloud has a silver lining. Although in this case, in true Trumpian fashion, the lining may turn out to be gold. Traditionally apolitical CIA officers are responding to Trump's calumnies, attacks on our institutions, and debasement of the office, by running for political office themselves. I have no doubt that my former colleagues will continue to put country first, and Congress and our nation will be better off as a result.

"And ye shall know the truth, and the truth shall make you free." Trump's willingness to destroy our nation in order to protect himself is in keeping with his instinctual tendency to rule like history's other illegitimate tinhorn despots. Despite Trump's best efforts to hide the truth about his lifetime of likely criminal and treasonous behavior, I predict America's battered institutions and the free press will withstand his reckless and relentless attacks. Trump will fail in his mission to pervert the truth, and that will make America free again.

EPILOGUE

I realize that I declared up front that I'm all Iraq'd out. I really meant it. You may recall that I also said with conviction that there was no way I'd go through jump school following SERE training, and we all know how that turned out.

Tarek and I just met up for another fun and Lebanese-food-filled week in Beirut. The day after a wild drive to and from the Beqaa Valley for some amphora wine tasting at the stunningly beautiful Château Kefraya (incongruously located five minutes away from a truly depressing Syrian refugee camp), we flew from Beirut to Baghdad to meet with our Iraqi colleagues and key Iraqi business contacts.

As always, I have some good news and some bad news to share.

I am happy and more than a little astonished to report that Baghdad has clearly turned a corner, and for the first time since the unwarranted 2003 invasion, I have real hope for Iraq's future. For Iraqis themselves, that is, and not just for foreign oil companies. Accompanied by Tarek, Hassan, Omar, and my other beloved Iraqi colleagues, I spent the past week driving around the sprawling, chaotic city, walking the streets, eating in restaurants, and hanging out in modern shopping malls. I even spent some quality time in the office. Much to my pleasant surprise, not once did I feel threatened as I had during previous trips to Baghdad. (Tarek has been insisting Baghdad is safe now for some time, but I'm a natural skeptic and I needed to find out for myself.) As far as I could tell, I was the only gringo on the streets, but I suspect westerners of all stripes will begin to pour into the city once word is out that Baghdad is secure and really open for business. Private enterprises abound, including luxury car dealerships, and glitzy, modern shopping malls are springing up all over Baghdad like California poppies after a wet winter.

Another sign that Iraq has shed its violent past in favor of a better future is the quasi-comical hipster invasion of Baghdad. Almost every young man under the age of thirty wears skinny jeans, meticulously groomed (non-ISIS) beards, and the most outrageous spiky hair ever coiffed on the planet. The hair literally stands straight up, sometimes as much as ten inches. (My daughters will no doubt roll their eyes at the fact that I even find this trend remarkable.) A few years ago, young men in Baghdad were being killed by the dozens by Islamic extremists "because they looked gay" for daring to dress or style their hair differently. A vast majority of young Iraqis now feel free to dress and look as they choose. This is a very positive sign that bodes well for Iraq's future. It's an indication of real change and real progress.

As for young Iraqi women, many still cover their heads with hijabs, but at the same time a significant number wear much less conservative and more revealing clothing than in the past. This has prompted some Iraqis to crudely quip that these women's "heads are for Allah, but their bodies are for Abdullah." Openness toward change is a slow process and only extends so far, but at least the young women are no longer being harassed, threatened, or killed for their sartorial choices. Hopefully this trend will continue.

Part of the reason for this refreshing makeover of Baghdad society is that former prime minister Haider al-Abadi and his successor Adel Abdul-Mahdi, both Shi'ites, have gone to great lengths to treat Sunnis fairly and include them in the new Iraq. Further institutionalizing freedom, equality, and equal treatment under the law for all citizens will be the key to Iraq's peaceful and prosperous future.

Yes, Baghdad traffic is still maddening, by any measure, but because of the inherently good nature of the Iraqi people, it is somehow less stressful than one might expect. Mind-numbing Baghdad traffic jams defy reason or explanation. There is constant honking and cutting off of other drivers, but no one gets truly angry. I saw no examples of road rage, even though we were bombarded by outrageous behavior that would have resulted in multiple Tasings if not mass murder had it occurred on one of America's many congested freeways. To venture out on Baghdad's streets is to participate in a daily game of chicken that Iraqis seem to relish playing. Baghdad traffic flows in fits and starts like a gargantuan school of fish, if the fish were smoking, looking at their cell phones, and eating breakfast, while talking animatedly with their passengers, other drivers, and any passersby simultaneously. More shoaling than schooling. Like switching to soy milk, Baghdad traffic takes some getting used to. There really is a certain sweetness and civility to ordinary Iraqis, and I believe this explains the anger-free controlled chaos that reigns on the streets of Baghdad.

Although I am now cautiously optimistic about Iraq's future, I also recognize that ISIS and AQI can and likely will rear their very ugly heads again at any time. As of April 2019, ISIS has lost all of its territory in both Iraq and Syria, but there are thousands of radicalized ISIS fighters, wives, and children with no place to go and an overabundance of hatred, ignorance, and bloodlust in their souls. ISIS leader Abu Bakr al-Baghdadi is still out there. All of this makes it highly likely (in my estimation) that these craven murderers will again resort to suicide bombings and other attacks in Baghdad and elsewhere in Iraq, in order to again incite fear, hatred, and violence among the country's Shi'ite and Sunni populations. We can probably expect the same in Western Europe and the United States. Like smoldering embers in a seemingly doused campfire, tribalism remains a dangerous threat until fully extinguished.

In addition to the lingering menace posed by Islamic extremists, endemic corruption persists in Iraq, at every level of the government. Corruption may actually pose a greater threat to Iraq's future than ISIS or tribalism. It is clear to me that virtually every government employee in Iraq views his job as an opportunity if not an obligation to crassly extort money out of fellow Iraqis and foreigners alike. My Iraqi colleagues deal with this scourge on a daily basis, whether seeking government permission to run a generator (because the government fails to provide electricity) or a business license that will result in a boost to the Iraqi economy. These shameless Iraqi officials quite simply do not care that their greedy, corrupt behavior is doing possibly irreparable harm to their country.

To cite but one recent example, I was prevented from leaving Baghdad this week by an airport immigration official who decided on a whim that I needed an "exit visa." What's an exit visa, you may ask? It's an unnecessary bureaucratic nuisance required in a small handful of backward totalitarian countries, like Russia and Saudi Arabia, to control and harass foreign visitors and workers. Even Cuba, hardly a paragon of freedom of movement, did away with this vile practice, but it persists in Iraq. Saddam Hussein may be dead and gone, but his authoritarian practices live on.

One cannot simply apply for and receive an exit visa at Baghdad International Airport. No, that would make too much sense. In order to obtain an exit visa, I first had to offload my Hallab 1881 baklava–laden luggage from my Turkish Airlines flight and return to Baghdad and find a hospital and get a blood test (I am not making this up). I never did find out the rationale for the blood test. After the blood test—the results were irrelevant to the process—I would normally have to spend several days waiting for a bureaucrat to do his job and issue the aforementioned exit visa and blood test stamp in my passport, before returning to the airport to try again. Imagine going on a week-long trip to any country on earth with a valid visa, for business or pleasure, and then being told for the first time at the airport minutes before departure that you must get a blood test and an exit visa if you wish to leave the country. (In retrospect, I'm pretty sure this was belated payback for my handling of Yuri Jerkov's visa case in Belgrade many years ago.)

No Iraqi bureaucrat would even think of actually doing his job without demanding and receiving sufficient baksheesh (bribe payment) in advance. If I wanted to depart Baghdad only one day late (as opposed to several days late), I would have to pay nearly one thousand dollars in cash for the privilege. (I did not say this out loud, but at that point I was thinking it would have been a bargain at twice the price.) Not every foreign businessperson is as patient as I am, and this type of brazen corruption that permeates literally every aspect of Iraqi society will undoubtedly impede Iraq's future growth and participation in the global economy. I wonder if this is what the Eagles had in mind when they penned their haunting epic "Long Road out of Eden" song about the war in Iraq and the folly of empire building.

This book has covered its fair share of difficult ground, but I'm going to conclude on a positive note. You may recall the situation that I described in the preface, in which the Iranian-backed Shi'ite militia arrested our key man in Basra in an effort to extort large sums of money out of Babylon Inc. in exchange for a "license" to operate. They threatened to shut down our entire business in southern Iraq, which now accounts for a very large percentage of our company's Iraqi business. We could not and would not pay the bribe, for a variety of reasons. We were at risk of going out of business after fifteen strong years in Iraq, thanks to a band of Iranian-backed thugs. (I am beginning to seriously consider the possibility that I may be an Iranian-thug magnet.)

Then a funny thing happened. Omar, our erstwhile Sunni driver who was kidnapped, abused, and then released by AQI in Mosul after we paid more than market price for his freedom, is married to a Shi'ite woman. Her father is a high-ranking military intelligence officer in the Basra area, and he was able to make our existential threat disappear. Tribal connections are always key in Iraq. Always. Our potentially disastrous run-in with the Shi'ite militia had an unforeseen happy ending.

When we paid $50,000 for Omar, it was a simple humanitarian investment in his life. Little did we know at the time that quiet, dependable Omar would go on to save our entire business, a feat worth considerably more than the $50,000 we handed over.

Some might say this story perfectly exemplifies the wishful concept known as karma. I'd like to believe that, although I can't say for sure whether karma is at work or if it's just plain old good luck. Either way, I know that we did the right thing for the right reasons for our terrified employee and his family many years ago, and we have been unexpectedly rewarded one-hundred-fold in return. Sometimes good things happen in this world.

SPOOKSTOCK AND H. K. ROY WEBSITE

A word about Spookstock, a charity with which I am actively involved. Spookstock is an annual battle of the bands fundraiser for the CIA Officers Memorial Foundation and the Special Operations Warrior Foundation. Spookstock is a private, invitation-only, and senior executive–only event, with no press or PR. Past celebrity judges have included Robert De Niro, Harvey Keitel, Dan Aykroyd, Admiral Bill McRaven, and Paul Shaffer. Headliners have included ZZ Top, Peter Frampton, John Fogerty, Ronnie Dunn, and the Steve Miller Band. Lenny Kravitz is scheduled to appear at the 2019 fundraiser. Beneficiaries of Spookstock are the children of fallen CIA and special ops warriors. Dozens of new beneficiaries are added to the list each year.

To make a donation, please visit the following:

https://www.ciamemorialfoundation.org/
https://specialops.org/

To access additional photos from the author, a soundtrack for the book, and other "state secrets," please visit www.hkroy.com.

Also, connect with H. K. on Twitter @HKRoySpyWriter.

ACKNOWLEDGMENTS

I would like to give a shout-out and extend a sincere "thank you," "shukran," "gracias," "spasibo," "grazie," and/or "hvala" to the following people, without whom I could not and would not have written *American Spy*:

To my parents for your love and for raising me to value hard work, honesty, integrity, fairness, and equality, concepts that led me to my career with the CIA. I'm sorry you had to learn from this book that, unbeknownst to you, I regularly smuggled illegal knives and low-grade explosives into the United States from Mexico under your car seats. I'd actually been meaning to tell you about it for some time. I promise it won't happen again, so please don't make me go to confession.

To my brilliant, kind, and beautiful "spy kids" for your unconditional love and encouragement throughout the book-writing process. I love you more than you will ever know, and not just because you always pretend to find my dumb jokes as hilarious as I do. Did I ever tell you the one about the grasshopper that walks into a bar?

To my siblings for putting up with me all of our lives and for unwittingly contributing to some of the funny stories in chapter 4. Thanks also for not ratting me out to Mom and Dad about that Mexican smuggling thing. Or about the time when I was fourteen years old and I took you all on a joyride in Dad's Ford Galaxy around our fair city somewhere in the American Southwest. To our youngest brother: it's time you knew the truth—you were not actually given up at birth by the Ranchero family for adoption.

To Stacy for your love, patience, and support for much longer than I deserved. While I've got your attention, would you mind if I took our second daughter—oh, please, I know her name, but I just can't reveal it here—to Baghdad for New Year's? What could go wrong?

To "John," "Dan," "Nate," "Charlie," "Rodd," "Lance," "Mac,"

"Scott," "Amy," "AK," Ted Price, Burton Gerber, and dozens of other CIA colleagues, instructors, mentors, COSs, DCOSs, branch chiefs, division chiefs, fellow case officers, and others in the CIA—including SERE guards and interrogators—who patiently and selflessly provided guidance and training to me and my colleagues.

Mark Kelton, I probably would not be alive today if it were not for you. But for your quiet professionalism and dedication to duty, I would likely be represented by a star on the Memorial Wall and my daughters would have joined the growing ranks of beautiful beneficiaries of Spookstock.

To "R. J.," "Big Dale," "Jesuit Joe," "Jack," "Army Jim," "Carol," "the Interceptor," "Heather," and my other CT classmates: I'll never forget you or our CIA training exploits and hope I did our training (and you) justice in this book.

To the US military's secret special operators with whom I worked in the Balkans and in Iraq, thank you for risking your lives on my and our nation's behalf and for silently supporting the agency's mission in defense of our country.

To 00HITCH, "Jovan," "Sasha," and countless other unnamed foreign agents and witting contacts with whom I worked and who risk(ed) their lives and those of their families to support the noble cause of freedom. You are the unsung heroes of this book.

To my former foreign service colleagues: thank you for your service, your professionalism, your thankless support to the CIA, and for not playing "spot the spook" overseas when the walls had ears. Dink: if you're reading this, kudos for acting like you didn't recognize me when we unexpectedly crossed paths at the Jolly Hotel in Rome.

To R. J. (and supervisor) for your decades of friendship, cigars, p(ivo)-rations, football, Diet Mountain Dew, Yorkshire terrorist(s), wise counsel, and for an endless string of inexplicable life coincidences. Also, thanks in advance for agreeing to serve as acting president of my new pet project, the Deep State Alumni Association.

To "Buey" for a lifetime of laughs, for always being there, and for 24/7 help with vocabulary, syntax, and grammar. I'm just happy that your English degree has finally paid off for me.

To my Iraqi friends and colleagues at Babylon Inc., who knowingly risked their lives to support American troops and unknowingly risked their lives to enhance security in both Iraq and the United States.

To Ceca for your thirty years of professionalism and friendship. I'm pretty sure you'll recognize yourself in the book, *jebiga.*

To "Homebeebti" for your humor, your scary brilliance, and your insights into Iraqi culture and the Arabic language.

To "Señor Doug," principal pilot, mechanic, and procurement officer tasked with the acquisition of frosty beverages and crispy fried snack treats for DougAir (aka AeroDoug when in Mexican airspace), thank you for helping me find my long-lost box of Balkan war photos for inclusion in this book. We need to go to Mexico ASAP; it does not suck there. In fact, according to the forecast, today it will not suck even more than it did not suck yesterday.

To family friend, neighbor, and dentist "Dr. Lou" for introducing me and my family to Mexico when I was eight years old. Your enthusiasm for life and for Mexico was contagious and led to my own lifetime of adventure.

A la bonita Porteña: Gracias por creer en mi y por las ricas enchiladas de pollo. Un día tendrás que aprender a decir más en inglés que "Pancho, you fat fuck." *Y no me llames* "Pancho."

To Joan for decades of friendship, for help with the DC bar exam, and for encouraging me to write. I can't wait to read your first novel.

To "NSM" for your friendship, your broccoli recipe, and your patient work editing and improving my Russian intel reports. I also can't wait to read your first novel.

To "La Bellina" for your heart, humor, Amaretti, and your enthusiasm for my writing. I'll finish the novel, I promise!

To "Tarek" for your friendship and years of devotion to Babylon Inc. and our Iraqi colleagues. Without you, there would be no Babylon and no Babylon stories. My trips to Beirut are always perfect since you clearly own that town.

To "Bueno" Dave for your decades of friendship. I'm just sorry the publisher rejected your proposed cover art for *American Spy.* I personally thought that a dreamlike photo of Fabio on a white horse—with both Fabio's and the horse's eyes obscured for the sake of anonymity—perfectly captured the spirit and essence of the book.

To Ms. Ortega for your support and advice and for believing in this book. Your Spookstock selfie with your favorite actor is still on my phone.

To my patient literary agent Claire Gerus for believing in *American Spy* early on and for taking the time to provide insightful "big picture" guidance, which was, without fail, spot on. When you told me bluntly, "Nobody cares about your life story," I actually knew what you meant and that it was said with love. Without you, there would be no *American Spy*.

To former Prometheus Books editor in chief Steven L. Mitchell for taking a chance on this unusual "animal" of a book. I wish you well in your much-deserved retirement and hope I was not the cause.

To Jeffrey Curry, copyeditor extraordinaire. I may not be as stupid as I look, but you make me look smarter than I am. Thank you for your professionalism and attention to detail and for allowing me to tell my stories in my own voice.

To Hanna, Jill, Cate, Lisa, Jade, Nicole, Jake, and the entire team at Prometheus Books. Thank you for your consistent professionalism, for humoring me, and for patiently and thoroughly answering this novice author's many questions about the writing business. I especially appreciate your and Jeff's concern about protecting my safety and that of others in the book.

To all the musical artists named in the book, and hundreds of others not mentioned: you not only provide the soundtracks to our lives, but your passion for creating music also makes life better for the rest of us. Even while conducting SDRs in denied areas.

To Pack Fancher and everyone behind the fundraising phenomenon known as Spookstock: thank you for all you do for the grieving and deserving children of our fallen CIA and special operations brothers and sisters.

And finally, to Donald Trump, Vladimir Putin, and Kim Jong Un and his secretive twin brother (and heir to the throne) Kim Jong Dos: I'm eternally grateful. Without real-life villains, there would be no need for the good guys.

NOTES

CHAPTER 1: BETRAYAL IN THE BALKANS: HILLARY SENT ME, BUT BILL NEARLY GOT ME KILLED

1. In CIA circles, the name is spelled "Usama" over the more widely used "Osama."

2. Kyle W. Orton, "From Bosnia to Guantanamo: How War in the Balkans Shaped Al-Qaeda and the Global Jihad," *Medium*, January 23, 2016, https://medium.com/news-politics/from-bosnia-to-guantanamo-94b804c467ea.

3. Marcia Christoff Kurop, "Al Qaeda's Balkan Links," *Wall Street Journal*, November 1, 2001, https://www.wsj.com/articles/SB1004563569751363760.

4. James Risen, "Bosnia Reportedly Told Iran of U.S. Spy," *Los Angeles Times*, January 15, 1997, https://www.latimes.com/archives/la-xpm-1997-01-15-mn-18698-story.html.

5. Adam Goldman and Ellen Nakashima, "CIA and Mossad Killed Senior Hezbollah Figure in Car Bombing," *Washington Post*, January 30, 2015, https://www.washingtonpost.com/world/national-security/cia-and-mossad-killed-senior-hezbollah-figure-in-car-bombing/2015/01/30/ebb88682-968a-11e4-8005-1924ede3e54a_story.html?utm_term=.757879e82289.

6. Fred Burton and Samuel Katz, *Beirut Rules: The Murder of a CIA Station Chief and Hezbollah's War against America* (New York: Berkley, 2018), p. 334.

CHAPTER 2: CIA LEAK

1. James Risen, "Bosnia Reportedly Told Iran of U.S. Spy," *Los Angeles Times*, January 15, 1997, https://www.latimes.com/archives/la-xpm-1997-01-15-mn-18698-story.html.

2. James Risen, "Report of Bosnian Spy Network Stirs Concerns in U.S.," *Los Angeles Times*, February 6, 1997, https://www.latimes.com/archives/la-xpm-1997-02-06-mn-26055-story.html.

3. H. K. Roy, "Betrayal in the Balkans," *World & I Magazine*, August 2001.

4. Central Intelligence Agency, "Yugoslavia Transformed," *National Intelligence Estimate (NIE 15-90)*, October 1990, https://www.cia.gov/library/center-for-the-study-of-intelligence/csi-publications/books-and-monographs/csi-intelligence-and-policy-monographs/index.html.

5. Perm. Select Comm. on Intelligence, Investigation into Iranian Arms

Shipments to Bosnia, H.R. Rep., No. 105-804 (1998), https://www.congress.gov/congressional-report/105th-congress/house-report/804/1?r=51.

CHAPTER 4: DON'T GET ME STARTED

1. Jerry Knight, "Tylenol's Maker Shows How to Respond to Crisis," *Washington Post*, October 11, 1982, https://www.washingtonpost.com/archive/business/1982/10/11/tylenols-maker-shows-how-to-respond-to-crisis/bc8df898-3fcf-443f-bc2f-e6fbd639a5a3/?noredirect=on&utm_term=.16c48547e855.

CHAPTER 5: CIA PARAMILITARY TRAINING

1. Joseph Finlay, "Five Years to Freedom," *American Thinker*, June 9, 2014, https://www.americanthinker.com/articles/2014/06/five_years_to_freedom.html.

CHAPTER 6: SECURE YOUR CHUTES

1. "The Closer You Get," track 1, on Alabama, *The Closer You Get*, RCA, 2000, compact disc, originally released in 1983.

CHAPTER 8: CUBAN OPS

1. Anthony Faiola, "From Riches to Rags (Venezuelans Become Latin America's New Underclass)," *Washington Post*, July 27, 2018, https://www.washingtonpost.com/news/world/wp/2018/07/27/feature/as-venezuela-crumbles-its-fleeing-citizens-are-becoming-latin-americas-new-underclass/?utm_term=.66247d4bcf5a.

2. Lewis H. Diuguid, "Cuba Exults That CIA's Men in Havana Were Double Agents," *Washington Post*, July 27, 1987, https://www.washingtonpost.com/archive/politics/1987/07/27/cuba-exults-that-cias-men-in-havana-were-double-agents/a4db4946-0ed2-45b9-9757-2337a6d0c407/?utm_term=.02dfdd891d5a.

CHAPTER 10: MESSING WITH CHINESE SPIES

1. "Nicaragua: Report by Independent Experts Affirms That Government of President Ortega Has Committed Crimes against Humanity," Amnesty International, December 21, 2018, https://www.amnesty.org/en/latest/news/2018/12/nicaragua

-report-by-independent-experts-affirms-that-the-government-of-president-ortega-has
-committed-crimes-against-humanity/.

CHAPTER 11: MOON OVER LIBYA

1. Steven Erlanger, "4 Guilty in Fatal 1986 Berlin Disco Bombing Linked to Libya," *New York Times*, November 14, 2001, https://www.nytimes.com/2001/11/14/world/ 4-guilty-in-fatal-1986-berlin-disco-bombing-linked-to-libya.html.

2. "U.S. Bombs Libya," *History*, February 9, 2010, https://www.history.com/ this-day-in-history/u-s-bombs-libya.

3. Office of the Historian, "Foreign Relations of the United States, 1964–1968, Volume XXVI, Indonesia; Malaysia-Singapore; Philippines: Note on U.S. Covert Action Programs," US Department of State, https://history.state.gov/historicaldocuments/ frus1964-68v26/actionsstatement.

CHAPTER 12: CIA VS. KGB

1. Ian Shapira, "'Rick Is a Goddamn Russian Spy': Does the CIA Have a New Aldrich Ames on Its Hands?" *Washington Post*, January 26 2018, https://www .washingtonpost.com/news/retropolis/wp/2018/01/26/rick-is-a-goddamn-russian -spy-does-the-cia-have-a-new-aldrich-ames-on-its-hands/?noredirect=on&utm _term=.8699add3e662.

CHAPTER 13: HOW—AND WHY—TO RECRUIT A RUSSIAN SPY

1. Laura Mandeville, "In Dresden, Putin Is More than a Fading Memory," *Gulf News*, March 14, 2018, https://gulfnews.com/culture/people/in-dresden -putin-is-more-than-a-fading-memory-1.2187888.

2. *Wikipedia*, s.v. "Federal Security Service," last modified April 12, 2019, 15:21, https://en.wikipedia.org/wiki/Federal_Security_Service.

3. Armin Rosen, "The Soviet Union's Fall Led to an Alarming Nuclear Failure That Informs Today's Nuclear Crisis," *Business Insider*, May 26, 2015, https://www .businessinsider.com/irans-hunt-for-nuclear-components-in-soviet-union-2015-5\.

CHAPTER 14: REAL HOUSEWIVES OF THE CIA

1. Milt Bearden and James Risen, *The Main Enemy: The Inside Story of the CIA's Final Showdown with the KGB* (New York: Presidio, 2004), p. 5.

2. Dexter Filkins, "The Shadow Commander," *New Yorker*, September 30, 2013, https://www.newyorker.com/magazine/2013/09/30/the-shadow-commander.

3. James Glanz, "G.I.'s in Iraq Raid Iranians' Offices," *New York Times*, January 12, 2007, https://www.nytimes.com/2007/01/12/world/middleeast/12raid.html.

CHAPTER 15: SPY KIDS

1. "30 Years of Remembrance," Central Intelligence Agency, May 23, 2017, https://www.cia.gov/news-information/featured-story-archive/2017-featured-story -archive/30-years-of-remembrance.html.

CHAPTER 17: DENIED AREA OPERATIONS

1. *Dr. Strangelove, or How I Learned to Stop Worrying and Love the Bomb*, directed by Stanley Kubrick (1964; Culver City, CA: Sony Pictures Home Entertainment, 2016), Blu-ray Disc.

2. Zach Dorfman, "Botched CIA Communications System Helped Blow Cover of Chinese Agents," *Foreign Policy*, August 15, 2018, https://foreignpolicy.com/2018/08/15/ botched-cia-communications-system-helped-blow-cover-chinese-agents-intelligence/.

CHAPTER 19: KOMANDANTE GIŠKA

1. Steve Balestrieri, "Operation Halyard, One of the Great Rescue Stories of WWII," Special Operations, February 28, 2018, https://specialoperations.com/32596/ operation-halyard-forgotten-500-one-great-rescue-stories-wwii/.

CHAPTER 21: LIFE IMITATES ART IMITATES LIFE— HUNTING BOSNIAN WAR CRIMINALS

1. Apologies to Amazing Rhythm Aces.

2. Jack Hitt, "Radovan Karadzic's New-Age Adventure," *New York Times Magazine*, July 22, 2009, https://www.nytimes.com/2009/07/26/magazine/26karadzic-t.html.

3. Julian Borger, "Radovan Karadžić Sentenced to 40 Years for Srebrenica Genocide," *Guardian*, March 24, 2016, https://www.theguardian.com/world/2016/ mar/24/radovan-karadzic-criminally-responsible-for-genocide-at-srebenica.

4. "Radovan Karadžić Complains of '19th Century' Jail Conditions," *Irish Times*, https://www.irishtimes.com/news/world/europe/radovan-karadzic -complains-of-19th-century-jail-conditions-1.2600716.

5. *The Hunting Party*, directed by Richard Shepard (2007; Weinstein Company, 2008), DVD.

6. **Synopsis:** First line: Vowing to avenge the horrific death of his Bosnian girlfriend, Caruso [an American] returns to his Bosnian nightmare in pursuit of a notorious Bosnian Serb war criminal.

Movie: Plot: The American protagonist Simon Hunt (played by Richard Gere) vows to avenge the death of his Bosnian girlfriend, and returns to his Bosnian nightmare in pursuit of a notorious Bosnian Serb war criminal called "the Fox."

Synopsis: Justice, revenge and five million dollars in reward money motivate Caruso and his daring team members.

Movie: Justice, revenge, and five million dollars in reward money motivate Hunt and his daring team members.

Synopsis: Neither Mladić nor his victims expect that he will ever face justice for his crimes.

Movie: Neither the Fox nor his victims expect that he will ever face justice for his crimes.

Synopsis: Mentions mass murder at Srebrenica, but takes place in Sarajevo.

Movie: Mentions mass murder at Srebrenica, but takes place in Sarajevo.

Synopsis: "Balkan Justice" is testament to the thesis that unselfish acts of love, sacrifice, and courage can prevail over hatred, barbarism, and cowardice.

Movie: This movie's plot is testament to the thesis that unselfish acts of love, sacrifice, and courage can prevail over hatred, barbarism, and cowardice.

Synopsis: Marked by realism, humor, and historical accuracy.

Movie: Marked by realism, humor, and historical accuracy.

Synopsis: A seasoned yet idealistic CIA officer plies his trade, first on behalf of his country and then for other, more personal motives.

Movie: A seasoned yet idealistic journalist (believed to be a CIA officer) plies his trade, first on behalf of his network and then for other, more personal motives.

Synopsis: The story opens on the deadly backstreets of war-ravaged Sarajevo, a modern-day hub of espionage and intrigue. Most of the story takes place years later, when the protagonist returns to Bosnia to avenge his lover's death and hunt the responsible war criminal.

Movie: The story opens on the deadly backstreets of war-ravaged Sarajevo, a modern-day hub of espionage and intrigue. Most of the story takes place years later, when the protagonist returns to Bosnia to avenge his lover's death and hunt the responsible war criminal.

Synopsis: Caruso reports on secret Bosnian government plans to bomb a Sarajevo marketplace and attribute the act to the Serbs, in an effort to accelerate NATO's engagement.

Movie: Hunt flips out on live TV when he is asked about a secret Bosnian government plan to carry out attacks on its own people and attribute the act to the Serbs.

Synopsis: Caruso's Bosnian girlfriend, who has one child, is raped and killed by the notorious Bosnian war criminal. This is the basis for Caruso's revenge.

Movie: Hunt's Bosnian girlfriend, who is pregnant with a child, is killed by or in the presence of the notorious Bosnian war criminal. This is the basis for Hunt's revenge.

Synopsis: Later, Caruso's sources on black-market crime provide intelligence on the Bosnian war criminal.

Movie: Later, Hunt's sources on black-market crime provide intelligence on the Bosnian war criminal.

Synopsis: The CIA gets wind of Caruso's (private) activities and solicits his cooperation against the war criminal.

Movie: The CIA gets wind of Hunt's (private) activities and becomes involved.

Synopsis: Caruso hatches a secret plan of his own to capture the war criminal. Team includes trusted friends.

Movie: Hunt hatches a secret plan of his own to capture the war criminal. Team includes trusted friends.

Synopsis: The novel's climax is a surprise, since the usual three outcomes during the hunt for a war criminal are (1) captured and turned over to The Hague, (2) killed, or (3) escapes / never captured. In the novel, the war criminal is set free by the US government as part of a cynical strategic geopolitical deal. The war criminal goes free, and the Serbs agree to the Dayton agreement. But Caruso exacts his revenge by having the war criminal castrated by a Bosnian veterinarian whose own daughter had been raped and murdered. Both Caruso and the Bosnian victims get their revenge.

Movie: The movie's climax is a surprise ending, not one of the usual three outcomes. The war criminal goes free as part of a cynical strategic geopolitical deal with the Serbs. But Hunt exacts his revenge by capturing and turning the Fox loose in downtown Sarajevo, where he is recognized (and presumably lynched) by his angry Bosnian victims. Both Hunt and the Bosnian victims get their revenge.

CHAPTER 22: THE ROAD TO BABYLON

1. Andrew Testa, "Kosovo Finds Little to Celebrate After 10 Years of Independence," *New York Times*, February 15, 2018, https://www.nytimes.com/2018/02/15/world/europe/kosovo-independence-anniversary.html?mtrref=www.google.com.

2. "Hillary Clinton Hears Kosovars' Tales of Tears," CNN, May 14, 1999, http://www.cnn.com/WORLD/europe/9905/14/kosovo.refugees/.

3. AFP Reporter, "Kosovan Death Toll Is Its Argument for Independence," *Telegraph*, November 30, 2009, https://www.telegraph.co.uk/expat/expatnews/6692257/Kosovan-death-toll-is-its-argument-for-independence.html.

4. Andrew Higgins, "Not the Worst Hotel in the World, Perhaps, but 'the World Is Very Big,'" *New York Times*, March 1, 2018, https://www.nytimes.com/2018/03/01/world/europe/kosovo-grand-hotel.html.

CHAPTER 23: MISSION: IMPROBABLE

1. Duncan Mackay, "Torture of Iraq's Athletes," *Guardian*, February 1, 2003, https://www.theguardian.com/sport/2003/feb/02/athletics.duncanmackay1.

CHAPTER 24: TRIBALISM

1. "The Origins of Shiite Islam," *Christian Science Monitor,* June 6, 2007, https://www .csmonitor.com/2007/0606/p13s01-wome.html.

2. John Harney, "How Do Sunni and Shia Islam Differ?" *New York Times,* January 3, 2016, https://www.nytimes.com/2016/01/04/world/middleeast/q-and-a-how-do-sunni -and-shia-islam-differ.html.

3. For more information on how *hawala* works, see *Investopedia,* s.v. "Hawala," last modified April 9, 2019, https://www.investopedia.com/terms/h/hawala.asp.

4. Scott Neuman, "Hijacked Driver Helped Police Track Boston Bombing Suspects," NPR, April 26, 2013, https://www.npr.org/sections/thetwo-way/ 2013/04/26/179296836/driver-hijacked-by-tsarnaev-brothers-helped-police-trace-them.

CHAPTER 25: TRAVELS IN ARABIA

1. "Syrian Refugee Crisis: Facts, FAQs, and How to Help," *World Vision,* November 19, 2018, https://www.worldvision.org/refugees-news-stories/syrian-refugee-crisis-facts.

2. Max Greenwood, "Air Force General: 'If You Can't Treat Someone with Dignity and Respect Get Out' of Academy," *Hill,* September 29, 2017, https://thehill .com/homenews/news/353058-air-force-gen-if-you-cant-treat-someone-with-dignity-and -respect-get-out-of.

CHAPTER 27: BREAKING BAD IN TIJUANA

1. Evan Valletta, "How 'Syriana' Almost Killed George Clooney," SBS Australia, April 19, 2018, https://www.sbs.com.au/movies/article/2018/04/07/ how-syriana-almost-killed-george-clooney.

CHAPTER 29: IGNORE MY INTELLIGENCE AT YOUR PERIL (I AM NOT AS STUPID AS I LOOK)

1. "1998 US Embassies in Africa Bombings Fast Facts," CNN.com, July 31, 2018, https://www.cnn.com/2013/10/06/world/africa/africa-embassy-bombings-fast-facts/ index.html.

2. "USS *Cole* Bombing Fast Facts," CNN.com, March 27, 2019, https://www.cnn .com/2013/09/18/world/meast/uss-cole-bombing-fast-facts/index.html.

3. Bill Powell, "Donald Trump Associate Felix Sater Is Linked to the Mob and the CIA—What's His Role in the Russia Investigation?" *Newsweek,* June 7, 2018, http://www .newsweek.com/2018/06/15/sater-963255.html.

4. "Is There A Link Between Al Qaeda and Iraq?" PBS, https://www.pbs.org/ wgbh/pages/frontline/shows/gunning/etc/alqaeda.html.

5. Dana Priest, "U.S. Not Claiming Iraqi Link to Terror," *Washington Post*, September 10, 2002, https://www.washingtonpost.com/archive/politics/2002/09/10/us-not -claiming-iraqi-link-to-terror/71466a05-ff7e-45bd-94a9-428c5ad38fd5/?utm _term=.5131b7262935.

CHAPTER 30: IRAQ INTELLIGENCE FAILURE

1. Peter Baker and Eric Schmitt, "Many Missteps in Assessment of ISIS Threat," *New York Times*, September 29, 2014, https://www.nytimes.com/2014/09/30/world/ middleeast/obama-fault-is-shared-in-misjudging-of-isis-threat.html.

CHAPTER 31: THE SPY WHO CAME DOWN WITH A COLD

1. Adam Entous and Jon Lee Anderson, "The Mystery of the Havana Syndrome," *New Yorker*, November 9, 2018, https://www.newyorker.com/magazine/2018/11/19/ the-mystery-of-the-havana-syndrome.
2. John 8:32 (King James Version).
3. Caitlin Oprysko, "Trump Tells Intel Chiefs to 'Go Back to School' after They Break with Him," Politico, January 30, 2019, https://www.politico.com/story/2019/ 01/30/trump-national-security-1136433.
4. Derek Hawkins, "Trump Called It a 'Very Special' Wall. For the CIA, It Is Sacrosanct," *Washington Post*, January 23, 2017, https://www.washingtonpost.com/news/ morning-mix/wp/2017/01/23/trump-called-it-a-very-special-wall-for-the-cia-its -sacrosanct/?utm_term=.5a779d7d72e2.